PRAISE FOR
NEW MOON MAGIC

With their first book, Amy and Risa invited us all on a journey of story and magic that followed the rhythm of the Sun. Now we are invited to make another journey; to see ourselves, others, and our tools through the ever-changing and potent phases of the Moon. Come join us, join Risa and Amy, and let us all make magic together!

—JINKX MONSOON, Queen of All Queens

Missing Witches weave together magical history, the potent present, and futurism to offer us inspiration and resources. This is a beautiful guide to healing that emphasizes that healing comes in many forms and that reminds us that we are not alone.

—SARAH FAITH GOTTESSDIENER, creator of *Moonbeaming*, the *Many Moons* workbooks, and author of *The Moon Book*

This book is more than a book. It is an ecosystem teeming with modern Witches, ancestral agitators, anarchic seeds, and embodied practices. This book channels the moon's medicine of mutability and movement. There is a medicine available for every type of weather and every type of body.

—SOPHIE STRAND, author of *The Flowering Wand* and *The Madonna Secret*

Imagine, for a moment, entering a portal where you are encircled and empowered with the words, the magic, and the wisdom of historical and modern Witches. By holding this book in your hands, you hold the key. Open the portal of the pages of *New Moon Magic* to embrace ritual, to unlock the stories of spellcasting, to rejoice in rising up together to create change. Amy and Risa's book contains the juicy secrets and stories of personal Witchcraft to cultivate your own practice in a way that is authentic to you. In *New Moon Magic*, you are the spell!

—VERONICA VARLOW, author of *Bohemian Magick*

This book is a welcome reminder that we need neither products nor permissions to make meaning, to build community, to exercise our power to shape our spiritual and physical lives. From celebrating our connection with nature to reaffirming our fundamental right to occupy space in the world, *New Moon Magic* is a timely message of empowerment and resistance.

—JAROD K. ANDERSON, creator of *The Cryptonaturalist*
and author of *Field Guide to the Haunted Forest* and *Love Notes
from the Hollow Tree*

We are at a point in history where, once again, resistance is necessary. Laws, science, nature, policy, equity, inclusion, and freedom are being challenged more than ever. It can be easy to get wrapped up in the veil of "purchasing power," wanting or needing to buy the "right" tool for your magical tradition. *New Moon Magic* helps you understand why this isn't so, how this belief only soils the freedoms we all should enjoy, and how to get results while respecting the traditions of fellow healers, artists, and writers, from all different cultures and experiences. Risa and Amy give you an introduction with tools, stories, and substantial reference points on and for each tool, by those who are in and not in our community of healers. There is something for you in here. Whether you enjoy ritual, nature, geometry, poems, chants, or just want to learn more, you can find what you are looking for or store away the information in a book of shadows or vlog for later. The authors' truth comes honestly as they tell you about their own lives in ritual and supported by ritual. This helps you to see for yourself the true life of a practitioner—in times of mourning, joy, doubt, hope, and need.

This book is a call to action for those who want to be change agents without increasing the chasm between the social and political. I say this as a coven member, a Patreon contributor, a guest on the *Missing Witches* podcast, and a fan of their first book. As a practitioner of my own beliefs, I can attest to this book's wisdom and that it can be used by and shared with any magical tradition. The guidance is gentle—like a friend pulling you aside to share a great secret—but comes with backbone and research behind it. Research that is shared and bared from activists, authors, educators, practitioners, and healers from many other walks of life in addition to Witches. The tools themselves are as vast as the stories that are interwoven in the journey through the text. Bodies, tarot, art, needles, knives, geometry, journaling, poetry, brooms, crayons, and so on. Even though I do not practice in the same way as Risa and Amy, I can use these thirteen tools in a way that is familiar to me, respectful of my needs and ways, without diluting the message. I can't wait for you to experience this book for yourself and to learn and grow in your practice and join the cause of resistance to capitalism.

—SHERRY SHONE, author of *The Hoodoo Guide to the Bible*
and *Hoodoo for Everyone*

New Moon Magic

New Moon Magic

13 ANTI-CAPITALIST TOOLS FOR RESISTANCE AND RE-ENCHANTMENT

RISA DICKENS AND AMY TOROK

North Atlantic Books

Huichin, unceded Ohlone land
Berkeley, California

Published by
North Atlantic Books
Huichin, unceded Ohlone land
Berkeley, California

Cover art © Arina-Ulyasheva, ElenKoss
via Getty Images
Cover design by Jasmine Hromjak
Interior illustrations by Amy Torok
Book design by Happenstance Type-O-Rama

Printed in Canada

New Moon Magic: 13 Anti-capitalist Tools for Resistance and Re-enchantment is sponsored and published by North Atlantic Books, an educational nonprofit based in the unceded Ohlone land Huichin (Berkeley, CA) that collaborates with partners to develop cross-cultural perspectives, nurture holistic views of art, science, the humanities, and healing, and seed personal and global transformation by publishing work on the relationship of body, spirit, and nature.

North Atlantic Books's publications are distributed to the US trade and internationally by Penguin Random House Publisher Services. For further information, visit our website at www.northatlanticbooks.com.

Library of Congress Cataloging-in-Publication Data
Names: Dickens, Risa, 1980- author. | Torok, Amy, 1977- author.
Title: New moon magic : 13 anti-capitalist tools for resistance and
   transformation / Risa Dickens and Amy Torok.
Other titles: Thirteen anti-capitalist tools for resistance and
   transformation
Description: Berkeley, California : North Atlantic Books, [2023] | Includes
   index. | Summary: "In New Moon Magic, authors Dickens and Torok reclaim
   witchcraft as resistance in a time of commodification and capitalism.
   The authors create a book that offers wisdom and guidance, using
   witchcraft as a channel to resist systems of oppression and in turn
   transform and nurture our own spirituality and agency"-- Provided by
   publisher.
Identifiers: LCCN 2022040362 (print) | LCCN 2022040363 (ebook) | ISBN
   9781623177904 (trade paperback) | ISBN 9781623177911 (ebook)
Subjects: LCSH: New moon--Religious aspects. | Witchcraft--Anecdotes. |
   Witches--Anecdotes. | Astrology. | Materialism.
Classification: LCC BF1623.M66 D43 2023 (print) | LCC BF1623.M66 (ebook)
   | DDC 133.4/3--dc23/eng/20230217
LC record available at https://lccn.loc.gov/2022040362
LC ebook record available at https://lccn.loc.gov/2022040363

1 2 3 4 5 6 7 8 9 MARQUIS 28 27 26 25 24 23

We dedicate this book to the radical
spirit of mutual aid, revolutionary
acts of love, and playful dissidence.
To Cathy Simard, Mothers-in-Love
everywhere, and to the ancestor web.

CONTENTS

ACKNOWLEDGMENTS

Amy and Risa want to thank Andy, Marc, and May for everything, always.

In humble gratitude, we thank every Witch who sits in circle with us and shares their perspective.

Special thanks to Christena Cleveland and to our contributing astrologers for illuminating our dark moons: Eliza Robertson (director of content at CHANI, author), Monefa Walker (creator and founder of *Sekhmet's Visions*), Thea Anderson (director of production at CHANI, author), and Jasmine Richardson (producer/cohost of *Kosmic Tonic* podcast).

We thank our families—chosen and blood—for every lesson, and our Missing Witches coven, whose tears, laughter, and support fuel us.

Note on the Illustrations

For *New Moon Magic*, we wanted to envision ourselves among a family of practitioners who aren't linked by DNA but rather by their usage of our ancestral tools. Imagine placing yourself in these anachronistic family portraits—a part of a long lineage of Witches who are our kin. A family tree with vast, deep, and mysterious roots invites us to sit at the table.

FOREWORD

Magic snatched my breath away and returned it to me in a spicy gust laced with liberation. And by magic, I mean *gestalt psychology*.

At the time, I was a young justice dreamer and doctoral psychology student enrobed in a Black and female body—and my entire being was fragmented. I was too Black for the white feminists and too feminist for the (predominantly male) Black liberation folks. Further, I was too spiritual for the academic folks and too academic for the spiritual folks. I quickly learned that in order to "connect" with these groups, I had to splinter my identity. Like a stolen car is dismantled so that its individual parts can be sold off at a higher profit, I learned that to be "effective" in the world, I needed to break my sacred intersectionality down to simplistic, palatable components. By my early twenties, I implicitly understood that oneness with my whole self was impossible, much less oneness with others and the earth. I felt that my only option was to dismally resign myself to a life of total disconnect.

So, it's not surprising that when I encountered the early twentieth century concept of *gestalt*, meaning that the whole is greater than the sum of its parts, the idea stole my heart. Gestalt psychology offered the enchanting promise that oneness is the precursor to wholeness. It taught me that, despite what our splintered and segregated society had taught me, I am most fruitful when I embrace and engage *all* of who I am. By applying the concept of gestalt to my life, I experienced for the first time what Amy Torok and Risa Dickens describe in this glorious book, "Self-acceptance became both a healing spell and a prosperity spell."

Gestalt is magic.

But (thankfully) gestalt isn't just about me or the lone individual; it's also about the larger world. Gestalt invites us into the astounding interconnectedness of the world by teaching us that we are intimately and mystically connected to all people and things. As we awaken to, honor, and embody those connections, we begin to see how we nourish and empower others, and vice versa. As we awaken to, honor, and embody this *gestalt magic*, we participate in the flourishing of the world.

New Moon Magic: 13 Anti-capitalist Tools for Resistance and Re-Enchantment is astonishing gestalt magic. Within these profound pages, Amy and Risa invite us to embrace the liberating truth that "we are full of unconscious harmony." At our very core, we are one—with our bodies, our intersectional identities, the whole of humanity, this lush and bitter earth, and the intricate world around us. But perhaps you are like me and our capitalistic society has programmed you to believe and practice the exact opposite. Indeed, Black geographer and prison abolitionist Ruth Wilson Gilmore defines capitalism as a *technology of antirelationality* precisely because it breeds unconscious *dis*harmony by inducing us to divide and conquer our bodies, each other, and the earth. Rather than cultivating sacred oneness, capitalism fosters competition and cuts us off from the magical expanse that theologian Matthew Fox calls "the unfurled divine tent that exists in all creation and in every human being" (as quoted within this book).

We were made for more than this.

Yet, the *problem* of capitalism often feels so global, so ubiquitous, so normalized that it seems insurmountable. And this is why we need magic—for magic doesn't see things in binaries like problems and solutions, nor does it grant anything the power to be insurmountable. Magic *sees* creative flourishing everywhere, and in the places where the oppression of antirelationality feels insurmountable, magic *seeds* creative flourishing. Magic summons another way. Though capitalism furiously labors to disrupt our connection to our birthright harmony, magic has the power to mend the broken strands and re-weave them into an intentional, conscious harmony with all.

New Moon Magic is a timely and insightful clarion call to re/claiming our oneness—with the earth, with seemingly mundane objects such as knives and compost, with our bodies, with all bodies, with pain and grime, with music, with the ancestors, and more. Guided by holy curiosity and gestalt magic, Amy and Risa offer us a technology of relationality that combats capitalism. By giving us the practical tools that help us to embody the truths that "all our magic is a homecoming to the bodies we've been missing" and that "all our bodies and the body of the earth are interpenetrated," *New Moon Magic* helps us to encounter a wholeness that is greater than the sum of its parts. In the company of a virtual coven of fellow readers, we can allow this book to wisely guide us as we practice liberation from capitalism by binding ourselves to all that the bountiful world holds.

Don't be fooled by the moon motif guiding this book. *New Moon Magic* is not linear, nor can it be broken down and sold off in parts. Rather, the book is an unpredictable, uncontrollable, encyclopedic spiral of autobiographical parables, historical anecdotes, wisdom bouquets, quixotic research findings, provocative musings, and deepening rituals—all held in harmony by the illimitable, all-encompassing, and magical gravity of relationality. *New Moon Magic* summons us into the gestalt wholeness amid vast difference that can save us from binaries, from antirelationality, from capitalism, and from the type of death and decay that does not plant seeds and replenish the soil. It beckons us to cast our own anti-capitalism spells—with both our bold and mundane actions, our luminous words, our germinal hope, and our embodied lives. Indeed, it beckons us to *be* the prophetic spiral that conjures gestalt magic in all things.

CHRISTENA CLEVELAND, PhD is a social psychologist, activist, and public theologian. A weaver of Black liberation and the divine feminine, she is the author of *God Is a Black Woman*. Christena makes her home in Boston where she leads the Center for Justice + Renewal.

INTRODUCTION

*We claim the discursive space of Witch as a useful location
for building mycelial connections of solidarity and resistance,
to imagine new ways of being, and to manifest our discoveries and
creations with specific attention to dismantling systems of oppression.*

—BIOART COVEN MANIFESTO

Lunar living is in direct opposition to capitalism and linear time.

—SARAH FAITH GOTTESDIENER

THIS IS A BOOK ABOUT THE TOOLS OF MAGIC. But it's not a how-to guide, nor is it a checklist of things you need to buy to be a Witch. We take up our tools, turn them in the light, and think about what it is we really use to make magic in our lives. What do we use to craft possible futures? What actually works?

The material and aesthetic tools of magic are sold in more places than ever before. Witchcraft is a multibillion dollar industry. You can get crystals, wands, and potions made by children and delivered by drones, but you don't need to. You can support local artisans and buy only fair-mined stones, but that assumes privilege too. This book was written to remind us all that we have identities and power beyond consumption.

We don't need to buy a single thing to connect with our own phenomenal magic. These tools are the birthright of our humanity.

> *The common stones you see lying on the street or dig up in your yard, those tumbled up on riverbanks or beaches, or lying scattered as if a giant hand threw them onto the countryside, are possessed of powers."[1]*

We believe that our bathroom mirrors are as prophetic as any crystal ball. Mud puddles hold whispers of the ocean. A birthday candle speaks the language of first fires. The sky is yours to behold for free. This club has no cover charge, and all our stones have souls.

You can use tools you already have—tools that are both material and conceptual—to disrupt the way capitalism co-opts both magic and craft. Silvia Federici claims that "the revival of magical beliefs is possible today because it no longer represents a social threat."[2] Capitalism is very happy for our crafting of the world to become another flavor of the month, another illusion of choice; happy to sell us another horoscope while the machine bends our bodies again and again to its labor. But, in a quote we always come back to, Federici also gives us back this hope:

> *The very sense that we are living at the edge of the volcano makes it even more crucial to recognize that, in the midst of destruction, another world is growing, like the grass in the urban pavement, challenging the hegemony of capital and the state and affirming our interdependence and capacity for cooperation. . . . This is the horizon that the discourse and the politics of the commons opens for us today, not the promise of an impossible return to the past but the possibility of recovering the power of collectively deciding our fate on this earth. This is what I call re-enchanting the world.[3]*

And so this is a book of tools for collectively deciding our fate. This is a spellbook full of instruments for spiritual monkeywrenching. This is a grimoire for our collective re-enchantment.

This is a book for all those hatching their own individual relationships to a new kind of praxis. *Praxis* as in the actions by which a philosophy or theory is embodied. Praxis as in the craft. How we do what we believe. How we make our beliefs manifest. How, step by step, we bring our ideas into our bodies, and the world. As the owner of HausWitch shop in Salem, Massachusetts, Erica Feldmann told us, "like Witchcraft, anti-capitalism is a practice."[4] Here, we weave these praxes together.

Small causes have large effects. As lesbian activist, academic, and poet Judy Grahn, with eighty-two years of experience behind her when we spoke, said, "the steps will feel small but they add up." And she told us, "our bonding is what makes a revolution happen."[5] Step by step, we affirm our interdependence and co-craft the revolution with collaboration.

Use these tools to put a spanner in the works of late-stage capitalism. Because for us, Witchcraft isn't just a trend; it's a praxis for the pre-utopia. It's a word we find useful to describe the meeting point of our politics, spirituality, and art. A discursive space, a way of both imagining and creating a world of posttraumatic growth, flourishing in the cracks, and charting a path beyond the violence of capitalism, patriarchy, and white supremacy.

In our wildest dreams you find this book in a local library and use it to help disrupt the machine. Pick up these stories and use them to release your astonishing power and to join forces with all those who are undertaking this wild, enchanting, collective work of claiming common spaces and weaving flourishing communities. Because no matter how often we are demonized and turned against each other by liars using sleight of hand to rob us, the truth is we are in this together. "We are at stake to each other," as Donna Haraway writes in *Staying with the Trouble*, and "our job is to make the Anthropocene as short/thin as possible and to cultivate with each other in every way imaginable epochs to come that can replenish refuge."[6] Here, in the midst of destruction, in the heart of the trouble, our job is to replenish refuge.

In a poem called "For George Floyd: Fire" adrienne maree brown writes:

> we will never be convinced to be expendable.
> alchemize every death system, liberate
> our divine lives[7]

We are at stake to each other. We dedicate all our work, words, and tools to alchemizing every death system, alchemizing the death cults of white supremacy and late-stage capitalism into our divine lives, singing out with every divine life that we are not expendable. Audre Lorde taught us that "the master's tools will never dismantle the master's house," so we craft and carve new tools out of these old boards and beams to find that vein of magic in ourselves, in our loves and communities, to conjure forth our power to resist and re-enchant.[8]

With this book we send out into the circle stories of women, people of marginalized and expansive genders and sexualities, Witches, and all those who have been persecuted for a spiritual philosophy that resisted the destruction of the natural world and our connection to it, people who have forged their bonds in the fire. Because the stories of people whose knowledge was occulted hold power. We share stories of the tools these ancestors used to amplify and extend their power so that you might amplify and extend your own.

After writing *Missing Witches: Recovering True Histories of Feminist Magic*, tracing the immutable Wheel of the Year, we were left with a feeling that what came next was to look for things we could control. To look through the lives of Missing Witches for stories of their tools, tools that could be put to the work of feminist, antiracist, decolonized, and unsettled utopian-world-building. We have no say in the turning of the wheel, but we can turn our plowshares to the planting of new seeds.

As Layne Redmond wrote, "Cultural transformation begins with individual transformation."[9] The tools you'll find in this book might not be able to change lead into gold or water into wine, but they can transform the mundane into the sacred. They can transform us, our lives, and—with the rippling effect that we know magic has—our culture as a whole. As above, so below. As within, so without.

This book is not about the conventional tools you'll find in your local Wiccan shop. Though a cauldron might appear in the "Potions and Poisons" chapter, a wand in "Ritual and Ceremony," an athame in "Needles and Knives," these specific objects are not the focus. We love the Witch aesthetic, the pentagram-etched mortar and pestle, velvet cloaks, stacks of tarot cards, and oracle decks. They bring us joy. Supporting the makers who create them connects us to them, and it feels like this heightens the magic that we bring from within ourselves. But these accoutrements are not the magic. You are the magic.

The tools you'll find in this book are those that you can access, free or cheap, at any time. These are tools that need not, and often cannot, be bought. They are action items, modes of conversation between yourself and nature, between all of us and the divine, however you define or observe that.

For us, sometimes the divine is our collective, interspecies ancestry. Sometimes the divine is an emergent property of the complex network that is life and all its stories and archetypes. Sometimes it is a shared sense of self, of awakeness. Sometimes it is the wind. Whatever you believe, the tools in this book contain power for atheist practitioners and Gaia worshippers and Christian servants of the Lwa alike. These universal tools are gifts from the totality of human history that help us process trauma, pain, love, and joy and make meaning. They can connect us to an ancient, pulsing web. Sanctified.

Think of a hammer. It's a simple tool our ancestors would have made with stone; you still could if you needed to. You can use a hammer to build a house. Or you can use it as a weapon of violence. It is up to each of us to inform our tools of their meaning and purpose and to use those tools to channel both rage and joy, to create and destroy, to sleep, dream, imagine, and craft. You may have purchased, borrowed, or stolen this book, but it doesn't come alive until you read it.

In each chapter you'll meet the historical and contemporary Witches we've found who act as role models for us on the usage of these tools, making world-changing magic from pencils, dirt, and math. For our *Missing Witches* podcast, we've had the tremendous, mind-bending privilege to interview over one hundred people about their practices, research, art, activism, craft, and magic. This book is woven like a magpie's nest full of insights we've gathered from those interviews and from our own investigations into the lineage of Witches' past. We are still looking for the Witches we've been missing.

In our first book, *Missing Witches: Reclaiming True Histories of Feminist Magic*, we wrote that Missing Witches for us doesn't just mean *missing* as in not there, but as in the French for missing, *tu me manques*, which translates directly as "you are missing from me." You are a piece of myself that I lack. Over time we've realized that *we* are the Missing Witches. And the word *Missing* in this context is a verb. We are the ones who have been missing you. We come from a place of longing and lack. We are Witches driven by our sense that we are missing people, missing perspectives, stories, and possible worlds. And so we see the Missing Witches project, including this book of New Moon magic, as an act of science fiction and speculative futurism: What will our worldviews and world look like when we reintegrate marginalized, obscured, violated, missing wisdom? What kind of community and identity can we find if we follow our own longing? We are searching always for a philosophy, identity, and relationship with the natural world and with the universe. We have been longing for kinship and a way of relating that speaks to a void in us. We have been missing you, all of you; none are expendable. So we go looking.

We offer these true stories of real Witches to conjure the magic of possibility. Possible worlds. Because sometimes the impossible is just waiting for someone to be first. No one could run a mile in under four minutes until Roger Bannister did it. Once a rival saw that it could be done, it took him less than six weeks to beat Barrister's time. Over the next twenty years, over 200 runners officially achieved the impossible. The story is the same for the 720 in skateboarding (doing two full circle rotations in the air before you and your board hit the ground), and it's the same for bringing gardens back to Brooklyn, bringing the wolves back to Yellowstone, and for changing the world with the magic of the circle and the pen. It's easier to do when you know it's been done. It's easier when we can place ourselves in a web, a framework of magical, intersectional, physical people doing metaphysical work. We offer these stories of Witches we've found in books and in our own circles for us all to be awed and uplifted: how infinite our possibilities.[10]

We made the decision to include people in the first book—and in the stories we tell in this one—who did not and do not self-identify as Witches. This is not to say that they are Witches—they can choose their names and labels for themselves. But for us, their ideas expand how we understand the possible magics of resistance and of re-enchantment. They help us understand this place where our politics and spirituality intersect, where self and other intersect, where knowledge and dreams intersect—a space we choose to call *Witch*. Because this word has been used to burn us for generations and now we hold it up like a shield.

As Lindy West wrote during the height of the #MeToo movement, "Yes, this is a Witch Hunt. I'm a Witch, and I'm Hunting You."[11] We claim this word and flip the tables. We are hunting those who have persecuted us, ravaged our earth, and stolen land and culture, and we are spinning and crafting, incanting and conjuring and mapmaking a version of the world that we can celebrate. The women and people of marginalized and expansive genders you'll find here give shape to our ideas about what it means to be Witches today. What is wild and beautiful and weird, what has refused to be expendable. These voices give us power and a sense of possibility. We come to them from a place of longing and of thanks. We use their insights to make the circle of protection bigger. Step inside.

We chart our way through these chapters following the potent, gentle darkness of the new moon. The dark moon time is vast, quiet, and nurturing like black, rich soil. It is a perfect time to see the unobvious, look beneath the surface, discover something new. To see things differently. To look at the tools around you and—in the dim light of Witch history—to see how you might turn them to your power.

The moon doesn't belong to any of us, it belongs to all of us. It's not owned by any culture, any class (for now at least). We can all connect with its cycles as an open practice. To notice the magic in the moon is to be self-initiated into a most ancient form of the craft. Thea Anderson, an author who uses astrology to chart new dimensions to Black stories where the archives are bereft, told us that when she lived in Bed-Stuy, in Brooklyn, with her family, when they couldn't see many stars, she would still take her daughter out at night to follow the moon.[12] To fill cups with moon water and fill them with their hopes for the future. Because no matter where you are, the moon and their cyclical dance with our earth and sun always encircles you, includes you, and keeps you in their celestial heart.[13] And on the darkest nights, when the dazzle and reflection of the sun are off their face, the moon is most fully with us. They are most powerful when unseen. In the dark of the moon, we unmask and let our wildest wishes enter the world. And we call forth the possible.

We encourage you to read these chapters during the new moon and take them with you as the light of the moon begins to grow. Turn them over in the brimming light. Weave them into your life along with the waxing moon, and watch as the possibilities they contain for you open and grow, increasing and inviting in new ways of moving, practicing, and being.

We hope you'll embrace the stories, tools, and ideas in this book in the nonlinear way they were created. Because this was written in spirals and dedicated to the moon's spiral through the Milky Way, there's no right way to approach this, and you can't fuck it up. Whatever skill or knowledge you bring is enough. Witch or non-Witch, person of any gender, every body, you are welcome here: "if you are a dreamer, come in."[14]

We just want to tell you stories about some powerful, real people who make real magic. We just want to share some of the ideas and objects that have been used to resist the delusion spell that capitalist patriarchy has cast, the one that endlessly asserts that we are powerless.

We just want to light you up with ways to find yourselves and find each other, to flourish, to call forth joy and possibility, to resist the beckoning, consumptive disease of the status quo, and to re-enchant the world.

Blessed Fucking Be.

1

New Moon in Aries

Needles and Knives

This circle is led by Risa
with expansions by Amy.

The New Moon in Aries is the edge from which we can hurl ourselves from and through darkness. It is The Fool in the Tarot. We may fall. We may fly. It's a match stick lighting our way into possibility burning for the self within.

—THEA ANDERSON, ASTROLOGER

WE BEGIN WITH THE NEW MOON IN ARIES—the great warrior burnished by flame glinting in the dark. We begin by taking up needles and knives, stories of cutting and piercing. We prick our fingers on the sharp edges of Witchcraft and begin with a blood ritual. Because as Callie Little, tattoo artist and emotional support Witch, told us: "your blood is the most real currency, other than time. It is mortality."[1]

Consider this your content warning for this book going forward. Because we can't talk about how people have used these tools to resist and re-enchant without also telling true stories of oppression and violation. Of how our blood has been taken from us. Of our mortality.

After I was sexually assaulted in 2019, I was catatonic. I was just in my bed and silent and didn't speak to anybody. I got to the point where I was like: I have to feel something other than this. I asked my friend if she could tattoo me, and she made time, and I do remember it was painful and it was exactly what I needed. It helped so much that I got to have this reminder of being in control of my experience.[2]

We start with the sharp edges. We call our blood forward to remind ourselves that we have agency. Needles and knives are tools of violence, destruction, revolution, and also of stitching, weaving, delivering essential medicines, piercing through to something new. Our fates are not determined by our tools, or by our traumas. This is fundamental to the philosophy of Witchcraft and of activism both: your life and your will matter. Your choices cut and shape the fabric of the world. As Callie said of her assault, "I'm not grateful for the experience, but I am grateful for myself."[3] She woke up in her body, and she took up the needle.

In the Scottish Witch hunts, Witch prickers were well-paid torturers who used needles, pins, and bodkins to stab any mark on a woman's body. They stabbed the accused's skin until she didn't react—because she was disassociating or just wanted the torture to stop—and then claimed that as evidence of her pact with the devil.

Needle magic is about taking up the tools that have been used against us and piercing our will, our life force, through this world and into the next to make our changes. Even if this is just a way to bring you back to a sense of agency and control over fate, or over those who have tormented you, sometimes that's enough. The feeling of power is powerful.

Emily Goodall—traditional Witch, member of the Missing Witches coven—uses needles in her craft, especially knitting needles. "My magic is rooted in self-empowerment and trauma processing and reclaiming my sense of self and power."[4] She told us, "The energy that I really wanted to bring forward was going into the dark moon to grasp these threads of fate and weave them into what I wanted to have happen. To use that void and chaos of the dark moon, of being unobserved and being under the mound and being outside of physical time and space to weave my will. And it worked." In the new moon darkness, Emily cast a spell that worked. This is the magic at the needle's point; it pierces and it draws forth, it collaborates with the other side.

I like to embroider. For years I would hand sew strange alterations to my clothes with brightly colored thread. My mendings would walk off the seam and into freehand embroidery, drawings of buildings and faces. When I began to practice Witchcraft more intentionally, I read about container magic—a basic principle that recurs in many traditions of focusing your will by gathering resonant items together within a container. I spent days selecting fabric, herbs, and stones and drawing symbols and writing out the dream: a soul-mate editor, a soul-mate publisher, a way to write the strange books I envisioned about feminist ideas. A life so totally different from the one I lived I could barely imagine it. I hand stitched all my gathered symbols with silver thread into a bag I wore from new moon to full. Five years later, here we are. You and me and Amy, in a circle, in the dreamworld, always becoming real.

Amy: I learned how to knit a few years ago and took on a perhaps ill-advised first project: a giant blanket scarf, two feet wide and ten feet long. I made a deal with myself that I wouldn't correct any errors, wouldn't pull my work apart to fix a hole or bump. I would embrace imperfection so I could watch myself learn. In this way, my first knitting project became a book of shadows. I poured my anxieties and hopes and spells into every loop and pushed the needles back and through, to take a story, a yarn, and turn it into something warm, comforting, and protective. As the scarf got longer, I could see in its shape as my confidence grew, as I settled into the rhythm. I learned to make hats too, and with every stitch, I marveled, "Look what two needles and a piece of string can do!" Witches can take this idea into our work of unlearning capitalism. Making something out of nothing, taking needles and knives and yarns and, with actions, efforts, and persistence, creating a blanketing protection spell. Our friend Sherry Shone's grandmother would lay her handmade Pink Ladies quilt across Sherry when she had nightmares. And Sherry would sleep peacefully. And there is so much magic there.

A needle pierces to stitch, to deliver medicine, to draw forth new worlds.

A knife is a different kind of thing. And different Witches have different ideas about knives. For Wiccans, the black-handled athame is used to channel and direct power. Its point can be called upon to draw the circle, to consecrate offerings, to call the corners, to close a circle, to thank and send the powers of the four directions home. Then there's the white-handled boline for cutting herbs and cords and for carving candles. In many traditions a ritual knife is kept away from the mundane world; the tool gains in its power as you consecrate it to a task.

For Emily, the power in a knife is to be used sparingly.

I'm not Wiccan. I understand a lot of traditions will use a knife to cast a circle or use an athame more or less in every ritual. But for me, I feel like iron, that edge controls Spirit, that's a controlling thing because of the magnetism of that tool. Using a magnetic tool lays a path and you can control spirit with that edge. So I use it sparingly because I want to interact with Spirit. I don't want to control. I want to be witness to wherever Spirit wants to go in that moment and work with Spirit. But if I do a seance, if I need to draw a line, or close down a session, if I can't ground or something, then I will pull out my blade . . . Sometimes you need to draw a line. Boundaries are important in all areas of life, and in magic, especially.[5]

These days, personally, I am working on both my boundaries and my skill with a blade.

I am working on what Christena Cleveland calls my holy No.[6] I have become a woman who carries a knife, and slowly its magic is making itself known to me.

No is a boundary, and it's a sharp edge. It's not one that has come easily to me. And a knife has been harder for me to take up than art, writing, music, or divination. Given the choice to fight, flee, or fawn, I have often used my magic to conjure dream worlds of pleasure and comfort. This was a coping mechanism that served me well. But in doing so, I sometimes hid from painful truths. I stayed in bad places too long. I cut myself off from my body. I refused to cut the cord. Over the decades, step by step and often protected by my enchantments, I had to learn to chisel out my strength. I cut narcissists out of my life, raised up my boundaries, and made choices nobody gave me approval for that brought my life huge leaps in new directions.

And then, in the kind of correspondence Witches love, the first gift Marc—eventual father of our kid, fiery Aries artisan—ever gave me was a wood-handled knife. He had burned my name onto it. My eyes glinted and I stood a little sharper.

There is a magic particular to the sharp edge. Maybe it's in the hairsbreadth between helping and hurting. Lancing a wound or severing an artery; freeing a captive or taking one. Delivering a vaccine or feeding an addiction. Carving something new where there was only potential before, or brutalizing that potential away. This is a tool of magic that requires muscle memory and practiced care to walk its edge. Intuition alone is not enough; you have to put the time in.

My knives now exist for me in an unexpected, sacred set of three: two in the kitchen, one on the hip. They are practical, not expensive or ceremonial. I keep them honed and always at hand.

My knife skills in the kitchen are slow and awkward still. I am acquiring the rhythm, learning where to hold my fingers, listening for what the speed should sound like, feeling for which blade fits best for each task. I explore the magic of making food and drink more in the "Potions and Poisons" chapter, but it resonates with this: before we transform and transubstantiate, first we make a hundred unmendable cuts.

We keep two very sharp knives on the large slab of wood on the oversized counter that makes up most of our kitchen. Marc hones these daily and taught me the rhythm of the long, quick slide down the blade. Honing a kitchen knife puts the blade minutely back to center, and when centered, the blade will seem sharper. If you are listening to—and taking metaphors from—your tools, you might hear this in the scraping swipe of honing your blades: find your alignment, again and again, before coming to tasks that require incisiveness and precision. Do the work to come to center before making a cut in the fabric of the world.

It turns out, weirdly, that honing prefers a rhythm taken directly from Fibonacci, so this tool weaves into the "Geometry" chapter too as we make this fine triangle: five strokes on each side, then three, then two, then one, with the one repeating ten times. Use the counting and the scrape of steel and the balancing rhythm as part of your own honing. This is not a simile; you are not like a knife. This is a metaphor: you *are* a knife, coming back into balance in order to cut clean. If, like Emily and so many of us, you come to craft to reclaim your power, then begin by building up a steadiness with sharp things. You are capable and worthy of this responsibility.

The kitchen counter is our family's living altar. The chef's knife and the paring knife are never put away; they always sit clean and sharp at this warm heart, and they keep me firmly in the quick-ticking, blood-ready present. Don't get lost in the kid-world, or in the wind in the trees when holding these; they are very sharp. I have cut myself more than once. Every knife eventually gets bathed in blood.

The knife Marc gave me is a sturdy Opinel, which I carry on my belt loop. This is the daily knife for life in the woods. It cuts secret messages into candles and driftwood, strips fallen branches into walking sticks, trims and splices new additions to our ramshackle art shelters nestled throughout the woods. I'm still awkward with this one as well. One day, I watch Marc open his with one hand while driving 100 kilometers an hour down a northern road, flick a tomato seed stuck in his gum out with its point, fold and twist it back, and sigh in relief, "that's been bothering me for an hour!" and I have to admit, I want that. I want to be a woman with that ease with a knife, a Witch who is fast, deadly, and practical. I want that confidence and that knowledge of the knife-edge of the world. I want both the praxis and the symbol of the knife.

I realized, while writing this chapter, that I have, many times in my life, been described as a knife. I've been told that I cut to the heart of things, and also, that I am cutting. I'm trying to walk a line. I work to keep that edge folded away until it is called for, but also not to dull myself, as I have at times in the past. I work to keep clearing my way to the truth. I have become a woman who carries a knife, and it's teaching me how to use it.

I pull my pocket knife out slowly to help our daughter May strip twigs off a green switch. I'm proud to have her see me make use of a knife. I am building my daily, hourly relationship with this sharp danger restrained, this pent-up power and quick ability. As far as I can tell, the last woman in my life to have skill with a blade was my maternal great-great-grandmother who ran a struggling farm and slaughtered and butchered her own animals. At times I feel her in my knife hand, feel her severity, and her need, the reaching and slipping, the things she had to sacrifice in herself and for her children in order to survive those winters on that farm that only ever grew rocks. Settlers blind to the knowledge of the land white ancestors had stolen, cut from their own heritage by the great distance they had come into the "New" World. Cut from roots, scrabbling in the dirt.

Those women are in my DNA and sinews as I turn over the knives I am working with. Our needs are different. We're vegetarian, peeling fruit and vegetables to boil up our stock and stews and homemade juice. We are constantly deciding which plants to encourage and which to cut back as the edge of the woods pushes closer, trying to eat the garden, to reclaim the house. I carve my sorrows, shadows, and dreams into apples and plant them, into driftwood, and cast them back to the stream. I work to be honest without unnecessary hurt. I take my lessons where I can: from Marc and May, as we build our life in the chopping, nurturing, splicing rhythm we are finding here. And from the stories of Witches, and Indigenous knowledge-keepers around the world branded Witch by colonizers, who used knife and sword in ways that gave them power, that defended their people, and that helped them cut a shape for themselves in a suffocating history.

Humans have a complicated history with knives. Our first encounter with this world is at a knife's edge: most of us are severed from the body that birthed us by a blade cutting the cord. Birth and death straddle the blade. It is our oldest tool; it's the start of how we made a place to live, made a space for ourselves. It's a tool we built with cunning about the different ways of stones; about the ways stones are formed over millennia. Flint defined the Stone Age as people found it in deposits often marked with fossils and learned to chip and grind it to an edge, to make sparks in the process, to skin and butcher and make fire. Knives like the Gebel el-Arak, dating to 3500–3200 BCE, have a flint blade and ivory or bone handle and are carved with recurring depictions of a "Master or Mistress of Animals" and symbols of the Morning and Evening star, Venus/Lucifer in both their guises.[7] Testing shows the Gebel el-Arak was never used to butcher or spill blood; these knives had a different purpose.

Inuit ancestors used iron that has such a specific chemical signature that we now know it came from "the core of a primeval planetoid large enough and hot enough to have a molten metal core."[8] Our species' first tools, honored here at the start, came from the fires of our own Earth, and also from the fires of distant worlds meeting their end.

Ultimately all our tools and selves come from the first fire, the great cauldron of the universe exploding. That is the heart of the power in the division of cells, the splitting of atoms. It's why we sanctify our knives with fire symbols and strengthen them in flame, and it's the fundamental power we can connect with in our magical practices. Our strength has been formed under pressure for millennia.

Early blades are still a source of mystery. They disappear into the archeological record, lost in centuries of sediment and other stones. What people needed to do and make, how they lived and what they believed in, how they connected and what they severed, is an open question. What we know about those ancestors and their relationships with their tools and their environment is largely thanks to the people who still care for this kind of bushcraft today. Let your knife remind you of this: Witch's craft and bushcraft, the spirit-muscle-memory of artisans, craftspeople, hunter-gatherers and nomadic people, are profoundly intertwined. Building a relationship with an ancient tool like a knife can help us approach that interconnected craft with practicality and power, with reverence and with play.

Over time the combined pressures of patriarchy, racism, and capital combined in different ways on different bodies to take many kinds of power away (and many possibilities for play). Homogenized power changed our relationship to craft and to tools. In response, as the blade grew distant and our relationship to it was constrained and controlled, the blade also became an important metaphor, a symbol of rights. We can see tiny traces of this in the way the idea of a right to defense, and a right to vote, are tied together by the suffragists.

The right of self-defense is one of the natural rights; everybody concedes it, and to take from me the natural and effective means of defending myself is to take from me the right itself. Government is the means of securing natural rights, and should depend upon the consent of the governed. Therefore the right to give or to withhold my consent is a part of the natural right . . . To say that I have the right of self-defense, but that I have no right to use the knife or any instrument necessary to protect my life against the assassin is nonsense.[9]

We have a right to self-defense, and that is tied to a right to vote. The vote is the extension of our self-defense and in places where our vote isn't counted, the knives come out. These are sides of the same triangle of power. We have a right and a duty to be strong and sharp and loud, to protect ourselves and fellow beings, and we have a responsibility to use our tools to nurture Earth and each other.

We live in a traumatic and traumatized culture. Trauma distorts memories and the way we experience time; trauma makes violence repeat on a loop like a record skipping.

The Witch hunts were a season of fire in our communal memory, an act of violence against a complex, polyvocal worldview that saw holiness in the living world. They were also a weapon in the global violence of capitalism and of colonialism. As we work to disrupt androcentrism (the framework that sees masculinity as normal and all else as other) with feminist history; to heal from the violence of colonialism; to resist the worst of Earth-eating capitalism however the fuck we can; it's useful to go looking for diverse places where women were and are called Witch. Not so we can perpetuate another trauma, or repeat the colonial crime of taking what isn't ours, but so we can honor their lives and stories and skill. We call out their names and pass around their stories so we can cut the spirit bindings, find parts of ourselves that have been missing, and learn to put our shoulders and our weapons to their common cause. Trauma is a trap, and maybe it's one we need to cut ourselves out of.

Dihya al-Kahina was a seventh-century warrior Witch priestess. Dihya was a Black Indigenous Woman who was a hero. She was champion of the native North African Imazighen people. Her name means "the beautiful gazelle" in the language of the Imazighen. Imazighen—Amazigh singular, Tamazight feminine—means the "free or noble people."[10] Among outsiders, the more common name for Imazighen is Berber, which comes directly from the word *barbarian* or *barbary*. *Berber* is a colonizer's word.[11] A word to diminish and destroy. The Amazigh or Berber people are also sometimes called the Tuareg.

> *It can be argued that the very notion of a people called "the Tuareg" is an invention of 19th century explorers and anthropologists, who adopted this supra-tribal and alien (i.e., Arab) collective noun with which to group together the Amazigh or Berber speaking nomadic tribes of the southern Sahara.[12]*

Like her people, Dihya is largely known to the world now by the name given to her by colonizers. Conquerors wrote her history for generations and they are the ones who christened her "al-Kahina" or The Kahina, meaning "prophetess," "seer," or "Witch."[13]

Arab records describe Dihya as having "dark skin, a mass of hair and huge eyes."[14] It was said she had supernatural powers; she read the movements of desert birds and the messages of the wind on leaves and sand to predict the future. Whether or not she was a sorceress, she was a warrior hero who could pierce the veil and read the world, and she had deep knowledge of the blade. Both the saving edge, and the life-ending one as well.

Dihya was a religious and military leader who led Indigenous resistance to the Roman and Arab Muslim conquest of the Maghreb, the region then known as Numidia. The greater Indigenous land of the Imazighen is called Tamazgha, and it stretches across borders—imaginary lines cutting like knives, controlling Spirit—between lands we know today as Morocco, Algeria, Tunisia, Libya, the Western Sahara, Mauritania, the Canary Islands, and parts of Egypt, Mali, and Niger.

Dihya exists in a continuum. Before her, an Imazighen warrior queen known as Tin Hinan was so central to their legends that the foreigners who first recorded their history thought she was fictitious. They believed Tin Hinan was a mythic mother created from folktales to serve as a source of guidance and a representation of the tribes' social, political, and spiritual stability.[15] According to tradition, she saved her people from starvation by finding the grain stored in ant hills. She possessed knowledge of herbs for healing and medicinal practices. Her name means "she of the tents" and also something like "president," and so Tin Hinan is interpreted as "mother of the tribe" or "queen of the camp." She remained fictional in the colonizer's view, dismissed despite the carefully nurtured oral histories of the people, until she was found. Lying in her pear-shaped tomb at the crossroads of two dry riverbed valleys, she was buried with her jewelry, a mother goddess figurine, and an iron knife.[16] According to the oral history, she taught her people poetry and the Tifinagh alphabet, traces of which were found on her 1,500-year-old tomb.[17] She carved out her markings, told her story, brought her people safely into this world. All hail the mother queen.

This is a story about warriors and writers. About generations of powerful women called Witch. And it's about history and how it gets written. The ways stories—spells in their own right—claim and create what happened, to shape a version of the truth that becomes like a weapon. "It matters whose stories get told; it matters how we tell them. Imagination matters."[18] In the utilitarian histories crafted by colonizers, the Witch's real life goes missing. But the Witch herself remains. And her life still rings with power.

The Inhæd͡æn (Inadan) were a bonded caste of blacksmiths, artisans, and traditional storytellers among the Imazighen. They made the knives and kept the poems, and though they could be owned by a family of the ruling class, they were the ones who were able to lead rituals, and they were feared for their relationship with sharp and molten iron. "They were also often musicians and played an important role in many ceremonies. Their origins are unclear, one theory proposing an original Jewish derivation. They had their own special dialect or secret language. Because of their association with fire, iron, and precious metals and their reputation for cunning tradesmanship, the ordinary Tuareg regarded them with a mixture of awe and distrust."[19] Craft, including the crafting of words, can seem magic; it can give us power that makes us dangerous to those who benefit from the power staying where it is. And so, sometimes, the craft becomes occulted and the craftsperson is enslaved, or branded Witch.

Medieval Arab Tunisian historian Ibn Khaldun recorded many legends about Dihya al-Kahina. They refer to her spectacular hair and great size and strength, all apparently characteristics of sorcerers, as well as descriptors of powerful Black women in those texts. One legend claims that in her youth, she freed her people from a brutal tyrant by agreeing to marry him and then murdering him on their wedding night.

Dihya became the war leader of the Imazighen tribes in the 680s (CE) and continued their opposition to the encroaching Arab Islamic armies of the Umayyad Dynasty. The Imazighen had lived through multiple waves of migration and colonization already: the Carthaginian, Roman, and Byzantine Empires had stretched their long arms across the land with acts of violence and destruction; also bringing new science and culture and ideas, some of which were inspiring to the Imazighen and which they adapted for their own use. Jews had been deported from Jerusalem for resisting the Roman Empire and many Imazighen converted to Judaism in this period. Many Imazighen also converted to

Christianity in Numidia of the fourth century. But the overall pattern seems to be that a wave of "civilization" would hit and then, in the face of resistance, wild weather, remoteness, terrain, the wave would slip back, lose hold, and the Imazighen would remain, bearing new tools and new scars, still tending to their people and their land.

In the seventh century, the Imazighen of Northwestern Africa were under the control of the Exarchate of Carthage, at that time a division of the Byzantine Empire. Umayyad General Hasan ibn al-Nu'man led the Arab Islamic armies as they took Egypt and then marched from Egypt and captured Carthage and other cities. When the Byzantine capital of Carthage fell, Dihya rallied the Imazighen tribes under her leadership.

She was so successful that when General Hasan went seeking his next conquest, he was told that the most powerful monarch in North Africa was the "Queen of the Berbers," Dihya, and so he led his armies into Numidia looking for a fight. In 698 CE, the armies met near Meskiana in present-day Algeria.[20] Dihya defeated Hasan so soundly that he fled Ifriqiya and holed up in Cyrenaica, licking his wounds for years.

Dihya's life is mostly known to us through Arab historians writing on the Muslim conquest of Africa, and then later through French historians and novelists who use her story to justify their own colonial stranglehold in Algeria.

Some historians claim she was a Jewish sorceress who descended from the Beta Israel community of Ethiopian Jews. She is said to have been a royal member of the Jarawa tribe within the larger confederacy known as the Zenata Tribe; a princess who became queen and ruled over an autonomous state in the area of the Aures Mountains in modern-day northeastern Algeria. Some sources claim that Dihya was a Christian and that she derived her power from a Christian icon she carried with her.

It's also been argued that she practiced the ancient Indigenous religion of the Imazighen, which centered around the veneration of the sun, moon, and ancestors. The stories of her prophetic powers are in keeping with Numidian ancient belief in which the gods, or the spirits of the dead, could communicate with members of the tribe who had the gift of prophecy.

Pomponius Mela, the earliest Roman geographer, reported that Imazighen considered the spirits of their ancestors to be like gods. After making requests, sending their questions over to the members of their family who stood along the other shore, they slept in their tombs to await responses in dreams.[21]

Herodotus wrote:

. . . they divine by visiting the sepulchral mounds of their ancestors and lying down to sleep upon them after having prayed; and whatsoever thing the man sees in his dream, this he accepts.[22]

And so a priestess with both the strength of will and skill to take the lives of those who would erase her—husbands or colonizers—and with the ears to hear and the sight to see the unknown country, might spend nights resting against the family burial mound. Watching the stars. Listening to Earth dream. Listening, in dreams, to the long line of people who brought her there, and listening also to the stones themselves.

If you knew the blade like Dihya did, would that give you a different kind of insight? If you live your life at the knife's edge and you learn to wield it to protect your life, does it cut a new seam for you to step through in your dreaming?

Yesterday, after writing about Dihya and knives, I took a break in the dreaming space, the otherworld space I have been making for myself in my mind and meditations. This is a core practice of hedge Witchcraft: you make a space in the unknown realm across the hedge, this is how hedge Witches go riding through the thin spaces. Going there in your mind makes a needlepoint stitch between overlapping worlds. In my meditation/imagination/travels yesterday, I saw small sparrows turn into bright yellow birds. Where they landed, flowers made of light sprouted from the ground, encircling me.

Then later, I was back in this room, in the real world, playing with my daughter, and the zipper on her lifejacket was stuck. I pulled out my knife to pop a small stone out of the stuck clasp and pull the zipper free.

Then I looked up. And there, just outside the window, in the branches at the edge of our lake, sat a tiny yellow bird, the likes of which I've never seen before. Except yesterday, across the hedge, in an ancestor dream.

We know that Indigenous ancestors in North Africa erected huge monolithic stone monuments that tracked the summer solstice and Orion's belt. Archeologists think that these sites brought people back together each year to a place in the desert where there once was a lake. People would come to make offerings, and share stories, and honor their ancestors, and perhaps meet them again, in dreams. Maybe these were places where things thin.

Dihya's gift of prophecy is said to have given her the ability to read the wind and the movement of birds. It gave her knowledge of how her opponents would gather troops, and what direction they would come from.

According to legend, during a battle, when she was outnumbered by the Arab forces and fell back, she ordered her army to set fires that were carried by wind directly into the path of the oncoming enemy. The Arab army was forced to retreat and the land was so badly burned that any future campaigns would have to cross an arid wasteland without resources to approach her.

According to the Arab historians and legends, her victory by fire gave Kahina the idea to initiate a scorched-earth policy on a larger scale. They say she believed that the coming army was only interested in the richness in the land, and so the smoking husk of earth left by her military ingenuity made her think that maybe if she destroyed the farms and gardens of what had been a granary of the Roman Empire, then the next wave of hungry colonizers would leave her people alone. According to this version, she therefore commanded her army to tear down the fortifications, destroy the cities and towns, melt down gold and silver. She ordered orchards cut, fields burned, and private gardens destroyed.

Some historians claim that this scorched-earth policy, which was designed to deprive the invading army, led to a loss of support from her people. So in the end she stood alone.

She allegedly engaged in this tactic to save her people, but for all those who lived in the towns and cities and relied on the fields and orchards, Dihya's policy would have been disastrous. In this version, resentment toward the queen replaced the loyalty and admiration, and her people turned against her.

But let's breathe here and feel the weight of a knife in our hands. Listen to both sides of the knife's edge. Think about who gets to carve history, and why, and what they will leave bleeding on the floor when they are done.

Because this story of Dihya's fires—told by historians several hundred years after the fact—raises doubts today. Arab armies repeatedly used the scorched-earth tactic as they moved across the region. In Egypt, Libya, and Mesopotamia, the invading Arab army routinely practiced this complete destruction to subdue the population. In fact, this was a common wartime tactic for colonizing armies. So maybe this destruction wasn't Dihya burning down her world out of fierce desperation. Maybe it was just another gaslighting act of colonization that later writers attributed to Dihya, using history for propaganda, blaming the widespread destruction on the Indigenous sorceress queen who led the resistance, in order to break the morale of her people and to cut them from her.

Either way, after the scorching of the earth, it's said that many of Dihya's former allies left her side, going over to Hasan, perhaps because they were broken-hearted and demoralized by the loss of all they had built, their homes and gardens, or because they were susceptible to bribery when they had little else left. One of her sons either defected or was captured. Under who knows what kind of pressure, he informed on his mother's battle plans.

In the early 700s CE al-Kahina again met Hasan in battle. Before the armies engaged, one story goes, she sent her two remaining sons to the enemy camp to be raised by Hasan as Muslim warriors. The battle went against Dihya from the beginning. She was badly outnumbered, and her children were gone.

Accounts vary concerning her death. She may have been captured and later executed, or she may have poisoned herself, but the most commonly accepted story is that she died in battle with her troops, still clutching her sword. I believe she died blade in hand, refusing to surrender.

Her head was cut off and brought to Hasan as a trophy. She was, according to Ibn Khaldun, 127 years old. Crone and warrior and queen.

Hasan supposedly respected Dihya as an opponent and so her sons, who converted to Islam, were well cared for and later led their own armies against others who resisted Arab aggression. Dihya's people, on the other hand, were brutalized. Between thirty and sixty thousand of them were sold into slavery by the conquerors and shipped far from home. Women killed themselves to avoid being taken into the kinds of prolonged torture, rape, and slavery that awaited them. Small pockets of resistance held out, but between 705 and 750 CE, North Africa was fully conquered and the people converted to Islam. Or, in the ways of colonized people, they crafted a syncretic faith to keep their secrets safe, woven within the elements of the settler faith they chose to keep. "The Tuareg retained elements of pre-Islamic cosmology and rituals, particularly Tuareg women. For example, Tuareg religious ceremonies contain allusions to matrilineal spirits, as well as to fertility, menstruation, the earth and ancestresses."[23] Religions and stories are tools, and we are very good at adapting them to our use.

After being used as a cautionary tale for what might happen to resistors, Dihya's story faded for a while into obscurity. Until, that is, she was seized upon by the French in the nineteenth century to support their own military maneuvering in Algeria. She was cast as a freedom fighter who could inspire resistance to Arab Muslim rule.

Imazighen history-tellers also reasserted their claim to her. She is their heroine, though others try to use her.

Since the ninth century, accounts of (Kahina) have been adopted, transformed, and rewritten by various social and political groups in order to advance such diverse causes as Arab nationalism, Berber ethnic rights, Zionism, and feminism. Throughout history, Arabs, Berbers, Muslims, Jews, and French colonial writers, from the medieval historian Ibn Khaldūn to the modern Algerian writer Kateb Yacine, rewrote the legend of the Kahina, and, in the process, voiced their own vision of North Africa's history.[24]

They used her life and resistance to lend themselves power. They used her in fiction and histories to voice their own views, rewriting the story of North Africa in the process. She became a conduit, a symbol, an icon, a weapon. A blade.

> *The French colonial experience in Algeria effectively cut off Algeria from its history. So the Kahina, in being politicized by various Algerian inhabitants in both the native and colonial populations, was evidence of an attempt to create a history that was becoming harder and harder to retain.*[25]

In the present day, Dihya al-Kahina's image is used by Imazighen activists to symbolize their own strength and independence. Her face peers at you from graffiti and sculptures around Algeria. She stands for the progressive ideals of the modern resistance—activists call for women's rights and claim secularism as an Indigenous value.

Tamazight activist Nuunja Kahina writes:

> *In both past and present, Imazighen have fought for the freedom to practice our culture and speak our language on our own land… The Kel Tamasheq, Indigenous to the Sahara, have risen up against the Malian and Nigerien governments in a quest for self-determination, which most recently culminated in the creation of a state of Azawad in early 2012. The secular Azawadien state, without outside support, fought against Islamist militants and was then invaded by French, Malian, and West African military forces . . . The struggle for Amazigh rights and to be recognized on our own land will continue until, as our name implies, we can truly be free people.*[26]

May Dihya the Kahina—Witch, organizer, freedom fighter—be a mighty ancestor for that struggle. And in that spirit, I'll add one more piece of the mythology to the altar. One contentious and little-known fragment about Dihya, one that sounds right to me, and so I'll keep it on the altar of Witch truths I've been missing, holds that she studied birds. Knew them intimately, advanced the people's knowledge of them, loved and honored them. A possible burial site of the seer queen shows evidence of these birds and her time spent with them. She was called Kahina—seer, priestess, Witch—because of her ability to see messages in the natural world that others couldn't predict, where armies would come from and how fire would move, so it makes sense to me that she had an intimacy with the hollow-boned and soaring. Creatures who migrated through the same lands her people had navigated for generations, and who, like her, had to rely on messages in the wind to make decisions about when to attempt dangerous crossings.

Desert birds have to be wise and far-seeing and adaptive to the wild edges of a hostile habitat. They are at the frontlines of system collapse as the surface water burns away, lakes disappear, hurricane seasons blow past all previous records, and the stretches of sand get too wide to cross.

Everywhere the fabric is thinning. The center cannot hold.[27] But buried in the sand, written in the margins of conflicting colonizer histories, there are icons for our healing and resistance. There are Witches who wield the blade to heal and to resist. Women who led by listening to birds, who knew their tools, who chose to fight, who died with their swords in their hands, and who speak to us still with that blade held high. Witches who stand like monoliths in the desert, symbolizing lakes that could return.

This figure echoes with another icon of Western Witchcraft and mythology: the Lady of the Lake, she who rises with the sword. She is a crucial figure, if only as an arm outstretched. She reverberates in Celtic and romantic traditions, emerging in Arthurian legend from her castle beneath the water to give Excalibur to Arthur, to learn magic from Merlin or to teach him, to find love and exact vengeance, and then to return beyond the edge. She is Nimuë and Viviane, she is part of a heritage of water priestesses and magical liminal women and goddesses like Brigid and Cerridwen. She is a hand extended from the place we cannot live. She lives in the world beyond, she pierces the veil, and she comes with a blade that changes the course of the world.

What we can see of Dihya's life is like looking through a scrapbook pasted together to serve other people's desires, or through a lake whose depths are obfuscated by reflections. The magic is that we know her at all. Her name slices through the archives like a knife exerting this: I exist. She is unbound by bias and history. She is one with the birds, and the Missing Witches and their sacred and daily knives, and with the deep wells and the disappearing waters. She still scares colonizers and gives her people hope. Murdered and used for centuries, we still speak her name.

Our lives are seeds, and even when we go back into the electric, pulsing, howling Earth and all her underground currents, we cannot and we will not be erased.

I want you to whisper her name to yourself and carry it with you. Dihya al-Kahina, Dihya the warrior, Dihya scholar of birds, Dihya the noble queen, Dihya the beautiful gazelle, Dihya the Witch with a blade. She is an icon for all those who would resist the death of diversity, the desertification of the world. Saying her name, whispering it to our knives, we sanctify them to be with us for our work, and this ties us to the struggle for the sacred lands of the Imazighen, and to the struggle for liberation for Black and Indigenous women all over the world.

She offers the wings of this truth: the stories others tell about you do not touch your fundamental power. You are a wave of light and sound. You can cut through the cords that bind you and carve your own life. You are unbound.

When I look up again, the rain has stopped and in the gray sky, a falcon rides the thermals of the mountains that make this small bowl of a lake. The razor-taloned falcons returned last year, maybe part of that great animal migration pushing at our edges as the borders closed, the curfew came down, and the people stayed inside afraid to be cut down by the virus that stalked us everywhere. Pandemics are an inevitable byproduct of the death of diversity. Viruses evolve quickly to rage through monocultures. The falcons make me gasp with joy, and they make me think of Dihya and all Witches called to contract with the knife, the sword, the blade, the needle. Sharp and cutting claws and beak, taloned beasts, linchpins in diverse ecosystems. Turn your back on us at your peril.

The knife channels our power and focuses it like a point of light and fire. Its message is that what's cut can't be uncut, pieces can't always be mended, a life can't be untaken, our power is real and thriving and life-giving and deadly. We choose every moment of our lives to weave and stitch and heal and defend all that is living and good, and to have hope and to stay on this side of the blade.

Maybe that's part of why some people start cutting themselves.

Under the immense pressure of trauma—and we are alive in a traumatized time—we can be choked, numbed, ensnared by an agony of emotion that can't find a voice or a way out of our bodies. We are like animals, wild in a trap. A knife, a sharp edge, calls to us to break the surface of things, even of our own skin when we know agony, rage, shame, fury lurk beneath. Fuck fake perfection; give me blood and scars.

But cutters know, at the end of the day, this route on its own offers no relief. Cutting without art, community, ritual, therapy becomes another infuriating trauma-habit on repeat. If this is you or someone you know, wanting to feel something, and looking for an outlet for your pain and for your power, know this: you can take up sharp edges to get free. Callie told us that the hand poke tattoo community emphasizes safety and cleanliness and that this practice can be a destigmatized way to experience embodying. Learn to tattoo by tattooing yourself and making its pain part of your practice of awakening and ritual making. Un-numbing. Reawakening to your blood and pain and agency. Tattoo needles, sewing needles, knitting needles, knives can all be turned to ritual purposes, world-building purposes, ways to emerge from trauma and clear a path for your voice and your power. Find your way home to the community you deserve. Whether you take up tattooing or a ritual sword, knitting, stitching, or carving, I hope that careful dance of muscles and sharp edges brings you home to your body, to your empowered self, to the altar of this one life.

Ritual

On the night of the April New Moon, Aries Moon, sanctify your blade. Head to the woods, or someplace in nature where you will be safe and uninterrupted. If that place is not available to you, just be safe somewhere. Take a knife or sharp implement that will be able to symbolize for you the ways you have been hurt and have caused hurt. Bring your cutting tools, and tools for writing, along with a few plants that speak to you of fire: cinnamon, dandelions, eucalyptus, pine. Bring aloe too if you can, or something that cools and soothes you, perhaps a moisturizer you like or even a piece of cucumber. Bring a bowl, clean water and a cloth, and a lighter or matches. Bring that deeply trusted friend who is always with you: Shadow You, who would burn the world down if they thought it was what you needed. They can be clumsy, but they love you with their whole self, and nothing you tell them can shock them.

Carve a circle in the ground big enough for you to sit in with your tools. Carve it with intention. You are turning this knife to its new life, and yourself too, and it begins with this act. You could chant to yourself: "In this womb works one so dear, naught but true can enter here." Make the circle, sit inside. Breathe.

Inside the circle, call out to Earth, Air, Fire, and Water; North, South, East, and West. Anchor your safety with the love and protection that the circle creates all around you. Remember: the circle is where the unseen sphere of protection meets the earth. The knife draws the meeting place between seen and unseen. It makes a meeting point for our mind and the lunar communal mind. But the sphere is beyond the circle, the sphere itself radiates above you and below. It contains you completely.

Picture the sphere of light and sing to it. Build it with your breath and resonance. Even if it's just a low growl, sound reverberates around the sphere, within your bones, down the length of the blade. Nothing can enter that does not have your greatest joy and most beautiful life at heart, and everything inside is harmonized to that purpose.

Burn a fire plant—like cinnamon or a sprig of dried pine or eucalyptus—in a safe way in a small cauldron or hollow in the soil. Bathe yourself and the knife and your pen in the smoke. Cut into the earth again, not deeply, enough to carve a symbol that compels you to tell the truth. I always use the sigil Raidho; for me she is horses running free and powerful, and she is tied to my own name—R for Risa—she is yours to use too if you like. Carve a symbol that works for you. You could say something like: "Spirit take the hand of my Shadow, tell the truth tell the truth tell the truth, lance it like a wound." When you are ready, invite your Shadow to tell the story that cuts you. She can write it with your hand, or speak it aloud with your voice. Either way she will be your witness. Inside the safety of the circle, let her tell the truth. Care for her as she finds the words, tend to her as they flow like so much blood. What your agony means, why it started, what is the source. The words have to come out, they are cutting you up inside, spinning endlessly like infinite arrows and needles and knives, death by a thousand cuts, a black hole, all-consuming. There is no judgment in the circle. Telling the truth is the only thing that will begin to relieve the pressure, and you begin by telling yourself. Don't assume you know anything about this until you put it all in words; let them pour out, strange and unfettered and sharp and gross and glittering, the circle can hold it all.

The secret I had to learn the hard way is this: You only learn how to hold a sacred boundary once you've cut through to the ugly horrible truth. You can't skip that part. I thought I would be safer if I kept it contained and controlled, but it was only as I freed my voice and told the truth to myself about myself and my world that I unleashed my sacred No. If you read *The Voyage of the Dawn Treader* as a kid, picture the kid cutting himself out of the dragon he had become; taking a sword to layer after layer of scales and leathery hide, until he has freed his vulnerable self again.

Write or talk until your words run out into howls or sobs, and offer those to the sphere of the earth and the sky as well. This is not a ritual that's one and done; this is a space you can come back to whenever you need to. A ring of fire that is here for you to burnish yourself like a blade again whenever you need it.

Afterward, if you wrote your truth out, you can burn the paper, or give it to the person who needs to know, or cut it into tiny pieces, or bury it within the circle grounds.

Then take the knife and place it in the bowl, and pour the water over it. Picture the water flowing through sky and stream and all of life, picture it holding your blood and pain and the whole truth of your story, and who you are and have been, and who you might be as well. The water goes everywhere, is in everything. Add your cooling ingredient—aloe, cucumber, fresh herbs or grasses—to the water to cool and heal the blade; rub it gently, and rub aloe on your skin too. Pour the water out upon the earth.

Lay down your tools carefully, gently. Sit in the circle and rest. Feel the wind, the breath of the world, touch your smallest hairs. Feel the pleasure that is possible on your skin, the gentleness in your hands. Feel all the Witches who love you and are protecting you across generations. Feel the spirit eyes of all your most loving kin across a hundred thousand generations. When you are ready to leave, thank the corners and sweep the circle away. Carry your knife with you whenever you can from now on, cool and sanctified, or leave it in a safe and loved spot on your altar. Hone and balance it whenever you can; you can hone it along the edge of another knife; nothing special is required. Use it, build up your confidence by cutting yarn, cords, dead branches for forest art, foraged medicine.

When you are ready—and this is crucial—go and find a Witch you can trust, a therapist or teacher or aunt or friend, and tell them the story too. Say what needs to be said out loud. And hold your head high when you do so. You are a beautiful and powerful Witch, one of generations of brutalized and traumatized beings, sitting at the cataclysmic edge of the world, calling your healing and heroism out from the mound, out from the dark of the moon. Hone your blades and your truths, and honor your warrior ancestors. You are a knife that will change the future.

Incantation

I cut the fabric of the world.
I carve the circle.
I craft the real.
I cut the bindings that are unseen.
My voice is sharp.
My hands are free.
I cut the fabric of the world.
I craft the real.

2

New Moon in Taurus

The Body

**This circle is led by Risa
*with expansions by Amy.***

*The Moon is exalted in Taurus, according to traditional dignity schemes.
That means Luna is held aloft in this sign, enthroned in a seat of honor.
(Really all that means is the Moon is empowered to do its job in Taurus—to
nurture, nourish, care, and feel things.) Taurus is an earth sign, so this
lunation has a tactile, sensual quality. It's the almost indecent scent of
oud, rubbed into the hollow of your elbow. It's placing a velvet square of
chocolate on your tongue and waiting for it to melt.*

—ELIZA ROBERTSON, ASTROLOGER

THIS CHAPTER IS AN OFFERING FOR THE MAY NEW MOON IN TAURUS.
Taurus rules the second house, a house of all that is material, embodied. And so we come home. For this new moon, we turn our attention to our bodies. How we move through the world and also how the world moves through us. The nervous system is a vast web of sensors. The lymphatic system is a network of vessels that carry a clear fluid called lymph toward the heart. This fluid that moves through us takes its name from lympha, the deities of freshwater. Lympha bring inspiration, even a creative frenzy, one that can overturn all acceptable behavior and social norms. We carry within us a vast network of sizzling vessels that alchemize what comes into contact with our porous selves and bring it inward, to the heart.

> *The heart itself has recently been discovered not to be a mass of muscle, but rather a "helicoidal myocardial band" that has spiraled in upon itself, creating its unique shape and its separate chambers. . . Pair this with discoveries that the heart functions as an endocrine gland, has its own nervous system that makes and releases its own neurotransmitters, and emits an electromagnetic field that is far stronger than the brain's, and we begin to move from the idea that the heart is simply a mechanical pump. It is a spiraling organ of perception."*[1]

Our bodies run with sacred water, they beat and thrum and inflate and spiral, they are the rider and the chariot. And no matter our age or state of wellness, they are absolutely ripe with power.

Begin with the most powerful body spell I know: love. Gently smooth your hand across your face to remove the masks you wear and love the self beneath. Smell your inner elbow and send love to your own unique perfume, the very chemical essence of your living body.[2] Cradle your belly and tell all the beautiful, animal forms within you how you love them, their softness, their strength. Love your knees and feet, love your thighs, love the geometry of you, all the work this body does, which would exhaust your poor brain utterly if it had to figure it all out consciously. We are full of unconscious harmony. No matter how sick or frail or traumatized we are, this body is our only home, and it is a home of companionship shared by beings numbering at an estimated 39 trillion—microbial cells including bacteria, viruses, and fungi.[3] Members of our coven told us they began to identify with they/them pronouns when the reality of that constant companionship sunk in. All across our skin and within, we are alive with diversity. Tend to them with love, and this love will be a spell that eases you through the body-numbing trauma of a world in crisis.

All Witches carry a body memory of trauma. "The burning of witches, heretics, and healers was a favored scene for discrediting feminine knowledge about bodies and terrorizing its healing effervescence, and its strength as a technology of friendship between women."[4] Knowledge of the body as a technology of friendship has been terrorized for women; Black, Indigenous, and all colonized people; Queer and Trans people; and for white men too, honestly: brutalized into often lonely lives as providers and/or weapons. But in the depths of our DNA, in our deep time memories, in our very bodies, we can come home to a different possibility. We flood with power in our dancing feet and pulling fingers, in the potency of breast milk, menstrual blood, sweat, cum, and tears.

I want to offer that although rituals are powerful and spells can summon the unexpected, there is no need of special instruction or initiation. All you need is your hands, your eyes, and the constant infinity loop drawn between your lungs and the churning, sporulated air of the entire world . . .

Your body is an ancestor. Your body is an altar to your ancestors. Every one of your cells holds an ancient and anarchic love story. . . . You are threaded through with fossils. Your microbiome is an ode to bacterial legacies you would not be able to trace with birth certificates and blood lineages. You are the ongoing-ness of the dead.[5]

The body is birth, death, and decay. It is the house of Spirit and of shit, and all our stories dwell here. Learning to work magic with your body is not a straight path, because nothing about the body is straight. We are curvy.

Sometimes this magic can mean raising up with joy a heart-pounding euphoria. Sometimes it can mean being dragged through remembered pain, shame, and humility to swarm in that feeling and burst out the other side. Either way, body magic works when we learn to listen to ourselves, replete with ancestors.

In 2017, Earthbound Futures formed around the idea of bringing new bodies and narratives into the wrestling ring. The founders, Skye, Tanya, and Marie, were drawn to the power of wrestling, its entangled bodies and epic narratives. As artists, they wanted to play with disrupting wrestling's usual use and understanding of human bodies—narratives so reliant on the same old two-dimensional identity of the male gaze. They wanted to explore the ring as a site for personal and cultural mythmaking. What does it mean to craft Queer futures for real bodies? But their progress was spun sideways. The call to change was undeniable, and the "call was coming from inside the house."[6]

Skye woke up with completely debilitating chronic pain, lost her apartment, moved across the country to be able to collapse into full-time family care. Skye says gender is fluctuating for them, but right now the pronouns they are feeling are they/them. When we spoke, they were in a mode of flux but also building new foundations. New growths, new tree rings. They mourned their life and autonomy, and they were rewriting their life story as a Queer wrestler and mythmaker in a body they didn't recognize. For Skye, this experience, while it brought with it monumental loss and rage and sorrow, also opened up new ways of understanding the kinds of story they could be telling with their body, both in the ring, and beyond:

> Something I am learning from disability justice advocates is that there's no healing for me if there's not healing for the larger systems in the world . . . That's the queering of the hero's journey for me: I don't want to fight something. I want to get together with other people and

creatively destroy the systems and the structures that are keeping the world inaccessible and keeping us sick and making us sick.[7]

Around the same time, Tanya broke a generational spell and decided to grow a beard she'd spent a lifetime hiding. She'd fought to keep the facial hair away, to fit in, and to keep her real, spectacular self hidden in straight lines for years. And it didn't work, and it made her angry and tired, and so finally she stopped. The stopping itself was exhausting. She had to slow down and feel her way through the exhaustion of being something new in almost every space she entered. But this radical mode of embracing her body exactly as it is, she says, connected her with a memory web of missing bodies.

I feel like I'm trying to get in touch with a body that society has tried to make me dissociate from in so many ways. Growing a beard at 11 was so confusing. It was such a big secret, a secret that I've been hold-ing on to, I was 32 when I started growing my beard and when I did that I feel like I unlocked all my queer ancestors. Be who you are. Smash that binary. I'm a bearded woman. I embody both energies.[8]

Tanya and Skye are in the great spectrum of people who identify as Witches. They center their art and performance and community-building practice around ritual and personal mythmaking. The ways their bodies turned their artistic practice inside out led directly to expo-nential leaps in growth and impact for Earthbound Futures. After these body rebellions, they received their first grant directly from the city of Montreal and launched an 2SLGBTQ+[9] youth summer camp in 2021 centered around queering the hero's journey, creating empowered new narratives from a place of body diversity and disability activism, and cre-ating a protective circle that they wish had been there for them; a ring of binary-smashing loving-kindness.

Self-acceptance became both a healing spell and a prosperity spell. All our work is ancestor work.

Their bodies led the Earthbound Futures founders to craft wildly new spaces of safety and creation, that respect difference and personal capacity, and that hold space for the truth of what happens to bodies beyond the harmful delusion of positivity thinking, love and light.

Sophie Strand writes of trying to heal from childhood sexual abuse with therapists who tried to help her remove the memories, forget the pain and trauma, scrub her mind as well as her gut where the trauma had found a body seat:

> *The turning point in my life came when I realized that the health-iest metaphor for me wasn't light, or soap, or ascent. It was compost. It wasn't "clean." It was everything. Refuse. Dirt. Fungi. Bacteria. Water. Grubs. Worms. And remarkably, it was fertile. It made soil. It supported new green shoots. My gut didn't need another dose of anti-fungal medication to remediate the problem created by antibiotics. Cleaning was killing me. I needed to compost my body. And I needed to compost my spirit. I needed to add more microbes, more foods to my diet. I needed to add herbal lore and indigenous knowledge and folk-tales and children's books and romance novels back into my philosoph-ically neutered world view. And I needed to approach psychological wounding not with a scalpel and hydrogen peroxide, but with flow-ers and joy and laughter. I needed to overwhelm the pain, not try to get rid of it. I didn't need to "integrate" the abuse. I needed to softly place it in dark soil. I needed to say, "Okay. You're nasty. But please make something grow."*[10]

We can't escape our trauma or our bodies any more than we can escape Earth by taking millionaires on trips into the atmosphere in phallic rocket ships stuffed with stolen taxes.

Amy: Judy Grahn told us, "This [movement] is Earth centered—we don't care if they want to rocket off to Mars. Goodbye."[11]

Hildegard of Bingen was a twelfth-century nun who lived with chronic illness and took her constant screaming pain and rode it like the wind to new vision. She gave us songs and visions of the unknown elec-tric that moves through our minds, cultures, and through flocks of star-lings and fields of honey mushrooms. She shone even in the dark with what she called the *Living Light.* Or in other contexts *The Greenness.*

Hildegard was walled up in a monastery and had funeral rites read over her when she was given by her parents to the church, a custom for tenth children that came with her dowry and her complicated, quiet pain. She doesn't tell us much about this time, but she would argue against the practice of child oblates later on in life, so we can assume it wasn't positive.

She was under the tutelage of a fourteen-year-old named Jutta behind those walls. I feel sympathy for Jutta; she starved herself and wore a chain against her skin that dug into her flesh. Hildegard didn't follow in her mentor's path of self-denial or self-harm, and I love that in a time when those body behaviors were popularized by the church, especially for women, this isolated young visionary took a different path entirely, one that loved eating and drinking and being in the world. She soothed her chronic pain with beauty and community. She gathered women and wrote music and books. Buried in the dark, she found a voice within her full of power.

Hildegard said she was anxious every single day of her life. Every single day.

Amy: This is me too. And it comes from my body and brain, waves of nausea, skies of impending doom. And it comes from my Grandmother, strands of DNA and a million years of ancestral information. I didn't know that Grandma had spent some time in "the loony bin" as it was eventually described to me. One didn't talk about such things back then . . . and when they did, they used terms like loony bin *. . . I inherited from her a dysfunctional thyroid, a brain exhausted from battling demons. It would have been useful to know, as I navigated my own path through the dark. My grandmother was psychic, though she tried to hide it, like her story had been hidden from me. One didn't talk about such things back then . . . As my mother tells it now, if Grandma was tired, she might let something slip. Mum arrived home one day to find Grandma napping. She said, "You'll never guess what I bought!" And without opening her eyes Grandma replied, "a tea set." I didn't inherit this power. The power I did inherit from Grandma is that I always know when someone is lying. It's a blessing and a curse. And maybe that's why Grandma and I are anxious. Because we know we have to face the truth at all times.*

When in need, I reach out to her to be with me, and I'm calmed. I know she gets it. It's in our DNA.

And it was from within this relentless body knowledge of anxiety that Hildegard knew the world.

Hildegard's theology is intensely incarnational . . . The human body is a microcosm of the cosmos, which Hildegard conceives as an ordered, harmonious whole. Her mystical vision of the universe is not a top-down hierarchy, but a cosmic egg with interconnected, nested layers—the earth at its heart.[12]

An incarnational theology understands the universe through our own body, and at the center of that body is the Earth-heart. Hildegard was punctured with eternity, attuned. Her anxiety didn't remove her from the world; it drew her out like nerves extending into the natural world, noticing how it weaves through us. As above, so below. Her transcendent noticing came from a particular experience of being in a body.

From my early childhood, before my bones, nerves and veins were fully strengthened, I have always seen this vision in my soul, even to the present time when I am more than seventy years old. In this vision my soul, as God would have it, rises up high into the vault of heaven and into the changing sky and spreads itself out among different peoples . . . I see them wide awake, day and night. And I am constantly fettered by sickness, and often in the grip of pain so intense that it threatens to kill me, but God has sustained me until now.[13]

She connects her vision, spread out into the changing sky and among different people, to her body's physical experience of constant pain.

And it makes me think of what occupational therapist, doula, and neurodivergent Witch Charlie Watts told us about her experiences with highly sensitive kids. I asked why she thought we were seeing more and more kids with Highly Sensitive Person (HSP) diagnoses. She cautioned that there may be a perceived increase in kids experiencing these conditions—feeling overwhelmed by lights, sounds, and smells; being bothered by their clothing tags or textures; noticing small changes in their environment or in people's attitudes; feeling intimately connected to the changing sky and other people—because of increased awareness and diagnosis. But with her Witch-brain, she also wondered if this increase in sensitivity is tangled up with the universe expanding: all of us, everything, being stretched thin. Minute spaces opening up between our molecules, letting more of the other pour in.

Those are the words I used to describe myself for years, funnily enough: stretched thin. Nerves pulled to the point of being porous. Every light and sound rushed in, and I was overwhelmed and nauseous all the time.

When we spoke, Sophie Strand told us:

I have a genetic connective tissue disease. I found this out after I had loved fungi and underground mycorrhizal systems for many years, which are the connective tissue of the soil. And for me it felt like this pivot point where I could become very solipsistic and feel very bad about myself or I could see how I could become a channel for something else that perhaps understood me. How can we become a channel for another species knowing that perhaps it won't be pleasurable . . . all we'll be able to know is like the carpenter ant, we are climbing up that piece of grass, we are sporulating something we aren't totally in control of.[14]

Sophie says that when she faced this death armed with this idea of sporulating, she started to share all her writing everywhere; it didn't matter anymore that she follow the conventions of going through literary journals and magazines. She just wanted to "make good soil." This reminds me of Hildegard, taken up into the vault of heaven and into the eyes of different people in order to write utterly new music, share an incarnational theology, and share something she wasn't in control of either.

How can we surrender to these bodies, to all our unknown companions and desires, to make of ourselves good soil for the re-enchantment?

I struggled for a long time, wanting to talk about chronic pain and what that experience had made me think about body, mind, and magic but not finding words. Because these thoughts don't take word shapes. I feel them in my small hairs when the breeze blows.

I had a migraine that lasted ten years. Like Hildegard, I experienced migraine auras, trails of light, and patches of darkness blanking out my vision; what Oliver Sacks describes as "a shower of phosphenes in transit across the visual field, their transit being succeeded by a negative scotoma," or, as Hildegard puts it, "a great star most splendid and beautiful, and with it an exceeding multitude of falling stars which with the star followed Southward . . . And suddenly they were all annihilated."[15]

Though the migraine stopped, sometimes the light show still happens. Once it happened as I walked through the farmer's market on my way to Amy's house when we both used to live in Montreal. I crept the final blocks hugging the shade and then sat in the dark and cried, terrified that the pain would come back. When the waves of light come these days, I want to find a dark and quiet place and curl up into a ball and hide from the paralysis that lurks, but instead, following the advice of another Witch, dancer, and occupational therapist, I move gently like waves, like leaves. I sway. I might curl up, but I will also unfurl. I come home to the inner cosmos of my body and all her unseen companions and follow them from sway to stand, to a slow walk, to feet in the grass, hands brushing trees, I walk the rosary of the lake and my breath eases deeper, and it feels like my mind comes home to the earth in my heart at the center of my cosmos.

In the Introduction to *Hildegard von Bingen's Mystical Visions*, Matthew Fox writes:

> *Hildegard does not lay out her theology of wisdom abstractly. It was won by her at the cost of great pain—physical, emotional, spiritual, psychological, political. Often sick, often misunderstood, often put down by males of privilege in a church that was sexist, Hildegarde knew what pain meant, she had tasted it. Her response included a mature anger, a moral outrage at what she called the multiple imperfections of the Church. And a second response was a personal recycling of pain. "One is able to be saved through the bitter price of pain."[16]*

Hildegard was saved through pain, not by starving herself like Jutta, but by being gentle with herself while traveling through the portal that pain opened into a perspective that vastly multiplied her vision. The great lesson that pain taught me was empathy. I see the way pain bends people's minds because it's like a mirror of that decade in my own mind. For me, this is at the crux of thinking of the body as a tool for revolutionary magic. Your body, in all its frailty and excess, leakage and renewal, is genetically as well as experientially tied to *every* body. Feel your way and you will find each other.

Pain isn't all grit-building visions and redemption, of course. It also fragmented my focus so I couldn't properly plan or handle logistics. Pain acts like hunger on the brain; we narrow to our snapping reptile selves. Skye of Earthbound Futures said what eased her pain was to revel in the senses. Listen to the body if it wanted to stop and smell the flowers. Pain connects you to all pain, and also all awe and pleasure. Hildegard wasn't a visionary just because of pain, but because she listened through it. It brought her to share a vision that had room for both pleasure and joy in a way that was completely challenging to the church and to patriarchy, and that vision gives us clues for enchanting a world beyond the violence and economic and environmental disasters of late-stage capitalism.

Matthew Fox writes:

The building of a house of wisdom in ourselves as individuals and in community with other humans and all other creatures of our earth is, for Hildegard, the essential task of personhood and citizenship. It is the setting up of the unfurled divine tent that exists in all creation and in every human being. Since it is the common task we are all called to, this enterprise and none other is the source of community—the communio—the common task which will render us a whole, living, breathing, celebrating, forgiving, justice making, compassionate and wise people. This is why we were born. It is worth the struggle.[17]

The building of a shared house of wisdom in community with all creatures of the earth is why we were born.

Burn this on my soul, make it the refrain for all my songs, encode it in my every spell. This is what my body is here to do, what it yearns for in all its breaths and heartbeats.

We were born to build a shared house of wisdom in community with all creatures of the earth.

Writing this chapter, I followed the light on the lake to the mountain on the other side. I spent a day up to my elbows in roots and soil and mycelium, digging plastic out of my neighbor's stream. I carried huge swaths of the stuff down the mountain. I came home and canceled an interview I had lined up for a high-paying job in advertising. I'm trying to listen. I repeat one of my few remaining prayers: oh my body, make me of service to Earth. "Oh my body, make of me always a woman who listens."[18]

I learn a lot from Hildegard, but let's cast that spell that is the truth: Hildegard is a problematic ancestor who would have been pretty unhappy to be called Witch. She was firmly on the side of the Church and its doctrine—her very safety depended on it. For example, she echoes some classically homophobic things, even while writing of her profound love for her female student, Richardis. Richardis died two years after leaving the abbey at the insistence of her brother and family, and she died wishing she had never left Hildegard's side.

Hildegard also used her voice and position to whip up crusades against the Cathar heretics in 1161 CE when the Church had already begun a campaign to associate their heresy—indeed all heresy and Witchcraft—and homosexuality.

> *The first explicit allegation of homosexuality against the heretics was made in 1116, concerning the Henricians. From that time onward we hear more and more frequently that the heretics copulated vir cum viris (man with man) and femina cum feminis (woman with woman). In 1209 Pope Innocent authorized the Crusade against the Albigensians in France, a policy which resulted in nearly total genocide throughout the southern part of the country, and by the time the Inquisition would finish its work in the seventeenth century, several million heretics and homosexuals had been burned at the stake.[19]*

The Church allied with early capitalism to enclose land and burn bodies, and Hildegard used her power to set that blaze alight. While she listened to the wind and transcribed what she saw when her body was used by Spirit, she didn't take that other step of putting her body on the line for the sake of community with all other beings. I don't judge her for it, but I want to find and sing out stories of women who did take their bodies to that further place.

~~~

Amy and I are happy tree-huggers. We are proud to be among those people who know the great calm of resting your heart and face against a tree, and who want to live out among them all the time, and blend our dreams with theirs.

The original tree huggers were Bishnoi women, leaders from a small spiritual minority in the Himalayan foothills. September 11 is National Forest Martyrs Day in India in their honor. This story of tree huggers, of women who used their bodies to make a portal to safety for the trees, is the story of Amrita Devi and Gaura Devi, who lived and put their bodies on the line for trees three hundred years apart in the Marwar desert region of western Rajasthan.

The Bishnoi sect was founded by Guru Maharaj Jambaji in 1485 CE. Of the twenty-nine principles laid down by Jambaji as fundamental for the sect, eight were prescribed to preserve biodiversity. For a Bishnoi woman, both prayers and service to the land and animals are part of daily ritual. They dig the soil and make sure that the nearby clean water remains in good condition to welcome birds. On every new moon, Bishnoi observed a collective lighting of holy fire. Other principles describe how to achieve healthy social behavior; live a simple truthful life; be content and moderate; avoid false arguments, don't criticize others.

The first of the twenty-nine Bishnoi principles, though, concerns women's bodies: they are prohibited from participating in rituals for thirty days after childbirth and for five days during menstruation.

I want to tell Amrita and Gaura's story with full awe and curiosity about their faith, but I also want to be honest about my gut-sense here:

if you are barred from connecting with Spirit when at any stage of your internal moon, blood, or birth cycle, or because you have a cycle, or certain chromosomes at all, call me Witch if you like, but I'm going to say that that particular regulation comes from man.

Your voice and offerings matter. Always. Your body and mind, wrenched open by the vulnerability of blood and pain, womb-world cracking open to unleash something new—all this is fierce and holy. You *are* that power that religion calls Nature and science calls God. Taking that power away from menstruating bodies and replacing it with shame has spiraling effects: keeping girls out of school and shaping how we think about what their lives are worth. Rajasthan holds the record in India for the highest percentage of married girls between the ages of ten and fourteen, which is below the age of consent and is child rape. This is not unique to the Bishnois. Child marriage is currently legal in forty-four American states, and between 2000 and 2018, nearly three hundred thousand minors were legally married in the United States. The vast majority of these marriages were between a minor girl and an adult man.[20] In some states, minors cannot legally divorce or leave their spouse, and domestic violence shelters typically don't accept minors, leaving these solitary, trafficked children trapped.[21] Patriarchy weighs its heavy choking hold everywhere. Nevertheless, we persist.[22]

In 1730, almost three hundred years after the twenty-nine principles were recorded, the king sent soldiers to fell timber from the forest near a village where Bishnoi villagers preserved and worshiped the acacia trees. When the soldiers began to chop away at the trees, the Bishnois protested but were ignored. Cutting or injuring trees, especially acacia, is against Bishnoi dharma. So Amrita Devi hugged a tree. She cried out that if she sacrificed her life to save just one tree, it would be a good bargain.

And the men axed through her body to cut the tree. They beheaded her in front of her children, and her three daughters wrapped themselves around trees to honor her in their grief, and they were murdered also.

The news spread; children ran to get help. That day, 363 Bishnoi people became martyrs to the forest. The soil of Khejarli is said to have turned red with their blood. When the king heard the news, he called for it to stop. He apologized to the community and issued a decree prohibiting forever the cutting of trees and hunting of animals within and near Bishnoi villages. That protection is still technically valid today, though Bishnois are constantly forced to fight to protect their rights and these small islands of biodiversity.

Hundreds of years later, the Bishnoi sacrifices became the inspiration for a much larger environmental movement in India. With Amrita Devi's last act, she imparted a wave of power that electrified Gaura Devi in her own fierce spell of tree protection generations down the line.

Born in 1925, Gaura Devi left her family and moved to a village named Reni after her wedding at the age of twelve. Her husband passed away by the time their son was about two, leaving her alone to raise her son and be the family's sole provider.

In 1974 the state government authorized the felling of 2,500 trees in Reni. Landslides were devastating the foothill regions because too many trees had been taken already. The forest was being partitioned with logging work sold to contractors from the plains who had no idea what was at stake.

The people held peaceful demonstrations, public meetings, and rallies. Frustrated, the government and contractors hatched a scheme to draw the local men away under the false pretense of a payout. While the men were gone from Reni, the state sent a group of forest officials and loggers to take the trees.

A young girl from the village saw them approaching and rushed to Gaura Devi, whose experiences had drawn her into community work and made her a leader in forest protection and women's rights in the region. Gaura had started campaigns in the nearby villages inspired by the Chipko Movement. Chandi Prasad Bhatt, a pioneering Gandhian grassroots activist, mobilized communities to stop the destruction of the forests under the banner of Chipko, inspired by Amrita Devi. He was joined by hundreds of women who were on the front lines of the resistance because they were on the frontlines of the devastation. Rallying to protect their community forests, they formed human chains to hug towering old-growth trees.[23]

That night in Reni, with all the local men gone, Gaura Devi mobilized a group of twenty-seven women and confronted the loggers. She tried to reason with them, but by then the officials were drunk, and they yelled and waved their guns at the women and kids and ordered the loggers to chop the trees. Gaura Devi called out to the people to hug their trees, and the women followed her lead and wrapped themselves around them.

And this time the men didn't murder the tree huggers. They were shaken, and they delayed. Gaura Devi spoke to the laborers, "Brothers, this forest is our mother's home, it keeps us alive and we run our lives through this. You can have your food and then come along with us."[24] The contractors tried to scare the women into changing their minds but the women stayed the night and guarded the trees.

After a four-day impasse, the contractors left. Shortly after, the state government complied with the villagers' demands and issued a ten-year ban on commercial deforestation in the area.

This incident would go on to define the Chipko Movement.

After the incident, Gaura Devi kept on mobilizing women to organize protests and rallies, but because she was illiterate, she was never included in conversations about the preservation of forests by policymakers.

Dismissed, disappeared, demeaned, excluded, we still have this: we can wrap our bodies around the lives we must defend. We can use our lives to find and resound with the voices we've been missing.

As Carol Padberg, founding director of the Nomad MFA, said to the audience we assembled for a 2021 Virtual Samhain Circle:

Notice what beings are calling you, are tapping on your shoulders, because I think we are living in a time when the tree ones, winged ones, water ones, and those who are no longer breathing are reaching out to us, so listen, respond and play . . . remember the capacity you have through your senses.[25]

How we interact with the world shapes it. Our bodies are universes. Our acts and gestures and impulses play cause-and-effect games with other bodies, caught in other drags and uplifts, slipping through other stages in the lifecycle of inertia becoming around us.

Witches listen.

Skye of Earthbound Futures told us that chronic pain and illness taught her to slow down and become a listening ally to her body, and in this way, to be with all bodies in pain or strangled by inequity. The constraint of pain taught her none of us is free until we are all free. The chronic pain body becomes a channeling body, a kind of instrument for hearing silent screaming.

We can practice listening to the singing within, and the voices beyond, and put our bodies in the places and states where we hear them. We can become a kind of door.

Lucille Clifton was a twelve-fingered woman, her mother and daughter too. Doctors removed their extra fingers, but those invisible extensions reached beyond the body into Lucille's imaginary world. From a house in Baltimore, Lucille began to hear the voices of her ancestors.

Lucille was the first poet to have two books up for the Pulitzer at the same time. Her grandmother was a child when she was taken from Africa and enslaved. Lucille was a warrior poet, a radical listener. She was from Dahomey women. Her book *Two-Headed Woman* tells the story of being born with a twelfth finger: "our wonders were cut off... now we take what we want with invisible fingers."[26]

Witches, we take what we want with invisible fingers.

I interviewed Marina Magloire in April of 2021, and it was in preparing for that interview that I first encountered Lucille. Magloire is writing the missing book on Lucille, and she shared a piece of her incredible story in this article for *Paris Review*:

> *In the seventies and eighties, the Clifton's Baltimore home became a spiritual way station through which a wide assortment of spirits apparently passed. Despite her fame as a poet, Clifton's trajectory as a self-described "two-headed woman" is a little-known part of her legacy. "Two-headed woman" is a traditional African American term used to describe women gifted with access to the spirit world as well as to the material world.*[27]

Two-Headed Woman is also the name of Clifton's first channeled book of poetry, written at the same time as her unpublished journals of spirit writing or automatic writing, where she received messages that became woven into her world view and her poems. Marina writes:

> *In August and September of 1978, for example, Clifton received a series of dire warnings about the fate of the human world from a mysterious group of spirits she called "the Ones.". . . They returned "to remind human beings that they are more than flesh," and to share a warning that the time is running out to save the world from a thousand years without the memory that life, love, truth IS."*[28]

Somehow these are connected: missing fingers, second heads, beings that are more than flesh, and the truth that *love IS*. This is a thought I want to use to think new thoughts with. "The children are repeating, we will wear new bones again."[29]

Lucille is mighty with her listening, she is a poet medium Witch who, in her very body, knows truths about the world. Lucille wrote that "writing is a way of continuing to hope," and that "perhaps for me it is a way of remembering I am not alone."[30]

Though we can feel so alone in our bodies, the body itself echoes with multitudes. The body is ancestor, an old house full of children and ghosts.

> *In her writing, being a Black woman is a way of listening, a radical form of receptiveness to the lessons that history teaches. And as her daughter Sidney puts it, "I think her actual gift was her openness and ability to hear." Clifton's theory of spirit does not succumb to fatalism.*[31]

Being a Black woman is a way of listening. A radical receptiveness that creates a theory of spirit that does not succumb.

> *There is solace in the idea that this brown skin and these wide hips were made for listening to the voices that could not be erased by time, history, or death. Oh my body, make of me always a woman who listens.*[32]

Marina and Lucille sanctify their own bodies with the idea that this body, in the way it has been pressure-treated by the world, and in its own electrical currents and specific shapes and resonances, is made for listening to missing voices. Generational trauma and ranks of murdered and missing ancestors grow loud, but so do the voices hollering that Light, Love, Truth, IS.

Lucille's poems are portals into each other's bodies. And all our bodies and the body of Earth are interpenetrated.

From the BioArt Coven Manifesto:

> We are not afraid to become intimate with our bodies and the organisms
> that inhabit us or move through us. We celebrate porosity, movement
> and contamination. We are vessels of eternal micro-knowledge that we
> accept as impossible to understand. Our goal is bodily autonomy, yet we
> acknowledge that our bodies are also part of a greater biome . . .
> We recognize processes like purification as problematic and segregation-
> ist, already infected with western-centric colonizing and exploitative
> values. There is no such thing as dirt, only not watching closely enough.
> There is no such thing as purity, only not looking at the entire picture.[33]

I want to follow Lucille and the work of the BioArt coven and treat my unseen cohort with care. I want to resist purity and celebrate porosity. Use modes of shifting to the in-between to become intimate with my own needs, boundaries, and gestures as they reflect and embody the vast web of needs, boundaries, and gestures that is the Greenness.

I take a vacation from my life when I'm writing this chapter. I book a hotel, wear full-length black velour, eat some green medicine, write, dance, and dance. I look out the window, and five floors and three blocks away, a little girl is dancing in the street. I laugh and we bounce together though she doesn't see me, spooky action at a distance. And then another kid joins in and another, blocks away, all of us riding the beat that's out there in the evening.

I go downstairs, and in the lobby of this hotel in Old Montreal, there is a bizarre and unexpected dance show. Bodies are standing on each other's shoulders, using each other to climb the architecture. I meet a covenmate and we watch, laughing, astonished, and then we plunge into the night. After a year and a half of quarantine, long days with young kids and little sleep, we are the bright nerve endings flickering all out around us. We are gulping in the wind, weaving around other groups walking these cobblestone streets.

We remember immediately how to do this. I put down some walls and weapons I didn't know that I'd been holding. I take back my own listening, and come back to my own body in concert with these night kin.

When we follow our bodies, we can slip through the locked gates of the action control center, back to our bodies as ancestors. We never really stopped being like mushrooms, every individual a fruit, a flower, with knowledge shared across the network. We just put that bigger-body self away, and individualism had its day. Now we find our exponential selves in dreamscapes, on trips, and in automatic writing.

All our magic is a homecoming to the bodies we've been missing.

Ritual

The water in your body is just visiting. It was a thunderstorm a week ago. It will be the ocean soon enough. Most of your cells come and go like morning dew. We are more weather pattern than stone monument. Sunlight on mist. Summer lightning. Your choices outweigh your substance.

—JAROD K. ANDERSON, creator of the *Cryptonaturalist* blog and author of *Field Guide to the Haunted Forest* and *Love Notes from the Hollow Tree*

In honor of Amrita and Gaura Devi, celebrate this new moon with a fast and a collective lighting of holy fire. Then, each day until the next new moon, make a ritual of walking a loop. It could be around your block, or around a park nearby. Bring a garbage bag and gather the trash you see. If you want, sing or incant under your breath as you go; lean into that wild Witch, mad hag energy. Walk your small stretch of the earth. Smile at the bodies you encounter. Look for ways in which you can heal the smallest stretches. Ask: How can I be a medicine?

In honor of Hildegard, break your fast with cookies and herbal tea or light wine.

In honor of Lucille, take up a pen and practice automatic writing to see what your unseen companions want to tell you.

From this new moon to the next, make a practice of seeding the earth with your body. Let your cells go like morning dew. Drop tendrils of your hair for birds to find, leave your nail clippings around your favorite tree, rub a little spit onto a rock and place it at your doorstep. Save a little bit of blood or cum and feed it to your garden. Each time you do, tell Earth that you are consecrating your body to the act of listening, of being porous, of making yourself a medicine to the fungi self.

Every night that you can, run your hand through moss or dirt or sand. Gently rub those worlds of organisms into your heartlines, love lines. Move your fingers through your own hair, along the fine pleasure sensors of your skin. Lift your arms, tip your head up to the sky, brace your legs wide. Take that shape that sings with Venus in her path across the night sky: that first and perfect pentagram.

Rest your head on your own shoulder, feel your lungs expand to welcome the atmosphere filling you over and over again with the unseen glittering webs of life in the air.

Call the corners of this round earth into the roundness and edges of you and know: the body is the first and last and most powerful magic. Take up your pen again, and ask them what they know.

Incantation

They are in me, They are of me
Oh my body.
They are in me, They are of me
Oh my body.

To Earth at the heart of my body,
Oh my body.
Love is.
Oh my body.
Truth is
Oh my body.
Beauty is.
Oh my body.
Love is.

3

New Moon in Gemini

The Garden

This circle is led by Amy
with expansions by Risa.

The Gemini New Moon is frenetic and curious. It's butterfly-winged speech and a darting mind. The Gemini New Moon is the trickster, the snake oil salesperson, the poet, and the class clown. It is the dance between umbrella, sunglasses, scarf in the liminal months between seasons. What it lacks in constancy, it compensates for in wit and a sense of humor.

—ELIZA ROBERTSON, ASTROLOGER

AS SPRING GIVES BIRTH TO SUMMER, we examine how Witches use and are used by our gardens to create magic, healing, and growth. The garden, like us, requires *and* provides both nurturing *and* nourishment. An ouroboros of sustenance, a small universe feeding and eating itself, originating from and returning to the soil, the garden is a window into the cycle of life. Magical herbalism and botanical therapeutics have their place in our stories, but creating and caring for a garden holds a magic all its own. There is medicine in plants and medicine in *planting*.

We can hear our human stories when we listen to our oddkin, those more-than-human companions. We can learn about our humanity if we listen to the roots and leaves. Get quiet, observe, and nurture the stems and blossoms.

My short time living in the woods has already taught me so much about what it means to be a singular being while also being a tiny part of a whole universe. How the growing season both begins and ends in yellow and purple—dandelions and irises in the spring, goldenrod and asters in the fall. In a thousand years, maybe I will begin to understand what that means and why. Until then, I put the clearer lessons to work in the seed and soil of every situation.

Gemini Moon calls out to our adaptability; it asks us to be ready for more than one possibility. It is playful, and multiple, and mutable. And as anyone who has ever seen a wild daisy poking its head through a crack in a concrete sidewalk knows, plants have a lot to teach us about both resilience and change.

We are connected to the moon and so too are our gardens. As long as humans have cultivated plants, we have done so in line with the waxing and waning of our moon. Schedules for planting, weeding, watering, and reaping were created within this cycle: Plant root crops just after the moon wanes from full. First quarter for fruits, waxing for leafy greens. The *Farmers' Almanac* tells us, "Those who swear by this ancient growing method say the water in both the ground and in plants are affected by the gravitational pull of the Sun and Moon, just like ocean tides are. Just as the tides are highest during the new and full phases of the Moon, this theory holds, seeds, too, will absorb the most water during these times."[1]

Germination begins in the dark, in the new moon of existence, and grows toward light.

Before we plant our very first seed, we are connected to something that glows and gets brighter. In the dark of the Gemini New Moon, we are sowing and sprouting. We are the grassroots of resistance, and the wildflowers of re-enchantment.

We are the underground.

We are grassroots.

In the twenty-first century, one of the greatest actions of revolutionary personal, political, and communal well-being is to grow our own food. Most of us don't have the acreage for self-sustaining food production, but this power can be tapped in any space we give it. A single herb in a two-inch planter is a powerful spell. It is a crack in our *dependence* on the systems of production—tiny, but maybe enough to plant a seed.

The garden is a space (a plot of land, or an upcycled yogurt cup on a window sill) in which we cultivate the miracles of nature; we tease nature toward our will with nurturing reverence. Earth, beyond our garden walls, is not our tool. Earth is our teacher, mentor, sometimes collaborator, sometimes tester of our will. But Earth is not for us to bend or tailor. The garden, however, is that tiny fraction of the universe where we make a deal with Earth to work together to produce something we can both enjoy.

"My way of looking at the world changed dramatically because of what I've learned from the plant world," writes Christi Belcourt. "Each plant has its own personality and its own spirit. Each has as much right to exist on the earth as I do. All plants are medicine. My own experience in getting to know the plants has helped me to feel whole and healthy. It has helped my relationship with others, and to be more respectful of the gift of life that we share."[2]

Witches turn to gardening as a means for growing food, ingredients for spells, and a deeper sense of connection to our world—people, animals, places, power. Soil is almost literally everything: a complex mixture of minerals, earth, heat, water, air, infinite living organisms, and decaying remains. A seed, once planted, breaks free of its shell, destroying the safety of this encasement to reach up to the sky with its leaves and down to the core of the earth with its roots. Beautiful, delicate, and strong. And when it has told its story, it returns to soil to sleep and dream of growing anew.

I can't tell you how to make a garden. For one thing, there are too many variables. Everyone reading this book has a different climate, different space, different lifestyle, and different circumstances to contend with; these will dictate the what, where, when, how, and even why of your magical gardening adventure.

Second, I'm still a beginner. My relationship to plants and soil is only starting to take root and sprout. I used to joke that instead of a green thumb, I had a black thumb of death. I didn't mean to, but I killed a lot of plants, mostly by over or under watering. I remedied this bad habit by routinely sticking my finger into the soil of my plants and gauging whether it felt dry or moist. Instead of assuming I knew, I, in my probing way, asked the plant what, if anything, it needed. This is a lesson we Witches can take from becoming gardeners: To ask what is needed of a situation before we jump in and try to "help."

As I picked up tips and tricks, I began to understand that a garden is like magic in the sense that no one knows everything. Science is only beginning to understand the complex workings of subterranean life. And the garden keeps changing. One year it's rainy and the next year it's dry. Maybe aphids are a problem one year and it's slugs the next. The garden transforms, and under our Gemini Moon we must transform with it, continually adapting to new situations. What is universal and timeless, however, is our physical and spiritual connection to our gardens, in that great, looping, mystical, mutual aid.

We can look to the garden as a real, literal mode of ecofeminist resistance to capitalism. Growing your own food or tossing seed bombs into vacant lots is activism. Seed bombs have many recipes but generally they are made of a mixture of clay, soil, and noninvasive native seeds— everything needed for a tiny patch of plants to enchant a neglected space. Seeds are ancient stories that reveal themselves as they grow. The garden is a rich source of nutrients, and a rich source of metaphors. In it, we find everything we need to know about birth and death and what happens in between. We can think of planting a seed to grow a tomato in the same way we think about planting the seed of an idea and nurturing it until it bears the fruit of manifestation. In a seed we find lessons to enact within our lives, even if the closest "jungle" is concrete and the closest "plant" is a factory.

"The basis of herb magic—and all magic," writes Scott Cunningham, "is the power. . . . The power is that which maintains the universe. It is the power that germinates seeds, raises winds and spins our planet. It is the energy behind birth, life and death. Everything in the universe was created by it, contains a bit of it, and is answerable to it."[3]

We see that all the information contained to produce an oak tree is in the tiny acorn and keep this in our minds as we pass, literally and metaphorically, through the notion of germination. We are all tiny seeds, already in possession of everything we need to bloom. And although it can be intimidating to flip through the hundreds of pages of Cunningham's *Encyclopedia of Magical Herbs*, Rebecca Beyer of *Blood and Spice Bush*, who you'll meet again in the "Potions and Poisons" chapter, told us that "It's a colonized mindset to think you have to . . . know all or nothing . . . You can know 10 plants deeply and be a wonderful healer."[4]

One summer my two windowsill succulents burst forth with one tall appendage each. Each had a long, skinny green arm with yellow fingers that towered over its short, spiky mother. I had had them for years and never witnessed this type of growth, so I asked the coven what was happening. I got two responses. One person told me that they were trying to spread their seed and getting ready to die. The next responder said, "They must be so happy, they're flowering!!" Knowledge, and especially plant knowledge, is not all or nothing. Most times, it comes down to wait and see.

Your life is a garden. Enchantment is a garden. Resistance is a garden. Social justice is a garden. We can't just buy a packet of seeds and hope for the best. First we research and learn what we can about climate, history, and technique. Then we till our soil, unearth and shed light on what has been buried. Only then can we sow our seeds. Water them. Nurture them. We pull unwanted, invasive weeds when we see them sprout. We watch for our mistakes and take advice from seasoned gardeners. Wait and see what happens. After bloom and harvest, we start again.

Growth is not a one-step process. As Witches and gardeners, we see the mutual aid and community care implicit in nature and take lessons from within. Lessons in patience, failure, and success. In adaptability.

The work never stops, but the bounty is beautiful and the magic is powerful.

As Marguerite Bennett wrote:

A garden is an altar. . . . Blood and bone meal and shit and decay—the gardener must clear out the dead, the dying, the withered, to make room for new life, cutting and cleaning and slicing, all sap and saplings and seeds, digging a graveyard steaming with rot and heat to feed the roots of something stronger. She nurtures what she please. She cuts down what does not earn her favour. She controls sun and shade, wind and water. Poisons and potions, elements and herbs—her hands are the scale of life and death. Here she is not only gardener, but guardian. Here, she is witch and priestess and god. A garden is an altar.[5]

When I moved to the woods and started my gardening adventure in earnest, I began with a patch of perennial wildflowers, luring pollinators to my little land. This garden is an altar. A gathering place for gratitude, spirits, and sprites. A symbol of hope that returns to explode in vibrant saturation every summer. Pinks and purples, oranges, yellows, and greens dance up from the ground to meet my winter-weary eyes, hungry for color. But this garden is also a grave. It's where I, alone, with only a spade and my memories, buried my father's ashes. In this plot I have laid my father to rest, watered the dirt with my sweat and my tears, sunk my songs and my silence deep within the soil. These flowers will remember me and keep coming back to tell my story after I'm gone.

Neighbor Fred needed a drainage ditch, which meant digging up the bearded irises his late wife planted decades before. He gave them to me for my garden, my ode to everlasting love. Their beauty blooms won't last the year, but they will be forever, working their magic in quiet darkness under a blanket of snow to return and face the sun again next spring. My garden is my altar.

Risa: We started with a bank that had been scraped dead, and we filled it with pollinators too. We pick up lupin pods and crack the seeds out on the hill, and every year, we get new tall flowers, purple and rose. We gathered every wild strawberry we could save from underneath where the walls came down and made a little plot, and they didn't flower that year, but the next year they were ripe with tiny, red, wild jewels. Before we began to scratch out a plot for food, I dug a hole and buried my placenta nearby (not too close). Covered her in flower rings. Dragged an altar stone over her. And every year we come and lay our braided grasses and wild fruits at her feet and thank her, that beautiful stranger whose wisdom comes from ancient retroviruses teaching us how to build a safe and nourishing place within.

The curl of your body, then, is an altar not just to the womb that grew you, but to the retroviruses that, 200 million years ago taught mammals how to develop the protein syncytin that creates the synctrophoblast layer of the placenta. Breathe in, slowly, knowing that your breath loops you into the biome of your ecosystem.[6]

You are a garden, and under the Gemini Moon you are more deeply twinned to other bodies than ever. Now all around my placenta wild poppies grow, and I like to think they are easing her dreaming.

"Given that a Neanderthal grave contained pollen, suggesting that flowers were sprinkled there," writes Judy Grahn, "the question arises of why human attention should have turned to such an odd thing as a flower?"[7]

Why did we turn to flowers? They are omnipresent in our emotional and ceremonial lives. They are mainstays at weddings and funerals, cross-culturally a part of festivals. They express love, lust, sympathy, grief, congratulations, and Get Well Soons. Bouquets serve as apologies, an olive branch in peony form. We give and receive them in times of triumph and in times of despair.

Navigating my own chronic illness led me to a practitioner of Ayurveda. After our first consultation, she suggested I put a vase of cut flowers in my kitchen. As a born cynic on a lifelong quest to open my mind to possibility, I was skeptical but willing to give it a shot. Entering my local flower shop with frugal trepidation, I was relieved to lay my eyes, first thing, on a big bucket of bunched daisies, four dollars apiece, for a bouquet reminiscent of Charlie Brown's Christmas tree. Perfect. Daisies are my favorite. They are so lovely and simple, elegant yet wild, like the sun bursting out from the clouds. I cradled them in my arms on the walk home, exchanging smiles with everyone who crossed my path—the flowers were already working their magic, doing their job of spreading joy like pollen through the air. I placed my precious nose-gay lovingly into the most vase-like jar I could find and, as instructed, put the daisies on the kitchen counter with the earnest specificity of a curatorial gallerist.[8] And it helped. The flowers were there to greet me or catch my eye as I passed. They were jolly and crooked and flawless. It helped. It didn't cure my chronic illness, but I felt better . . . happier.

> *Without our fully realizing it, flowers would become for us an expression in form of that which is most high, most sacred, and ultimately formless within ourselves. Flowers, more fleeting, more ethereal, and more delicate than the plants out of which they emerged, would become like messengers from another realm, like a bridge between the world of physical forms and the formless.[9]*

Years later, with a patch of land to call my own, I resisted the temptation to manicure and let the lawn, such as it was, run free. When daisies popped up everywhere, it felt like a reward for good work or a gift of gratitude. The same way that we humans exchange flowers, so too had Earth scattered bouquets around the house for me to discover.

There is a wisdom in the natural world, one that can be shared with us if we pay attention. We spoke to Joy Gray, Granddaughter Crow (GDC), about this wisdom of the natural world. As a member of the Navajo Nation (Diné), her father was a victim of the residential school system, and so it has become GDC's life's work to preserve and feed the ancestral knowledge of her people, to raise their voices and keep them alive "for the purpose of truth." She creates a circle and sets her ego outside of that circle. In her own garden, she sits in silence, watching and listening. Cultivating the ability to turn the energy of the landscape into a story she can hear, she becomes a translator. This is a power that all Witches can access, with attention, patience, and quiet. We can identify our personality traits with those of our plants, our sameness. We can abandon the religiosity of hierarchy.[10]

My stepfather responded to my youthful burgeoning vegetarianism by reminding me that the Bible says that man has dominion over the fish of the sea, and over the birds of the air, and over the cattle, and over all the wild animals of the earth, and over every creeping thing that creeps upon the earth (Genesis 1: 26–28). This Christian God told us that everything in creation is meant for us to consume, so it's easy to draw a very straight line between this idea and humanity's wanton consumption and destruction of our own ability to survive on this earth.

Goddess painter, global activist, and dharma gardener Mayumi Oda says: "The dharma wheel turns and turns, creating, changing every moment, yet continuing—why do we think we are different from plants?"[11]

The garden teaches us that we are not. Science tells us that we are not. We share *50 percent* of our DNA with trees, 25 percent with daffodils.[12] And in moments of doubt, I return to this thought. I am half tree. One quarter daffodil. And 100 percent Witch.

Sophia Buggs, owner and operator of Lady Buggs Farm, a small urban homestead, asks, "What if urban agriculture could heal not just our bodies, but our souls?"[13] As she waters her plants, performing her libation ceremony, symbolically giving her ancestors a drink, she thanks the ancestors, by name, who came before her.

"It is in my belief," she says, "that well-being is eminently tied to the soil and that urban agriculture is a spiraling movement that fosters relations with the mycelial landscape and human beings." She began this relationship with nature/food/plants with her grandmother. Her goal was to re-create her grandmother's zucchini bread from the literal ground up.[14] Aligned with ancestry and with purpose, Sophia noticed something she calls "magical"—plant medicine. For Sophia, for Witches, the medicine of plants is equally in their practical applications—peppermint tea for nausea, for example—and also in their spiritual teachings. When we use plant medicine, we gain a connection to our ancestors, to the cells of our bodies, and to the mycelial network.

Let's return to the soil. Let's get our hands dirty.

A contributor to the Queer Nature's *Critical Naturalist* blog foundered by Pinar and So Sinopoulos-Lloyd says:

> *The word "humility," meaning a "modest or low view of one's own importance," has a striking etymology. It comes from the Latin humus, which means soil. To be humble is to "lower" oneself toward the soil—toward the earth themselves—not out of self-loathing, but out of a desire to be in respectful relationship with another being. There seems, then, to be a paradox in humility—because what is more powerful, more full of potential and multiplicity, than the soil? What better model for so(i)lidarity than the ground that supports us all, and also decomposes our bodies after we die in order to share and redistribute our metabolic capital as nutrition for other beings?"[15]*

The practical, physical, and psychological health benefits of touching soil are well studied and well proven. Bacteria commonly found in soil activate brain cells to produce the brain chemical serotonin. Touching soil makes us happier. Another study suggests that microbes derived from nature might somehow contribute to training or calibration of the immune system.[16] Touching soil makes us healthier. Chris Lowry from Bristol University said, "These studies [also] help us understand how the body communicates with the brain and why a healthy immune system is important for maintaining mental health."[17] Once again, in the great everything of soil, we find life and death, the physical, psychological, practical, and mystical all at work in something that we flippantly call dirt. Let us Witches revere that which deserves our reverence. Glory be the dirt.

This is a fundamental part of Witchcraft. To sanctify the forgotten. To sanctify the underground. To go against the grain. To reclaim a defamed language. To regard with awe the complex beauty of dirt. To see the world in a lump of soil. Get emotional over the amazing potential of a seed.

"In the garden, I see life and death in the vegetables, always arriving and going, like a huge wheel of the cosmos," wrote Mayumi Oda, who is sometimes known as the Matisse of Japan.[18] Her paintings of goddesses embody paradoxical Witch energy by both glorifying and humanizing her deities. Goddess images informed much if not most of Mayumi's oeuvre as a visual artist. Rendering male gods as female, messing with time and space; having goddesses riding bicycles and talking on telephones, Mayumi allowed her imagination to reinterpret her traditions and her beliefs.

The colors she found in her garden echoed those of her palette. "These colours go right into my heart and dissolve into my whole being."[19]

> Through working in the garden, I felt the deep dharma moving through. We encountered impermanence and interconnectedness, nature's great teachings, as everyday truth.[20]

The concept of dharma can also be found in Jainism and Sikhism, but in its Hindu definition, Devin Kowalczyk wrote, "Dharma is a word without direct translation, but implies 'religion,' 'duty,' and 'righteousness.' Dharma derives from a Sanskrit root word meaning 'to uphold or sustain.' The concept behind Dharma is anything that upholds or sustains a positive order."[21]

In *Radical Dharma: Talking Race, Love, and Liberation*, Rev. angel Kyodo williams gives an even simpler definition of dharma: Universal Truth:

> Radical Dharma is insurgence rooted in love, and all that love of self and others implies. It takes self-liberation to its necessary end by moving beyond personal transformation to transcend dominant social norms and deliver us into collective freedom.[22]

Our dharma is rooted in love and also rooted in soil. This is what Mayumi found in her garden: Truth and Love. Self-liberation. An act of both rebellion and connection. Insurgence sprouted from care.

Let's pull from all this soil, up through our roots, and by osmosis, absorb dharma for our purposes as divine wisdom and goodness, purpose that flows, with our sweat and encouragement, toward justice and harmony. To take part, to uphold and sustain a stream of consciousness more ancient and complex than we can imagine. This is what Mayumi sensed running above and below the dirt.

"My earliest memories are of tremendous anxiety," she confessed.[23] Mayumi spent her early childhood terrorized by the constant threat of explosions in a bomb shelter that her father and grandfather had dug under their lotus pond. When evacuation became inevitable, the family went to stay with an aunt in the countryside, temporarily escaping the burdens of war. They left the city, Mayumi notes, on the spring equinox. After the bombing of Hiroshima, the Japanese emperor announced that the war had been lost. Her imperialist grandfather wept, but the emotion Mayumi recalls in that moment was relief. The war, she thought, is over.

Mayumi and her family returned to Tokyo, on the autumn equinox, to find the crumbling rubble of their former city. Resources were few, food was scarce. She recalls, "we were not good farmers, but we depended on that vegetable garden for our meals."[24] Her grandfather gave her an early example of mixing art and the garden by using his calligraphy brushes to collect and transfer pollen as bees do with their bodies, picking up the yellow dust with bristles and moving it from flower to flower.

She met an American man in Tokyo. They married, and had two children.

Mayumi wrote:

At a certain point, I realized the life I was leading was not right for me, and I decided to live truer to myself . . . It was no longer possible for me to live the life that I had been living . . . The urge to know myself became stronger and I read many books on psychology, spirituality and feminism.[25]

At age 38, Mayumi separated from her husband John, ending her marriage. She said:

I was raised in a Buddhist family in Japan during and after World War II. My childhood revolved around seasonal Shinto rituals and

Buddhist ceremonies. After the War we were very poor and had very little material comfort, but as a child I didn't know any different. Living in the outskirts of Tokyo, surrounded by Nature, I had a very rich life. The Buddhist ethics of compassion were very important growing up in my family. My father, who was a Zen scholar, always told me that I had a Buddha nature, meaning that I could always find the person and the place within myself that I could trust. How could I find that place now?

. . . For the first time in my life, I found myself living alone with my two sons. I was very sad, yet I also felt ready to know who I was. In my studio I sat for many hours watching the shadow of the walnut tree and my own breath, asking myself, "Am I all right?" Once in a while the woodpecker's pecking interrupted me, and I remembered I had work to do.[26]

The happiest parts of Mayumi's childhood were spent in those rural outskirts where a persimmon tree became a friend. "When I felt sad or lonely," she wrote, "I used to climb the tree and put my arms around its trunk. Sometimes the tree felt more like a mother to me than my real mother. It was always there when I needed it."[27]

Oh coven, I relate to that. When you're a kid, your space isn't yours. Under their roof it was their rules, but that tree in the yard, that was mine. Climbing that tree was like going home, my home. Thirty plus years later, I'm trying to remember what I did up there. I think I just sat.

When Mayumi asked, "How could I find that place now?" That's the place she meant, I think. In the arms of Mother Nature, who sometimes wants you to get to work and sometimes just wants you to sit in her branches and watch her shadows trace a path across the grass. An external place that mimics the internal place. A place you can trust.

The place she found was California's Green Gulch Farm. She and John had visited there before moving back to Tokyo. Mayumi began to sense reflections in her feelings about both her homes, Tokyo and John.

The frantic and fragmented city life of Tokyo and my own confusion made me miserable. I was no longer comfortable in my own country

. . . I was also beginning to realize, sadly, that my husband and I were on different paths. I felt that John was pursuing life outwardly in his successful career, and I became increasingly interested in my internal life. We no longer had the same values . . . I often thought about that peaceful zen farm I had visited in California. One day I dreamed I was living at the farm.[28]

As many of our Missing Witches have done, Mayumi had a dream, so she manifested it. She moved to Green Gulch Farm, built her studio, which she calls Spirit of the Valley, and lived there for many years. "Each day we noticed the changes of the moon," she wrote.

Now I understood why I was here in California, practicing Buddhism with American and European friends. In Japan, Buddhism for me was like the dusty sutra books on the altar. Here it is alive, taking new form. The ancient Buddhist teaching of inter connectedness is enriched by the Native American tradition of reverence for the earth. I want to see the blossoming of this new hybrid flower, and I know that we at the farm are all part of this process.[29]

There is a story in her book, *I Opened The Gate, Laughing*, that I carry with me, a tale called "The Deer's Path" that I feel truly encompasses Mayumi's message. It is about wildness and control, Nature's power and our own power—not as nemeses, but as collaborators. Watching and listening and *laughing*. Riding the wheel of dharma. Looking to our gardens as extensions of the earth that feed our bodies and souls in a different way than the untamed beauty of nature. We are forest, we are garden, we are artist, we are deer, turning meditation into action and dreams into reality.

Mayumi had made her garden the center of her life. A place she could trust. "With a secure fence around me," she wrote, "I healed. I became whole." But this was not the end of the story. One day Mayumi left the garden to explore the woods and found hoof prints of deer by a muddy pool in the creek. She followed the deer's path for a while and then, gazing up at her garden from this vantage point, what she saw seemed ridiculous, with the "self-conscious stuffiness of a proper English garden." In that place she had felt safe and protected, sewn her torn pieces back together. The *deer's path* led her to a sudden realization, and in that monument, she says, "The whole world became my garden."[30]

She decided to take the fence down.

As I write, Mayumi is probably harvesting daikon at her current home, Gingerhill Farm in Hawaii. There she holds Goddess workshops and continues her battle against the plutonium trade—Pearl Harbor, the dropping of the atomic bombs on Japan in 1945, and the Fukushima nuclear disaster in 2011 echoing in her personal and global history.

While we seek dharma in soil, we are also unlocking a real and practical survival skill. One that Mayumi Oda's family understood well. When *Small Purse Big Garden* blogger Lisa Pedersen's family fell on hard financial times, her gardening went from hobby to necessity. She grew food. She fed and sustained her family.

She told me:

I did not grow up in a gardening family—all of the house plants were plastic.

I lived my college years in Toronto in basement apartments, and spent any free time I had seeking out unpaved spaces, wild spaces, green spaces. Those spaces speak directly to our animal brains.

I was sketching scenes of forests, lakes and rivers, manifesting the life I have now.[31]

With her husband, she rented a home with a tiny bit of land that became their first foray into home gardening. She said:

It was a little haphazard and didn't make a lot of sense. I bought plants or seeds that sounded fun to grow. It was a lot of work and a lot of fun. Each growing season presented us with new learning opportunities and new challenges. One year, hail in June took out all of our tomato plants, but another year, our youngest learned his colors from watching the tomatoes ripen. Green, yellow, orange and red.[32]

During that time, Lisa was unemployed for over a year and had to make some drastic changes to her household budget. She experienced buying groceries with rolls of coins and along with that came intense feelings of shame. "Once, I came home from the store and saw eight jalapeno plants dripping with ripe peppers." she said. She saw food. A solution. Help.

It wasn't until that moment that necessity forced me to see the garden as an actual source of sustenance. Making our own meals with the food we grew helped me to learn how to have a more balanced nutritional approach as well as new appreciation for food and food production. I made a bunch of experimental recipes and some became family favourites. Some were definitely fails. And that's fine too. We learned.

We learned that pumpkin plants get lonely (you can't grow just one plant . . . their biology requires at least two plants to cross polli-nate). I learned about growing zones. I learned what grows well in our area and what does not. I learned we would never be great peach or cherry farmers while being located in eastern Ontario. Sometimes we have to accept our limitations. Sometimes we work within those boundaries with great success.[33]

In becoming the gardeners of our own lives, we Witches must assess our surroundings and ourselves. Are we in a fertile place or an arid one? Are we planting our seeds in rich black soil or dust and sand? Are we in a space that will nurture our growth or impede it? Are we surrounding ourselves and our thoughts with pollinators or invasive species?

Vietnamese Thiền Buddhist monk and peace activist Thich Nhat Hanh famously said:

When you plant lettuce, if it does not grow well, you don't blame the lettuce. You look for reasons it is not doing well. It may need fertil-izer, or more water, or less sun. You never blame the lettuce. Yet if we have problems with our friends or family, we blame the other person. But if we know how to take care of them, they will grow well, like the lettuce. Blaming has no positive effect at all, nor does trying to persuade using reason and argument. That is my experience. No blame, no reasoning, no argument, just understanding. If you understand, and you show that you understand, you can love, and the situation will change.[34]

We blame ourselves, suffer the weight of guilt, often for things that are or were beyond our control. We beat ourselves up when we find ourselves in bad situations, but perhaps that energy would be better used to adjust our fertilizers and make sure we're getting what we need. Look over the fence.

Lisa Pedersen engaged with local farmers and gardeners, discovering the Sisters of Providence at a seed sanctuary. The nuns told her stories about their gardening magic—how they stir the water to create a vortex in both directions—clockwise to add good energy and counterclockwise to release bad energy.

Lisa is emphatic about the symbiosis of Witchcraft and gardening—she feels her connection to this planet when she has her hands in dirt, claiming that once she became a homesteader, she saw the circle of life. She saw how death contributes to life and life ends in death. She saw growth from rot and growth turn back to rot. The magic of a flower becoming food. The magic of taste and smell. The alchemy that happens when we mix certain flavors together. Stirring the pot and the soul.

She sees her kitchen spice rack as her potion ingredients, creating spells of health and prosperity.

Lisa suggests that those of us without a fraction of the space required to homestead, or even grow zucchini in a kiddie pool, seek out local community gardens. Some cities have created green spaces in which residents without yards can grow. This is something Risa did when we lived in the city and it became somewhat of a gathering spot for our coven. We would laugh and dance as we sprinkled water from a rain barrel onto the tiny patch she shared with two dozen neighbors.

Risa: We crept in at night for candlelit ceremonies, whispering to the moon surrounded by plants, hemmed in by apartment buildings and an old folks home, where two old ladies always looked on, cackling, from rocking chairs on the balcony.

In her book *Feminist Weed Farmer*, Madrone Stewart wrote, "I was regularly interrupting my work with wild dance breaks. I had tons of fun and really connected with my garden and my plants. Yes, I gardened mindfully in silence too but the dancing I did that spring was memorable."[35]

In investigating these Witches' tools of enchantment and resistance, we often find that they work for both purposes at once. Deliberate, transgressive acts of jubilation. For Madrone, gardening is both joyful and revolutionary. "I especially believe that women, queer folks, and folks of color should grow our own psychedelic medicine because of how radically excluded we are from the emerging cannabis industry. I deeply believe that we need to empower ourselves with the skills and knowledge to grow the plants that help us to develop the wisdom that we need to liberate ourselves and our communities."[36]

Empower ourselves with the skills and knowledge to grow.

In the city, our spaces are smaller, so sometimes we have to think bigger. Reclaim public space for public good. And in these big thoughts, we find Hattie Carthan, a woman for whom a garden was too small an ideal. In her Bed-Stuy, Brooklyn, neighborhood, she planted a forest. Seeded a revolution. She made a place she could trust.

When she noticed conditions in her neighborhood beginning to deteriorate, Hattie began replanting trees. Throughout the 1970s, she founded groups with names like Operation Greenthumb, Neighborhood Tree Corps, and the Green Guerillas, so it was clear that Hattie came to her purpose with both an open, hopeful heart and a near military-level strategy. Her soldiers were her neighbors. They came armed with a need for green space in the inner city, armed with dreams and trees to plant. They started with seed bombs and eventually Hattie became the chairwoman of the Bedford-Stuyvesant Beautification Committee—a project that added over 1,500 trees to the neighborhood.

We've already lost too many trees, houses and people . . . your community—you owe something to it. I didn't care to run.[37]

Under the Gemini night sky, we see ourselves reflected in each other, we see our twin nature in everything, and it helps us to adapt. We don't run, we dig in.

In May 1998, a garden in Brooklyn was named in honor of Hattie Carthan; there, trees, flowers, and Hattie's legacy continue to grow. A hybrid yellow magnolia that was created and named in her memory and planted during a ceremony to honor her life now stands forty feet tall.

"People often ask me what one thing I would recommend to restore relationship between land and people," wrote Robin Wall Kimmerer in her book *Braiding Sweetgrass*:

> *My answer is almost always, "Plant a garden." It's good for the health of the earth and it's good for the health of people. A garden is a nursery for nurturing connection, the soil for cultivation of practical reverence. And its power goes far beyond the garden gate—once you develop a relationship with a little patch of the earth, it becomes a seed itself. Something essential happens in a vegetable garden. It is a place where, if you can't say "I love you" out loud, you can say it in seeds. And the land will reciprocate in beans.*[38]

In contending with my own body's infertility, I planted plum trees. Three little rooted twigs that with my love and care, will, I hope, outlive me, provide shade, sweet nourishment, and showers of white petals like nature's celebratory confetti on windy summer days for whoever might inhabit this place. For generations. The jolly wildflowers I grew from seed will keep coming back. They, like our actions, our spirits, are perennial.

I read that elderberries have more vitamin C than oranges, so I planted a few bushes. I didn't expect them to bear fruit the first year, so I was gleeful to see their tiny white petals turns to heavy red bunches. Elderberries are poisonous if taken raw. Much like Witches, you must understand their workings in order to reap the best benefits of their magic. That first year, I harvested maybe a quarter cup of elderberries, barely a handful. I was grateful. The bushes, the fruit trees, they make me slow down, exercise patience, turn away from instant gratification, appreciate tiny victories. Robin wrote, "This is really why I made my daughters' garden—so they would always have a mother to love them, long after I am gone."[39]

I have grown a mother to love me in this yard. I garden to reap the benefits of touching soil, the moist womb of all life. I garden to feed my body and birth ingredients for my potions and spells—lavender and purple mountain sage. I garden to foster my relationship with plants and note what we have in common. I garden to remember that I am one-quarter daffodil. I garden to enchant my space and resist its commodification. I grow for me. I garden to make a place I can trust.

I asked my friend, poet, Witch, Kate Belew, for a benediction for our gardens.

Look here, between our hands,
just green. This is what delight is,
wildness, whispers, the way that spring
seems to call and asks you to return.
A blessing on the garden
and a blessing on the gardeners.
Here's to the dedication
of dirt.
The Earth forms lessons under their very skin
and says all you have to do is pay attention,
and add a little bit of water, in some languages
it's called rain.

In a hegemonic space that pushes us to do and think and be the same, the mythical normal or all alike, remember that rosemary loves the sun, while hostas prefer the shade. Bunchberry needs acidic soil while lilies like an alkaline bed. Creeping thyme wants to spread, but an iris takes years to self-replicate. Mosquitos loathe catnip, while cats, of course, adore it. Cinnamon is a prosperity herb. Garlic is for opening the roads. Basil is a money herb. Bay leaves are for manifestation. In nature and in magic, differences are essential. What works for me may not work for you. What works for this may not work for that. We need not be the same to work together. And into our striving toward a better place, a place we can trust, it's important to remember that each one of us has a role to play in the revolution, and maybe, just maybe, we are, already, exactly who we are supposed to be.

We can grow for purpose—grow our herbs for our magical practices, grow ingredients for our spells, grow food to eat—but we Witches know that the most powerful magic is contained in the growing itself. In our understanding of cycles, the complex beauty of dirt and difference, our connection to the earth and rain. As Loretta Ledesma suggests, "I am not of the cosmos. I am of the primordial mud. My bones are not filled with sparkling dust from the stars, but with algae blooms and flora in decay."[40] If we are mud, if we are soil, then let us take hold of this infinite fertility and grow something that will last. Throw a seed bomb. An idea bomb. Grow a single plant where once there was none. Grow a new habitat, a new society, all nurtured from seed. Let us be grassroots. Let us craft our spaces into places we can trust, and in doing so, find that place within.

Let the whole world be our garden.

Ritual

One of my favorite spells is green onion regrowth. Also known as scallions, these little wonders are perfect for recognizing and manifesting the power of resilience and growth.

Scallion is known to help relieve nasal congestion, so let's work it for our vital congestion too. The garden teaches us about growth and change and forces us to respect each stage of the process. And so it will be for this ritual, this scallion.

Risa: Scallion is in the Allium genus along with garlic and onion. We grow garlic by the dozens here, multiplying our harvest every year; they hang

79

to dry in braids all down the dark hallway behind where I write. Amy suggested that we start putting green onions in jars in our window garden. This family of plants has deep medicine related to the heart—can't you see your own heart twinned in their little bulbs? They open passageways, they make us cry, they release stiff and blackened feelings from within us and they have antibacterial, antioxidant, anti-inflammatory, antiprotozoal, and antifungal properties.[41] *With this tiny window garden, where we provide nurturing love for the generous, quick-growing scallion, we open a door to a plant relationship that has deep healing at its heart.*

Lettuce works great for this too, though I've found that the noble scallion provides the fastest gratification.

When you replant a scallion, within just a few days, you should be seeing the regrowth of greens happen.

Procure a scallion. Touch it. Smell it. Run its leaves through your fingers. Note how the roots become a white bulb that extends into long greens. Cut the scallion about an inch above the roots, where white turns to green. Set the white, rooted bulb aside.

Lay your greens on a cutting board and select a ceremonial kitchen knife. As you chop your greens, taking these long strips and reducing them to smaller, more manageable parts, ask to echo this practice in your life. We unclog drains by breaking up big blockages, and so too it is with our lives. We chop so we can chew so we can digest. Take your chopped greens and add them to whatever you're having for dinner. Eat them mindfully.

Now, take your white, rooted bulb and place it in a small container with just enough water to cover the roots. This is a two-week ritual, so remember to replace the water as it evaporates.

Speak to your scallion. Tell it how you want to grow in your own life and what steps you're taking to achieve your goals as you top up its water. Watch the tiny miracle of growth happen before your very eyes. Ask to echo this power in your life.

Eat your scallion on the full moon. Repeat as desired.

Incantation

I open the gate, laughing.
I dig.
I plant.
I cultivate,
Bearing witness to birth, life, death, and rot.
I can't control the weather.
I adapt.
Learn and grow.
Let the whole world be my garden.
Let the whole world be my garden.

4

New Moon in Cancer

Dance

This circle is led by Risa
with expansions by Amy.

In Cancer, the new moon is the birthing canal adorned with
jewels of constellations. It reminds us to seed and to create.
In its waves, we undulate toward life and more life.

—THEA ANDERSON, ASTROLOGER

IF WE ARE LOOKING FOR TOOLS TO CRAFT NEW POSSIBLE WORLDS, maybe we need to approach this not sitting still and straight, not bent or prostrate. Maybe we need to move.

I want to think about dance as a tool for craft, as healing magic, as ritual, as a place where each of us can meet that surging electricity—the divine feminine, the divine masculine, our ancestor bodies, our kin— that living emergence that spurts and twerks through our muscles and nerves. I want to think about dance as an opportunity to move our minds in sync with our bodies, our shadows, and each other. As above, so below. As match strike, so conflagration.

I want to talk about dance as a tool of magic. And I want to ask why a history of colonization is a history of dances outlawed.

Dance researcher Rebecca Barnstaple, whose work with Parkinson's provides evidence for the way dance can restore ease and offer a kind of homecoming, told me:

> Dance has knowledge. Deep, powerful, free knowledge. It's a way of engaging in our deepest relationships with ourselves and the worlds we inhabit . . . colonialism and capitalism is all about circumscribing these things. How can we commodify things, how can we separate things, how can we create objects that can be exchanged? . . . Dance is a way that people have held on to their power and shared their power stories. In a history of oppression there's good reason to tamp out dance. I'm very heartened by its return.[1]

Let's connect with dance as a way to hold power. I want to entreat you, gentle reader, to pause and listen to your room. And in your room, your breath. And beneath your breath, your heart. Place your hand on your heart to hear the bass line that is with you all the time. Let it begin to move you.

Bring your awareness down to feel that internal rhythm in your pelvis, in between your hips. Feel the curling serpent of your spine, flock of bones, song of nerve endings. Let them move like a reed in a stream running deep. Sway, just a little private Salome. Worship, for a moment, your own Bastet, dancing goddess of both pleasure and health; or Nataraja Shiva, divine cosmic dancer who manifested the universe through dance and who is honored with a bronze statue of the dancing god at CERN, the European Organization for Nuclear Research in Geneva, Switzerland.

You are part of the pattern. Your particles are dancing all the time, so you might as well join them. Do it in the room or do it in your mind's eye; the neurons that fire when you dance or when you remember dancing are almost exactly the same.

> *When a person dances or imagines dancing, the area of the cerebrum that holds images of muscle movement is stimulated and sends messages to the hypothalamus . . . If the dance image is one of deep joy or release the body is put into a healing state through the hypothalamic pathways. The body can bathe every cell in the body with a hormonal flood as the imagery lights up the neural nets in the brain.*[2]

Imagine your hips rocking side to side like a boat that is safe in quiet waves, a warm breeze, beneath the vast dance of the cosmos. Imagine you are a tree in the summer wind.

Imagine you are holding a sleeping child in your arms and you are rocking, and you are beyond tired, but the movement comes of its own volition.

Rock your child—and by your child, I mean that unique spark of life that's in you to bring forth, whatever form it may end up taking for you. Rock this spark of potential in your mind's eye. Let your strict spine and tense wrists go soft. Feel the milk, bone, blood of your strength holding you long after you let go.

The space in your pelvis is full of the echoes of mothers who have rocked us, and the mother self who is one of our selves, who rocks us even when we are alone. Biome mother, Gaia mother, who gives air every time we hope to take a breath. Hold her safely in your belly and your heart and in your lungs . . . as we continue.

. . . Because we turn to the tools of magic in times of celebration, and in times of desperation too.

When we feel afraid and abandoned, at the end of rational action, we have resources of another kind. When we meet monsters, we can use the framework of ritual dance to build power in ourselves and ties in our community.

From 1979 to 1981 six women were raped and murdered on Mt. Tamalpais, across the Golden Gate Bridge from San Francisco. The trails were closed and the community lived in helplessness and rage. At the time, Anna and Lawrence Halprin were leading a community workshop called "A Search for Living Myths and Rituals." The participants decided to enact a positive myth in dance: the reclaiming of the mountain. That ritual, called In and On the Mountain, was performed over several days and included a walk along the very trails where the killings occurred.[3]

The Tamalpa dancers performed dance offerings that were guided and structured by the calling of the four corners. They danced story shapes to honor the waters, the winds, the earth, and fire. In the fire dance, they embodied the violence they felt stalking the mountain. They performed both murderer and victims, reversing roles until every member of the ritual dance embodied victim-killer.

After the dance, the ritual continued into the night as the audience and performers created smaller groups and made a "passage" to the next daylight. This passage ritual included a dream wheel in which members of the ritual body slept together in a circle with their heads close to each other in the center. In the dream wheel, members cocreate a new vision; they dream and bring the impressions from their dreams together in a story circle in the light of the new day.

"On the Mountain" completed the ritual, with the dancers and other participants challenging the killer directly by walking down the mountain. Each alone.

A few days later, police received an anonymous tip that led to the capture of the Trailside killer.

Don Jose Mitsuwa, a 109-year-old Huichol shaman, visited Anna Halprin and heard the story. He said, "This mountain is one of the most sacred places on Earth. I believe in what your people did but to be successful in purifying this mountain, you must return to it and dance for five years."[4]

And so the dance lived on, and the living myth grew. It continued for five years, and the dance went deeper into the dancers each time, and they left their marks on the mountainside. In 1985, they ceremonially renamed this annual dance Circle the Earth. "Where participants had once danced to reclaim a small measure of peace on the mountain, they now danced to restore health and peace to the planet."[5] Anna "claims the capacity for contemporary western life to create its own rituals."[6] And with Circle the Earth, she created a ritual for making peace with the world.

> *Circle the Earth is a peace dance. Not a dance about peace. Not a dance for peace. But a peace dance: a dance in the spirit of peace. It is a dance that embodies our fears of death and destruction, a dance that becomes a bridge and then crosses over into the dynamic state of being called peace ... In a world where war has become a national science, peacemaking must become a community and planetary art in the deepest sense of the word: an exemplification of our ability to cooperate in creation, an expression of our best collective aspirations and a powerful act of magic.[7]*

Dance slips past language to remind our bodies about what moving together through fear toward peace can feel like.

Contemporary Korean Shaman Eunmi says, "We pray for the mountains. We pray for the sea and for the sky. When we perform a ritual dance, we communicate with the spirits of our ancestors who serve as a bridge between us and God. We find solutions to problems people face with the help of the spirit world. Young Koreans see us as a sort of therapist."[8]

When we go looking for the Witches we've been missing, part of what motivates us is a need for feminist history—that is, not just a history of women, but of women's ideas, their spiritualities, their rituals, their methods of forming and healing communities. Approaching a feminist history of ideas means making space for knowledge that comes from different ways of being in different kinds of bodies.

Shaman Eunmi describes her experience of being hit with the spiritual sickness that would change the direction of her life:

> *I was 26 when I first showed symptoms of what we call "shamanic illness" or "shamanic crisis." I first started to experience facial paralysis. Every night was filled with terrifying visions and even visits from the spirits . . . After four months of visiting doctors for their consultations, my mother took me to a local mudang house. At the time, I thought only psychologically weak people visited the mudang. With just one glance at me, the mudang (the more general common term for mansin) said, "You need to accept your calling or else you are going to die."[9]*

You need to accept your calling or else you are going to die.

Witch histories repeat this pattern of spiritual sickness. "When Orishas make contact, attention MUST be paid."[10] Sometimes sickness has its roots in the soul or spirit; sometimes sickness is a call to change our lives, a magnetic pull from dance partners we've been missing.

How do we call forth a cultural transformation that resists the entropy of apathy? One way to do it might be to dance, alone and together. Because we need to feel the things we can't say anymore: that we are individual *and* collective, one and many, as within, so without. We dance to call back our power to act for each other, to burn away husks of greed, self-defense, and selfishness. In our personal joy and power, we can live for each other too. Living through that contradiction can be unimaginable, until we are dancing.

> *Religious anxiety about the body seems to perfectly sync up with the timing of the onset of industrialization and colonization. Wanting to believe that commercial prosperity would bring happiness and alleviate suffering, a lot of people became cogs in the industrial machine. As they did, their folk songs, stories, and dances diminished like endangered species. Decade after decade, as the new, industrialized,*

civilized, "progressive" values spread to other continents, they began to devastate many of the world's dancing cultures. Indigenous leaders like the Northern Plains shaman Wovoka, who dreamt and created the Sun Dance, saw the effects of this and warned his people, "All Indians must dance, everywhere, keep on dancing. Pretty soon in next spring, Great Spirit come . . . Indians who don't dance . . . will grow little, just about a foot high, and stay that way."[11]

We lose ourselves, our spirit, the part of us that stands tall when we stop dancing. Why is a history of colonization a history of dances outlawed? What does a culture dedicated to consumption and control know about the revelatory, revolutionary, re-enchanting power of our bodies in holy movement? What does it fear? What do sacred dancers know? "The soul is not really united unless all the bodily energies, all the limbs of the body are united."[12] What happens when we reunite our souls?

Anna Halprin said that seeing her grandfather dancing, twirling in the ecstasy of movement in his temple, lit the fire of movement within her. They couldn't speak the same language, but she understood something fundamental about how they were connected when she saw the ecstasy of his body in prayer. She was explicit in her work about her goal of creating rituals that are part of the great work of healing our communities, our Earth, and ourselves.

In her book *Returning to Health with Dance, Movement, and Imagery*, Halprin described the dance that reconstituted her own world, and her own body. This dance process began with a drawing she could not dance. She sketched a self-portrait and when she tried to dance it, got stuck at a dark spot in her pelvis. She went to her doctor and was diagnosed with rectal cancer. She went through traditional operation procedures, which left her with a colostomy and deep anxiety. After three years, cancer returned. At this time, she undertook a dance ceremony that brought her into the underworld meeting place of her mind-body.

When I first drew myself, I made myself look "perfect." I was young and brightly coloured . . . I turned the paper over and furiously began to draw another image of myself. It was black and angular and angry and violet. I knew this back-side image of me was the dance I had to do. When I did it, I was overwhelmed at the rage and anger inside me. I kept stabbing at myself and making howling noises, like a wounded animal. Some say I spoke in tongues.[13]

The dance of ourselves won't be all pleasurable release. Rage and sorrow are down there, and it festers. Rage of generations of holocaust, violence against Jewish bodies, Black bodies, Indigenous bodies, women's bodies, queer bodies, species genocides. Rage at our complicity, rage at our sense of powerlessness in the face of such astronomic wealth gaps, the rage and grief of every tortured and terrified living being. Anna Halprin encircled herself with her family, colleagues, and students to witness *this* dance, the back-side dance, the dance of the shadow lands.

They kept me honest, urging me to go deeper, reinforcing my sounds, calling out parts of the picture I was to dance. I danced until I was spent and I collapsed and began to sob with a sense of great relief. Now I was ready to turn the picture over and dance the healing image of myself . . . Something happened in this dance that I can't explain. I felt I had been on a mysterious journey to an ancient place.[14]

Anna found a way to cross the shores, to draw the sickness in the spirit body and then to dance it, and in doing so, to release it. "I often forget to tell my friends and readers that after this dance my cancer went into spontaneous remission."[15] So, Anna caught a serial killer and cured cancer with dance, if you choose to see it that way. But she insisted, "it is the healing aspects that interest me more than the cure . . . I have learned that we are all connected to each other and to the natural world in which we live. The power of dance to heal reaches its fullest potential when we are able to tap into this sense of wholeness."[16]

The power of dance to liberate, to heal, reaches its potential in our sense of wholeness. To dance our way to connection with all that lives requires a journey through the underworld of rage, terror, and grief.

Anna Halprin passed over in May 2021 and I see her now, in the great circle dance of the water cycle and in the spinning of winged seeds on the air. Her dances continue to move around the world. Whether we are seeking to heal ourselves, to heal the sickness of greed and poison in the world, or to flourish in the cracks of this troubled place even when healing isn't available, I think we need to do as she says and tap into the wholeness.

Dance researcher Rebecca Barnstaple told me, "I think of dance as a form of world-making."[17]

This isn't theoretical; ceremonial dance has changed the world before.

At the heart of a revolution unlike any other the world has ever seen, one story became a seed. A story of a secret ceremony, and a revolutionary dance.

There is a night meeting of people—enslaved people, and people who have escaped slavery—in the woods called Bois Caiman (the Alligator Woods) in what is now called Haiti. The colonizer's own words for revolution are hanging in the mist: *égalité, fraternité, LIBERTÉ*. Freedom, equality, and a universal family: not just for workers in Paris beheading their nobility, but for the people the empire has stolen too.

Into the circle of drums steps a Black woman dressed in white. She calls forth an almost unbelievable possibility: true freedom. A free, dancing body calling forth a connected web of power. She both is and symbolizes power beyond the colonizers' wildest, most greedy dreams.

According to some accounts, during the ceremony, a great storm rose over those gathered, and a mambo or priestess appeared and danced with a blade held high above her head . . . The mambo responsible for this vital element of the ritual is said to have been Cecile Fatiman, the wife of Jean-Louis Pierrot, a man who would eventually become the president of the small island nation from 1845 to 1846. Whoever the Mambo present actually was, she was elevated after her death to the status of Lwa, or Vodou deity, and was given the name Marinette Bwa Chèch . . . Known to ride those she possesses rather violently, she is feared, but also highly respected for her role in the fight for Haitian independence.[18]

Whoever was there that night, Marinette is with us still. She stands in for generations of women ancestors who led.

Vodou priestesses, Mambo servants of the Lwa, were leaders for enslaved people and for the Maroon communities in the mountains. They worked and danced and organized for freedom. Marinette is an emergent property of these dancing healer warriors.[19]

The archives tell us little about Cecile Fatiman herself. We know she was the daughter of an enslaved African woman and a Corsican prince, and we know that sex in an extreme power imbalance like this is rape, so let's call it that. Especially when the children are sold into slavery after their birth, as she was, as her brothers were.

We can't know, but we can imagine her fury at the loss and injustice. We can imagine how it fueled her. We can't come close to knowing her. But we can imagine. Imagine Cecile with an open heart and open palms and mind, imagine the power of her mind and hands and belief. Imagine her life and her anger and her calm and her magic. Imagine it all in her dance that wild night.

Dance your own picture of it in a flickering light. Conjure her memory to honor her alongside the other women of great and unending revolution. Because imagining these people whose stories and ideas we've been missing is an act of resistance in a war that still continues for our minds and for what's possible. "The war is the war for the human imagination," and in this war we dance to embody and incant possibilities beyond the hegemony of late-stage capitalism.[20]

She is a bitter spirit who prefers to be alone. People disappointed her. Rather than being celebrated as a heroine, she was first aggressively pursued by French colonial forces, then denied glory when Haitian revolutionary leader Toussaint L'Ouverture banned women from battle front-lines. Even now she is frequently dismissed as an evil spirit while her male contemporaries are lionized. She is a spirit of rage and frustration but also, in her way, a spirit of justice.[21]

Marinette emerges from Cecile Fatiman, out of the labor pains of the Haitian Revolution. This spirit-calling in the Alligator Woods is a ceremony that ties the people to each other, to their ownership of the land they are on, and to their ownership—crucially—of themselves.

In the ritual at Bois Caiman that helped conjure Marinette the priestess Cecile Fatiman transacted in some way with the Spirit of the place. Claudine Michel and Patrick Bellegarde-Smith write,

> *Vodou developed in the crucible of colonial life. Haitian Vodou is a neo-African spiritual system, philosophical construct, and religion whose core resides largely in Dahomey (presently Benin) and in Yorubaland, in Western Nigeria . . . Vodou also incorporated some aspects of the religion of the Arawaks, Freemasonry, and of course, Catholicism.[22]*

Marinette is connected to all the female warriors of Dahomey, The Mino, the Mothers, whom white writers would call Amazonians. This Lwa that emerges from Cecile Fatiman and the women of the revolution is a memory alive, adaptive, and expansive.

> *During ceremonies, Lwa mount their chwal, their horses, joining in the life of the living to deal with health and family crises and spiritual imbalance, to allow energy to flow better, and to advise, chastise, guide and restore balance and harmony, continuously opening channels of communication between spirits and humans; the Lwa also visit in dreams.[23]*

At the height of the ritual dance, the priestess both holds the bridles of wild horses and is ridden by something enormous. She can gather the life force around her, in the offerings and sacrifices, and send it swooning out into all who are present. With Cecile's dance, she calls forth a heroic wave that will stand alone in the history of the oppressed: Haiti's is the only uprising by enslaved people to result in regime change and democracy led by the enslaved people. It is the first and only slave uprising that led to a free state without slavery, ruled by non-whites and former slaves.

Haiti's history as an independent nation begins with Black people overthrowing their murderous oppressors. They launched into the world the somehow still-radical idea that Black lives matter, and that liberty, equality, and kinship are the rights of each living person. To be seen as family, kin, to be free and equal. We are still grappling to imagine systems that enact that promise.

In *Krik? Krak!* Haitian author Edwidge Danticat writes, "The women in your family have never lost touch with one another. Death is a path we take to meet on the other side."[24] Amidst so much loss, there are and always have been paths toward each other. Women who did not get to own their lives become ancestors, reaching out to inflame, comfort, haunt, and uplift you from the other side. Even without knowing their names or stories, you can feel their hands on your shoulders. You can honor them with your life and be with them in your dances.

Marina Magloire describes a moment when two protests meet on a Miami street. Marina was walking with Haitian Americans protesting the violent assault of François Alexandre by police, and she was there as this assemblage of mourners and protesters met and joined another protest singing out that Black Trans Lives Matter.

> *Somewhere around 36th Street and NW 2nd Avenue, something miraculous happened. We passed under I-195 and the rara band exploded in a burst of energy. All of a sudden the disparate protests seemed to be of one purpose. The chant of "Black Lives Matter" fell in time with the drums, and the unified voices were amplified in an echo chamber of concrete. A young queer man began twerking on a pole. We blocked a major intersection in a vortex of chanting and dancing, and I thought of the drumming and dancing at Bois Caïman in 1791, a Vodou ceremony that purportedly began the Haitian Revolution.*[25]

There is a possibility of common purpose. There can be a moment when the rivers of our pain and anger and activism run together to uplift and not subsume us; a common purpose, offering all of what we have to the dance of imagining freedom together; of actually hearing each other so we can pick up the rhythm. Under the right conditions, and a rara band certainly helps, we have the possibility of truly, finally, collectively becoming alive to our kinship. When we awaken from the lull and terror of capitalism's insidious and racist hallucination, a new dreamscape of possibilities can emerge.

Roxanne Gay, writes in her first book, *Ayiti*:

[Things Americans do not know about zombies:]

They are not dead. They
    are near death. There's
    a difference.
They are not imaginary.
They do not eat human
    flesh.
. . .
They can be saved.[26]

And if some part of you feels that capitalism, injustice, or violence has made you zombie-like, stuck repeating patterns, bitter and dry inside and not fully tasting life, maybe there's some hope for you here—in this memory of Cecile Fatiman, in the spirit of Marinette, in learning from a post-colonial spiritual philosophy that knows what it is to make a person into a zombie, and also how to save them.

Amber Sparks wrote for Roxanne Gay's *Gay Magazine*:

> *I believed in the power of believing in magic. I believed that a girl could switch paths, could make trouble instead of find it, if she only had the right set of spells to cast.*
>
>   *Witches are, with a few exceptions, the bad girls. They are closely associated with evil, with Satanism, though if you talk to any practicing Wiccan—concerned with positive magic, herbs, healing—they will of course tell you this is slander and dangerous nonsense . . . real witches, of course, are the kind of women who can make their own fate; they do not need men and they are wild with new feelings and ideas and spells. They may or may not have real magic, but they are the kind of women who can howl at the moon . . .*
>
>   *Maybe the best spell of protection was me.[27]*

There is power in being a spell of protection for your own damned self. There is power in believing in magic. For those of us interested in making "good trouble," truly owning our bodies and owning how and when we choose to use and synchronize them is a revolutionary act—a powerful magical act of energy and connection and manifestation.[28]

Amy: I had a day recently that was stacked with so much bad news that my brain stopped computing and my body started trembling. In a deeply intuitive act of self-preservation, I stood up, walked over to my stereo, put on a record, stood in front of my speakers, and just danced. My trembling body moved that energy into foot-stomping, hip-twisting, booty-shaking, hand-waving motions that tricked my whole system into feeling joy. Rebelling against a day, rebelling against cards stacked against me, I danced. It only took one song, four minutes of total realignment to renew my capacity to fight hopelessness.

Plantation owners tried to outlaw the dances of the enslaved people, but the people resisted. They hid their ritual dances in plain sight at weddings and funerals, and built up their communal power. And then there was the Danse a Don Pédre.

> *The dance was far more violent in its movements than other voodoo dances. With eyes fixed downward while drinking tafia, reputedly mixed with gunpowder, the dancers would enter into a state of frenzy, producing what observers described as epileptic-like contortions, and would continue dancing until near or total exhaustion. During the ceremony a pact was made among all participants, committing them to secrecy, solidarity, and the vow of vengeance.[29]*

Gather your most trusted cohort, even if that's only you and your ancestors. Begin by consuming something that puts fire in your blood. Move together with gestures that unleash the power in your body, go past the edges of political/social body control. Make a sacrifice. Feed each other. Make your dance a pact, a promise that together you will act for liberation. Call on your own gods, emergent properties, or archetypes of liberation, let them possess you. Let your body move like a being of total power.

The very real satisfaction to be gained by a poor peasant woman who becomes the vessel of a god and is able to parade about in silken dresses acknowledging marks of respect from the crowd has not been sufficiently underlined by studies of possession as a phenomenon. What a release for repressed bitterness and imprisoned hatred.[30]

There is magic in acting as if.[31] In letting our body take on new identities, in feeling our way toward new embodied possibility, and in witnessing that transformation in each other. In being possessed by a promise of liberation. In a time and place in which all religious observance was outlawed except for Catholicism, witnessing each other dancing, drumming, and chanting in this emerging syncretic faith shot the people through with the electricity of recognition. We resist. Vodou is itself an emergent and unifying rhythm, a coming together of bodies determined to fight. This is not religion as an opiate of the masses; this is something else entirely.

In their dwellings on the plantations and especially under the secret cover of the maroons, Vodou developed into "the leavening agent for their liberation from chains."[32]

Our dances can be a leavening agent for our liberation. Our words, our spells, our gathering together, even at a distance, can change the world. Dance can transform the ingredients of ourselves and awaken within us the ability to rise.

This insight from Haitian history is alchemical and speaks to why so many of us go seeking spiritual philosophies that connect us to our ancestors and specifically to ideologies that explode our loneliness, that connect us in a fundamental way to kin—spirits, humans, animals, trees—and see us as a part of the wholeness that is out there and also in here. We dance together to overcome the brokenness of an entire social-political system founded on slavery.

Cecile calls forth Ezli Dantò in her revolutionary dance:

A deity whose divine principle represents maternal love . . . She is also, in the words of Audre Lorde and other Black Feminists, a "woman-identified-woman," a lesbian. She is Black. This well-known song sung in ceremonies in honor of Dantò reveals a free flow between "me" and "us," between the singular and the collective.... "If you see me fall in the water, [it means that we are drowning.]"[33]

If you see me fall, we are drowning. Reach for me, and we rise.

In lifting up the drowning it's ourselves who are saved. Mambos, Witches, women, Queer people, people of expansive genders, all of us others with our other-vision have been caring for and weaving together families and communities. We have danced through the underworld and held the rhythm at the very center of vast networks; we provide comfort and support and carry the imagination of a better world forward. We have always been here and when we lift each other, we all rise.

Remember Marina Magloire and that 2020 protest with its rara band and echoes of Bois Caiman? She writes:

Like us, the participants of the Haitian revolution were Black people (and a few allies) of different cultures, languages, and religions. Like us, they danced their community into being. Black populations in America have so much to learn from each other. To miss this opportunity, especially in the multi-ethnic but divided city of Miami, would be just another way that, in the words of Audre Lorde, "We rob ourselves of ourselves and each other."[34]

She continues:

The possibilities of diaspora are fractured, fragile, and infinite. In Creole, the word for "protest" is "manifestasyon," a false cognate with the English word "manifestation." Let us dwell in the mistranslation to imagine how protest can be manifested across diaspora.[35]

How can we amplify our protests so that they manifest across space, time, diaspora? Let us dance our communities into being by resisting the pressures that would rob us of each other.

We dance together on busy streets to force people to stop and look us in the eye. We dance in the kitchen to summon deliciousness. We dance in the bathroom at night shaking off the dread and turmoil of the day before pouring ourselves into the water. We dance like the birds, like the summer blowing green. We will bring dance back into our lives and bring it to our manifesting. We dance to feel each other, all our others.

Because first and foremost, dance is a form of interspecies play. In our deep human history, dance has often allowed us to slip into the being-ness of other beings.

Artemis, Demeter, and Persephone all had priestesses called *melissai*—bees—or *mellisonomoi*—bee-keepers. From Minoan culture on into high Athenian society, up until the Roman empire violently suppressed pagan religions, women who celebrated and tended to the spirit of harvest, of fertility, of creation, were bound up with the dances of bees.

> *Throughout, there would have been much humming, buzzing or intoning of sacred songs. The dance would . . . have increased in frenzy until one of more of the priestesses was seized with the spirit of prophesy, and cried out words of dread import. Performed by "winged," "pollen-dusted" women, perhaps in the secrecy of a celebration of mysteries, it would have had a powerful effect upon all observers.*[36]

I love to imagine these prophetic, pollen-dusted, dancing women. They learned to come closer to the divine with fermented honey, they could heal with honey's antiseptic properties, and they danced in movements learned directly from the dances of the bees themselves.

> *The bee performs two dances—the "round dance" and the "waggle dance." Both are used by workers returning to the hive to report the finding of a good supply of food . . . The dance is spirited—even wild. The bee throws up its legs as high as it can and moves in dizzy circles. Other bees at first look on; then the frenzy of the dance seems to communicate itself to them also, and they join in.*[37]

I love to imagine these Witches devoting their lives to the ritual and resonances of bees. How much more could we learn from our local dances? The European honey bee is invasive, displacing over four thousand species of bees native to North America, each with their own intricate interspecies relationships and dances. The bee-dancing women offer a sketch for how we come closer to the more-than-human world. Maybe learning the dances of our bee kin and other ancestors can help reach back into mRNA memory toward a place where the lines between self and other could soften with the "grace of joy."

> *Play is the site of invention and creativity, the site of metamorphosis of same into other, just as much for beings as for meanings. It is the very site of the unpredictable, but always according to rules that conduct this creativity and its adjustments. In short, justice with the grace of joy.*[38]

Playing with dance magic has been, for me, a way of drawing in joy and shaking out fear. At a Valentine's Day protest remembering missing and murdered Indigenous women, Amy and I danced in the streets of downtown Montreal with all the other women present. We cried together too, but it was the dancing that brought us back into our laughing, powerful, generous bodies. Back into our power. Looking back, I think that dance started the rhythm that became the Missing Witches project, and our annual fundraiser for the Montreal Native Women's shelter.

We dance with past and future ancestors. We dance to remember painful histories and joyful ones too. We dance in defiance of killers and we dance to become peace. When we dance in rhythms that allow us to be transformed into the other, then our craft is a leavening. Dance can be a rising agent in us, calling out and within, to conjure more caring and equitable lives, and it can help us be possessed by the *magic* of people like Cecile Fatiman, all the women, all the brutalized and powerful people in our densely interconnected histories who have been standing at the margins of written history, but at the center of their own worlds, holding hands, spinning and kicking and shaking in circles in the woods, calling liberty, equality, and a true universal family into being. Drawing its shape with their energy. That act of imagining is our inheritance; picking it up and holding it high is our debt to them, it is how we rise, and it is our path together to true liberation from chains.

We are on the doorstep of a great journey . . . Imagine where we can go from here.[39]

Imagine the kitchen dances we all do with all our beautiful, imperfect bodies. Imagine the dance of your own self-portraits and shadowlands, and of your drawings of the world as it could be. Imagine the dances of all the species we love and need, the dances we will learn and remember and invent in order to be embodied by them and to listen to them and to labor for their lives. Imagine all of these and more and how they are part of how we will witness and imagine a choreography of re-enchantment.

Imagine the dance of celebration we will do when we are free. Dance it now, and send that shape out into the world, and know that we are there, dancing that future with you.

Ritual for the Collective

In a circle, take a minute to find your heartbeat. When you have it, turn to the person next to you and, with their consent, tap your heartbeat against their back. Tap near your microphone if you are in virtual circle.

You know the story, cells put into the same petri dish will quickly settle into a shared rhythm. We are these cells. Close your eyes and keep the beat. The beat of our collective hope, fear, illness, wellness, and life and life and life. Begin to move as you carry the beat, tapping against yourself, the walls, the floor, each other. Keep your eyes as closed as is safe, and move the rhythm deeper into the movements of your bodies, rocking, swaying, stomping on this beat that is uniquely yours, the beat of you together.

Use your bodies to draw up power from the earth, make gestures that are as big as what's available to you, add sounds that come from that deep beating place—maybe it's a keening wail of grief, a wrenching cry of rage—echo and witness each other. Keep your eyes half closed, look inward, keep the beat, let it take you into new body postures. Play with

Goddess power poses, play with postures of humility, play as animals, beat your wings. Lead and follow each other in a trance-dance-play that stays anchored by this beat you keep together. When you feel it's right, begin to whisper, "If you see me fall, then we are drowning. Reach for me, and we rise."

Let this sound travel through you, each pick it up when you are ready until you are repeating it together like a pact. Come back to the circle, come back to awakeness, continue to repeat this promise, looking each other in the eyes, until it rings like a new truth in your skin. If you see me fall, then we are drowning. Reach for me, and we rise.

See it in the eyes and gestures of everyone you encounter. May all your encounters become whispers of this truth. May you be cells bearing with you a rhythm of peace and of liberation.

Ritual for Solitary Crafting

Rebecca Barnstaple told us to notice the ways in which we are already dancing. Dance isn't outside us; it emerges spontaneously from us all the time. It offers us memory and metamorphosis.

From now until the next new moon, gently nudge yourself toward dancing. Choose an item you can wear all month to remind yourself: a pendant, a bracelet, an elastic band. Every time you notice it, think of it as an invitation to dance. Look up traditional dances from your ancestral cultures and identify one move, one twitch of the wrist, one stomp, and try it in the bathroom, on the walk home. Alone in the evening, put on a song you love and just play. Welcome the silliness and pleasure of dance, play into your sense of who you are and can be. Let it open up what's possible.

One last story:

I failed my driving test many times. I was a forty-one-year-old woman with a child living deep in the woods with no driver's license; the situation was unsustainable. I booked a test for the end of the summer and spent the summer practicing. And that summer I also gathered branches from the river near me, branches that had been shaped by the water. In a ritual space one afternoon, I bound them together around the longest one and made a Witches' besom. Not a broom for cleaning, but a tool for spiritual sweeping. A kind of dancing partner. The night before my test Amy wished me luck and sent me, laughingly, a song spell: the song "Man in Motion" from *St Elmo's Fire*. That night, I played it loud and danced, laughing in dizzying circles with my besom all around the living room, sweeping my fear of failure, my frustration with myself, and all the misogyny from past inspectors that had tripped me up before all out the door. I just laughed and danced, and passed my test with flying colors. And it's a silly story, but every time we make our own lives better, we liberate our power to re-enchant the world. My kid watched me pass my test and the other day she said she was glad I was old enough to drive now so I could take her to school. Reach for me, and we rise.

Incantation

If you see me fall, then we are drowning.
Reach for me, and we rise.

5

New Moon in Leo

Music

This circle is led by Amy
with expansions by Risa.

The New Moon in Leo is planting the seeds of courage,
setting a legacy from a place of regality, knowledge and pride.

—MONEFA WALKER, ASTROLOGER

OUR LEO NEW MOON IS NOT AFRAID OF THE SPOTLIGHT, not afraid of taking center stage and unleashing a roar. But maybe we're also feeling languorous in the heat and full from the fruits of the first harvest. So for this new moon, let's invoke a tool of Witchcraft that—meditative or frenetic—we are always using, in the air and in our bodies, but let's view it through our world-changing Witch lens. A tool that we can conjure with no prior preparation—while we're under stage lights, swaying in a hammock, doing data entry, reclining in a beach chair, while we are cooking, cleaning, or picking berries or while we're eating them: music.

The power in this tool of the craft is ancient beyond comprehension. Tones, older than words, older than humanity, are a primordial source of magic, communication, and resistance. We craft songs to charm our homes, our towns, our planet. We send out blessings and protests in melodic waves from our mouths, bellies, and hands.

Whether we get our girl power from Bikini Kill or Spice Girls, whether we sing in a church choir or only in the shower, whether we feel the pulse on stage, in the audience, or through headphones in our bedrooms, whether we scream thrash metal or find our voice through instruments, communicating wordlessly but expressively through a piano or guitar, we know there is power there. A resonance. An ability to enchant a moment or change the vibe with the push of a button or the warble of our vocal folds. All songs are sacred.

The "Official Witch of Los Angeles County" Louise Huebner suggests in her synth-backed spoken word album, *Seduction Through Witchcraft*, with her reverb-soaked voice drenched in mystical echoing delay, that "to be a successful enchanter you must be able to generate dynamic magnetic impulses at will and project easily emotional force with tremendous intensity. In order to obtain your desires you must leash the powerful forces of your emotions, and when you do you'll free your spirit."[1] So maybe music is our most powerful, yet profoundly accessible, tool.

There is a room in my house in which, simply by listening to electrical impulses and mechanical waves, I can conjure any emotion, leash it, unleash it, and feel it. As a performer, projecting "easily emotional force with tremendous intensity" was my stock and trade. I brought a smoky dive bar to tears singing "Crying" by Roy Orbison, a cappella, as an homage to David Lynch and *Mulholland Drive*. I was advised against it—you can't sing a cappella in a punk bar! But I had a vision. By the end, the game of billiards had stopped, and in a rare quiet moment, sniffles broke the silence, then applause . . . At Christmas, in that same dingy pub, I sang "Ave Maria" in Latin as part of a sermon-spoofing performance. I changed the energy. Made it sacred. That's just rock 'n' roll.

When Sly Stone sings, "you can make it if you try," I believe him. When Elsa sings, "let it go," I feel like I can. Arms raising theatrically with the big bold notes, I can let whatever it is go.

"Our hearts were ringing in the key our souls were singing" serenades Earth, Wind and Fire in "September," a song largely about the intangible, spiritual nature of our minds' and bodies' reaction to music. So much of our language and culture is based on this divinity of song. We say things like, "that's music to my ears" or "it struck a chord" when we like something. We play second fiddle or march to the beat of our own drum. As our blood and guts and neurons play syncopated rhythms echoing the drum circle of planets around us, Witches can hear the music, though those who cannot may think us insane.[2]

Music is math, art, science, and soul. It is personal, political, confrontational, and escapist, provocative and healing. Most religious and magical practices, and even sports games, begin or end with singing because this act has the power to unite us, transforming our moods, spaces, and minds. All the New Age buzzwords are there, inside music theory and the science of sound: Frequency. Vibration. Harmony.

Risa: In our coven, we slipped easily into a language of resonance; it's New-Agey, but it just feels right. We pick up and slip into each other's streams of thought by noticing what resonates. Our conversations always feel like they have a mind of their own, and I think it's because no matter what we start out with, we always just follow the frequencies.

Music gives us permission to feel what we are feeling. Grief, jubilation, and everything in between.

For me, writing about music as a tool of magic feels like a fish writing about water. It is where I swim and fly and sleep. Where I eat and pray. It is where I find and express the purest of joys and the deepest of sorrows. Where I learned to decode the mysteries of love and channel anger.

We spoke to self-described Sonic Witch, Brooklynn, who shared a similar memory—she recalls weeping over love songs as a kid when, in reality, she had no experience of romantic love. Somehow music allowed her to be overtaken by emotions that were windows into the complexity of human experience. As she spoke, I flashed back to being seven or eight years old, in my own backyard, absolutely wailing in heart-wrenched agony over "It Doesn't Matter Two" by Depeche Mode. Music was a spiritual teacher on a primordial level, this backyard breakdown predated my first crush, my first heartbreak, by years.

People often ask me why I still collect vinyl records when my thousand-pound music collection could easily fit on a pocket-sized hard drive. And this is why: I have almost nothing from my childhood—no stuffies, certificates, souvenirs, or mementos (my parents were not precious), but I still have records that I got when I was nine years old. They *were* precious, and I protected them, moving them between houses and apartments for thirty-odd years. Each one is a talisman, a time machine, and a teleportation device, a tool with which I can access almost any point in my life, and conjure the whole spectrum of human emotion. My record collection is a trusted friend who never judges me for my taste, or my tantrums, nor trivializes my triumphs. It gives me permission to feel what I'm feeling and/or change it. And if the world ends, the internet explodes, and the grid is lost, I can power my turntable with a hand crank and slip out of existence listening to my favorite songs.

I have been so lonely that I felt like I was floating in space. I have tethered myself to my humanity with music.

I have been in love with the miracle of life and have been swept away by the infinite beauty of it all. Music scintillates the joy. I have been angry, confused, frustrated, heartbroken, dignified, ecstatic, wild, and burdened, and at every turn, music has been safe harbor for who

I was and how I felt. It has been amplified and reverberated through my psyche, notes in ears through mind and body. Bass in my bowels and treble at the top of my skull, I have never been alone. I have Odetta, Madonna, Betty Davis, Tina Turner, Bjork, Jill Scott, Erykah Badu, Grace Jones, Grace Slick, SZA, Joni Mitchell, Kathleen Hanna, Buffy Sainte-Marie, Melanie, Cindi Lauper, Beyoncé, Cher, Sharon Tandy, Divine, Robyn, and Janis Joplin in my circle at all times.

As I was growing up, my mother taught me hymns while my father taught me jazz while my sister taught me punk, and each genre was a vast awakening to a universe of human experience. Reverence, irreverence, and experimentation. Rhythms and melodies became memories and manifestos.

I collect records and musical instruments in equal proportion. Creating and consuming.

When I found out that Risa wrote songs, I produced her EP, layering instruments to re-create the ways and waves I heard in my head as she strummed her tunes on the uke.

Risa: At some point in high school I realized I'd always been writing songs. I liked long walks and turning small melodies over and over in the back of my mind. In my twenties, I got myself a cheap purple ukulele and started learning simple chords and keeping myself company whisper-singing those simple melodies in circles for hours. This was a way into trance for me, a place I could never get to by simple meditation alone. My mind and body were always too busy. But playing with music was like drawing, gardening, or hiking. It took my conscious mind out of the driver's seat and let new voices emerge beyond the delusion of control. It brought new possibilities. Looking back, all those songs I wrote told truths my conscious mind wasn't ready to accept. And they were spells that conjured a future I couldn't yet imagine. They were ghost stories and ancestor stories. My singing voice burst through barriers of fear and control when I left a paralyzing place and couldn't talk about it but sang with Amy for hours until the truth and the tears came out. It's braver now, but it's still broken and full of cracks and whispers. It is imperfect, but perfect for the kinds of stories it has to tell. And so is yours. Amy told me everyone should record an album, she wants to hear every song every person is whispering to themselves, and I think about that all the time. Magic is brimming in all our secret songs.

In all forms, music has been with me, a part of me, a guiding force of soul connection, more familiar than even my own consciousness. I met Risa backstage at a ukulele showcase. I met my spouse when I auditioned to be the singer in his band. While Kurt Vonnegut claimed that music was proof of the existence of God, in my life, music is not proof of the existence of God, but more like a god itself. It is a materialized integral aspect of what it means to be human, where, much like how single notes combine to form chords and instruments combine to form orchestras, the layers and interactions hold limitless, exponential possibilities, continuously expanding and reforming to inform our culture, to influence and express how we experience our humanity. Music is the centerpiece for so much of what we do; its absence in our lives is unthinkable.

In his book, *The Singing Neanderthals*, Steven Mithen contends that prehistoric language evolved from a single sound, "a sophisticated communication system that was holistic, manipulative, multimodal, musical and mimetic in character: Hmmmmmmmm."[3]

The great hum of life, of humanity, of insects and tectonic plates. The hum of minds and wheels turning as we play with our Witchcraft, tapping into the hum and singing along.

Our ability to communicate is perhaps as equally rooted in our ability to sing as it is in our ability to speak. Our songs are powerful and come from the deepest parts of our DNA. That hum. We hear it. And under Leo's New Moon we can conduct the spotlight, embrace the energetic electricity of this larger-than-life fire sign and sing proudly along.

I've sung in church choirs, school choirs, concert choirs, musical theater, in bands. I've been a lead singer, a back-up singer, and a solo acoustic act. I sang the national anthem with my choir at a Blue Jays game on the AstroTurf of Toronto's SkyDome the same summer that my punk band had its first gig in the basement of a masonic temple, across the street from the church where my choir held practice. As a result of a lifetime of playing with this vocal instrument, I am a confident singer. And because of this confidence, many people tell me that they "can't sing." I always reply, "Preposterous. If you can speak, you can sing."

Singing is an act of magic; it is a reclamation of sacred knowledge, our sacred voice, a sacred path that has been professionalized for profit.

There was a time when everyone sang. Perfection in musical perfor-mance was valued and respected but not a requirement. We all knew songs and we all enjoyed singing. Then came radio, later records, audio CDs, television, movies and the internet. The realm of song became the domain of professionals and lay people became silent lis-teners. Today we have whole groups of people who never sing and never even think of singing as something they might do.[4]

We sing to enchant space and time. And we sing to break the spells that stifle our voice. Sing everywhere, whenever; raise that energy and soon you will sing without self-conscious judgment. Sing in the same spirit that you walk. There's no need to be "good" at walking. You're not training for a walking competition; you're not hoping for a shot at break-ing into the Walking Business. There's no TV show to find the country's best walkers.[5] We don't think about walking, we just walk. Witches sing like that.

Loudly! Ceremonially! With reckless abandon. Get unrepressed, gather your Witchiest self, your most powerful voice, and conjure the thunder that lives in your lungs and mouths.

In Judaism we find *zemirot*, sacred strains for sacred occasions, and in synagogue, we find a cantor whose job it is to lead prayer in song. In Christianity we find gospel music in many forms; most parts of Sunday service are punctuated with songs from the choir or the congregation. The call to prayer in Islam, the *adhan*, is performed in song and nowa-days pumped through loudspeakers into town squares. Hindus practice *kirtan* or *puja*. Where there is divinity, there is music. It creates culture.

"Singing is claiming space. Making your voice be heard is definitely a political act," Michaela Harrison told us. "Singing is inherently polit-ical."[6] In her Whale Whispering project, Michaela took to the sea to sing to and with whales—those ocean dwellers who bore witness to the transatlantic slave trade across waves of various types: marine, sound, brain. The message she received from the whales was "We are one."

> *What we need to be doing is singing to change the state of things. I'm convinced that singing together is the answer, that wailing together is the answer. I'm so convinced that setting our intentions to shift this vibration and jettisoning our voices out into the air, out into the waters, into the ether as a collective of folks who are joined in the intention of stopping the cycle of violence and harm that all these systems we find ourselves inside of are reeking on the planet as a whole, on women, on prismatic folks, on people of colour, on all the ecosystems, all the animals . . . that we can change this with our voices. I'm convinced of it.*[7]

Billie Holiday's song "Strange Fruit" is said to have kick-started the Civil Rights Movement in America. The death of "Over the Rainbow" songstress Judy Garland made its way into the history of the Stonewall riots for gay liberation when some people claimed that the grief had, in some small way, contributed to the anger, the need to throw the first brick and start a revolution.

We can make music at any time, in any place, with just our bodies. With our lungs and lips and throats, completely changing our breath, changing the vibration of our chests and necks, changing the air around us, and changing our environment.

Think of film and television. We know these as visual media, but while our eyes register what we see, it is our ears that often tell us how to feel about it. The musical score delivers the *emotional* information. Imagine a scene in which a person is approaching. Is the music menacing? Jolly? Tense? Romantic? A few simple musical notes might tell us more of the story than the pictures on the screen.

This is alchemical. The mixing of things to create other things. Witches pay attention. When we add music to any given situation, or even change the music that's playing, the effect is immediate and obvious, unleashing a complex mystery; yet the act in and of itself is so simple. It is the push of a button. Instant Magic.

A major chord sounds happy. A minor chord sounds sad. Wait. What? Musical notes, when combined with other musical notes, all at once or in succession, have emotions inherent in them!? This sounds like Witchcraft to me, so let's put a few of these spells into our toolbox by listening to songs that contain these chords, looking for music in these keys, playing them on instruments in great ringings out, and testing their effectiveness at changing the tone of our spells.

We can use Christian Schubart's *Ideen zu einer Aesthetik der Tonkunst* (1806) as a jumping off point:

C Major—completely pure. Its character is: innocence, simplicity, naivety, children's talk. D Major is the key of triumph, of Hallelujahs, of war-cries, of victory-rejoicing. E Major, noisy shouts of joy, laughing pleasure and not yet complete, full delight lies in E Major. F Minor— deep depression, funereal lament, groans of misery, and longing for the grave. B Major conjures anger, rage, jealousy, fury, despair. B Minor is the key of patience.[8]

I spoke to astrologer and classical pianist Monefa Walker about the link between magic and music. "Music," she told me, "is as old as the universe. One of the oldest and strongest forms of Magic. Beethoven said 'Music is a higher revelation *than all wisdom and philosophy*. Music is the electrical soil in which the spirit lives, thinks and invents.' He also wrote that '*music is indeed the mediator between the spiritual and the sensual life*.'"[9]

Monefa also quoted Nikola Tesla who said, "If you wish to understand the Universe, think of energy, frequency and vibration." And Brooklyn repeated this Tesla quote when we spoke. These two powerful, Black, neurodivergent Witches harmonized unintentionally across time, both tuning into a wave of sonic magic and amplifying it. It resonates for Witches, sonic or otherwise. It ties together the ancient and contemporary—all of our ideas that live in the space between what we know and what we feel. Through this lens—and with the backing of scientists, artists, and historians—music becomes a spiritual, sensual, and material tool for understanding the universe and our place in it.

Socrates said "When the soul hears music, it drops its best guard." Music is a potent charm with which to bewitch ourselves and others. Learn to use it and you can gather your communities and gently undo your enemies.

Musician Athena Holmes told us, "Music is witchcraft because Music is vibration, which is the heart of all life. It has the power to move people emotionally. It has the power to create change. Through song-writing we can channel our ancestors, we can channel messages. Music *is* life. You're accessing energy. You're accessing vibration. Where there's movement, there's life. You're changing these vibrations."[10] Athena has incorporated *body-percussion* into their practice, beating the chest in rhythmic ways as they vocalize. Athena accesses these original tools of music-making and also uses computers, electric, and electronic instruments.

Synthesizers are Witchcraft at work too, aren't they? They take mere electrical impulses and turn them into emotions, sounds poems, dance tracks, beats, and tones beyond imagination. Here we find Wendy Carlos, who built her own instruments, wired her own synthesizers, took classical baroque music and transformed it into disco bops with her game-changing 1968 album *Switched-On Bach*. A few years before the release of her experimental, yet Grammy-winning, album, Wendy had begun hormone replacement therapy. In an interview that appeared in *Playboy* magazine's May 1979 issue, Wendy said: "I was about five or six . . . I remember being convinced I was a little girl, much preferring long hair and girls' clothes, and not knowing why my parents didn't see it clearly.[11]

The proceeds from *Switched-On Bach* allowed Wendy to materialize her transition. She told *Playboy*, "[I had] always been concerned with liberation, and [I was] anxious to liberate myself."[12] Years later she remarked, "The public turned out to be amazingly tolerant or, if you wish, indifferent . . . There had never been any need of this charade to have taken place. It had proven a monstrous waste of years of my life."[13] Wendy's honesty with herself and with the public gave rise to new conversations about sex and gender, solidifying her place as a cultural architect. Wendy took to photographing eclipses, the layers of bodies that inform our views, and had her photography published by NASA. *Switched-On Bach* remains among the best-selling classical albums of all time.

"In all cultures we have our prayers that we sing," medicine woman and sound healer Annie Lamoureux told me. "And this is where we connect with the Great Spirit, and connect with the gods and connect with the higher self. Especially when we get into a trance mode."[14] Annie beat her hand on the table in an urgent tempo, conjuring a powerful and ancient act. Annie conjures the ancient with her hand, just as Wendy Carlos conjured the baroque with her synth. Music connects.

As Layne Redmond points out in her book, *When the Drummers Were Women*, "Handheld frame drums are among the oldest known musical instruments . . . The rituals of the earliest known religions evolved around the beat of frame drums." Music, as many ancients knew it, was a gift from Goddess. Inanna in Sumer, Hathor in Egypt, The Muses in Greece. "The drum was the means our ancestors used to summon the goddess and also the instrument through which she spoke. The drumming priestess was the intermediary between divine and human realms. Aligning herself with sacred rhythms, she acted as a summoner and transformer, invoking divine energy and transmitting it to the community." Redmond contends that drumming "answers a deep cultural need to reestablish our rhythmic links with nature and with one another."[15]

In group drumming, we experience synchronicity. It is both a spiritual and physical grounding. When we drum alone, we still get a taste of this magic of combination, our left and right hands seesawing back and forth with the beat, or we let off steam as we bang our sticks in left-right unison. In one study, group drumming resulted in significant reductions in anxiety and depression and an increase in overall mental well-being and correlated with a decrease in inflammatory markers in the bodies of the participants.[16] But before we go running off to our local music supply shop, let's take a breath and remember that this reestablishment of rhythmic links can also be achieved by clapping our hands, or by beating a wooden spoon against a cardboard box. I'm sure for many of us, our first drum kit was a stick dragged along a fence, a set of pots and pans spread (with or without permission) across the kitchen floor.

Singing, drumming, strumming, and tickling ivories can connect us to our spiritual centers, our primordial humanity, and our Witchcraft. It is healing in both spiritual and practical ways. Artist Emmie Tsumura told me that music was an integral part of her cancer recovery. Sounds pumped through her headphones as radiation pumped through her blood. Emmie memorized her playlist and knew that as David Bowie's song "Heroes" crescendoed in her ears, a nurse would enter the room and the treatment would end for the day. But music played another role in her recovery. A friend's band released an album as a way to help Emmie raise funds for her continuing care.[17]

The tradition of music-activism in fundraising, consciousness-raising, and song-writing continues to be a source of rich history and advocacy for Witches everywhere.

At Ghana's "witch camps"—settlements where women accused of Witchcraft can find safety and community—a set of field recordings was produced by Ian Brennan and Marilena Umuhoza Delli to raise money for the women, to amplify their stories, and to bind us to them.

"Belief in witchcraft is sometimes also used as simple scapegoating for the arrival of bad luck such as foul weather or illness," says Marilena. "More commonly, it is a justification for pre-existing hate and prejudice. A member of my own family was driven out of her village in Malawi as a child after she was accused of being a witch due to having a white father—a fate that could have been my own if our places of birth were simply swapped."[18]

Created with a community of singing, accused witches use objects from corn husks and a teapot, to tin cans, tree limbs, and a balloon left over from the political rally as percussion. Ian and Marilena condensed their six hours of Witch Camp recordings into the twenty-track album "I've Forgotten Now Who I Used To Be."[19]

I listen to these recordings often, and one of my favorite hooks plays on repeat like an earworm in my head: ehmmbadumbah edmbadumbadumbah ehmmbadumbah edmbadumbadumbah. Onomatopoetic.

Untranslated, indecipherable, but for me, the lines hold more meaning than many lyrics I've written or read. Through these songs I hear a whole history of persecution and persistence. It is, I hope, healing for them as it is for me.

Science is still catching up to understanding how sound heals, but the current research is promising. A review of 400 published scientific articles on music as medicine found strong evidence that music has mental and physical health benefits in improving mood and reducing stress. In fact, rhythm in particular (over melody) can provide physical pain relief.[20]

One study found that "an hourlong sound meditation helped people reduce tension, anger, fatigue, anxiety, and depression while increasing a sense of spiritual well-being. The sound meditation used a range of Tibetan singing bowls, crystal singing bowls, gongs, Ting-shas (tiny cymbals), dorges (bells), didgeridoos, and other small bells."[21]

If sound is sacred and healing, why is rock 'n' roll equated with the Devil? Why is music haram? Witches know: music stirs in us something before and beyond the rules of polite society, it connects us to the impossible-to-define rhythm of our planet, our universe, our bodies, and how those things combine to form the orchestra of existence. All of these feelings threaten the status quo. And that's what we are here to do. Threaten any system that serves to disenchant.

Princess Nokia raps about Orishas, KRS-One freestyles on the zodiac, Nick Drake sings of magic and the moon, George Clinton and Eddie Hazel conjure a deep mother goddess, Coven gives us black mass recordings, and Killing Joke formed their band around occult ritual, but when I think of the vast and expansive connection between magic and music, one voice fills my ears.

The story of Buffy Sainte-Marie is not just about a singer. It is a story about persistence, creativity, indigeneity, and ingenuity. She sang, "Magic Is Alive." She said that the core of her belief system is creativity. She was the first to incorporate ancient tribal sounds into a rock 'n' roll record and the first to use new digital technologies to record and send sound files in the creation of an album. Future, past, head and heart: Buffy Sainte-Marie is undoubtedly *holy*. Buffy is a medicine woman, with medicine songs through which we can trace how magic manifests as music through time. She teaches us that we can keep pace with technology while never losing our ancient roots.

Buffy's activism is relentless. Her music is incendiary. Her lyrics are provocative. Her energy for change seems limitless. But a kindness and a joy pour out of her glowing smile, something is comforting and playful about the tone of her voice. Even when her tears are visible, when her sadness and rage are palpable, amid her cries for justice, we can sense that sympathy is her guide. She radiates goodness . . . and magic . . . and love.

There's no official record of Buffy Sainte-Marie's birth. We know she was born in Saskatchewan. We know she is Cree, which often meant going uncounted at the time of her birth. Buffy was likely born in 1941, so she technically predated the epidemic of cultural annihilation known as The Sixties Scoop, when between the 1950s and the 1980s, it is estimated that at least twenty thousand Indigenous children were taken from their families. The Canadian Government kidnapped Indigenous children and adopted or fostered them out to primarily white middle-class families.

We know from Buffy's story and many others that this scooping actually began long before the 50s and continued long after the 80s. Starting in the 1800s, residential schools took Indigenous children from their families and placed them in religious indoctrination institutions. In total, an estimated one hundred and fifty thousand First Nation, Inuit, and Métis children attended residential schools. The stories of rampant abuse are devastating. The last residential school in Canada closed in 1996.[22]

As a baby, Buffy was shipped off to become a Sainte-Marie in whose family home she would, at least, discover a piano and the music within her. At three years old, she would patiently observe the piano lessons of her older brother, and afterward, she would run to the keys to re-create the lesson by ear and go on to compose by instinct. Andrea Warner wrote: "Every note she's ever played, arranged, composed or produced is by ear and memory, gut and feel."[23]

Ear and memory, gut and feel. Ear and memory, gut and feel. What do you sense? What do you remember? What does your inner Witch warrior advise? What emotions are arising? Ear and memory, gut and feel. Ear and memory, gut and feel.

Now, a warning—hold steady your heart lest it be shattered: Buffy also grew up being physically and then sexually abused by her older brother. And then by an adult man, a friend of the family. She took refuge in music and nature. Athena told me the same thing about their childhood: that music and nature saved them.

I don't like to quantify trauma, but I think it's safe to say that my childhood was a lot easier than Buffy's. Still, when I was a kid and needed an escape, I'd climb trees and sit in the embrace of their limbs for hours. Or I would put on a record and disappear, sinking into the tones like warm water. As I aged these things merged; that tree limb became a guitar neck, and I could clutch wood, sing, and play myself into another world.

Buffy was drawn to philosophy. She said, "I guess I fell in love with thinking in its limitless manifestations." Andrea Warner wrote, "Studying philosophy and world religions reinforced [Buffy's] church-less spirituality as well as the connection she'd always felt between herself and something bigger: the Earth, animals, ancestors and life itself. . . . Ultimately, it's creativity that is holy."[24]

Buffy, at heart, is a creator. Not just a thinker, a philosopher, but a maker and a doer. In an interview with the CBC she reaffirmed:

To me there's a spirituality to everything. If we're made in the image of the Creator, what that means to me is that we're creative. . . . the purpose and the sum total of our lives has to do with our creativity.[25]

Buffy had a unique voice, an ear for music, a creative spirit, and a political message, plus, she came of age in the 60s, so naturally, she became a folk singer. Having gained confidence through coffee house gigs and tiny concerts while completing her philosophy and teaching degrees, Buffy made the decision to move to the undisputed hub of mainstream American folk music at the time: Greenwich Village. There she would edge her way into open mic nights and share the stage with a young Bob Dylan in a basement venue called The Gaslight. When *Time* magazine called Buffy, "the most intriguing young folk singer to emerge in many a moon," a record deal was inevitable.[26]

In 1964, Buffy released her first album: *It's My Way!* She thought this would be her only album, so she felt compelled to include every important message she had. Some listeners and music writers compared this to Frank Sinatra's "I did it my way," with the emphasis on the word *my*, but Buffy explains that her focus is on the word *Way*. She said, "This is my path. Discover your own. They're out there. The paths to wonderfulness, to effectiveness, to joy, to living are generated everywhere! Project Your Path Outward From Where You Are Inside Yourself."[27]

The *debut* song on her *debut* album was called "Now That the Buffalo's Gone," and as I hear Buffy singing, I can imagine the strength of character required for her to insist that this song about broken treaties and Indigenous genocide be her introduction to the world at large.

Buffy wrote her song "Universal Soldier" as news of America's war with Vietnam began to spread. The more famous folk singer Donovan covered this song and many assumed he had written it. "Universal Soldier" was also covered by The Highwaymen who, in a case of cocktail-napkin contract fuckery ended up owning the publishing rights to the song. It took Buffy ten years and twenty-five thousand dollars to buy back the rights to her song; some websites still show Donovan as the songwriter.

I can't help but see the connection between songs and selves and land. Songs Back. Land Back.

Cree community organizer Ronald Gamblin wrote:

When I hear Indigenous youth and land protectors chant "Land Back!" at a rally, I know it can mean the literal restoration of land ownership. When grandmothers and knowledge keepers say it, I tend to think it means more the stewardship and protection of mother

*earth. When Indigenous political leaders say it, it often means com-
prehensive land claims and self-governing agreements. No matter
what meaning is attached, we as Indigenous nations have an urge to
reconnect with our land in meaningful ways.*"[28]

It's My Way—Track 5. "Cod'ine." The song is about addiction and
withdrawal and comes from Buffy's own experience. As she tells it, she
went to a doctor for a bronchial infection and he gave her what he told
her was a vitamin B12 shot, some pills, and a prescription for more pills,
which he said were antibiotics. For a few weeks, she received check-ups
and more shots. Then, luckily, she went on a trip. She started feeling
sick, so she went to a pharmacy on the road to refill her prescription. The
pharmacist told her she wasn't sick, she was going through withdrawal.
Horrified, Buffy spent the next several days riding out the hell of being
junk sick. Writing "Cod'ine" helped her process, but the experience still
haunted her—years later she heard a story and it all made sense. That
same doctor had been sent to jail for turning young, vulnerable women
into prostitutes by deceptively and intentionally addicting them to
drugs.[29] Buffy may have escaped this doctor's evil plan, but, encounter-
ing violence all her life, she did not escape the statistics. The missing and
murdered Indigenous women (MMIW) epidemic has been described as
a Canadian national crisis and a Canadian genocide. And in the United
States, Native American women are more than twice as likely to experience violence than any other demographic. She did, however, survive.

Buffy lived through the violence of displacement, was sexually abused
as a child, and as an adult, found herself in another violent, abusive
relationship—her marriage. This is the power of systemic displacement,
theft, and personal abuse. If it can convince a person of miraculous will,
like Buffy, even momentarily (she did leave him), that violence is what
she deserves, imagine what it does to us mere mortals. Predators are
drawn to the vulnerable, so when we as a society make an entire people
vulnerable, when Indigenous women are marginalized and disenfranchised both socially and economically, we create this epidemic. Emotional vulnerability is powerful. Systemic vulnerability is powerlessness.

Buffy has put out twenty-one records; we won't dig into them all here, but I do want to stop in 1969 to drop the needle on *Illuminations*. This record blew my fucking mind when I first heard it. It was punk before punk, goth before goth, prog before prog. Buffy has inspired musicians of every genre by discovering and following her own path.

On *Illuminations'* opening track, Buffy sings that God is alive and that magic never died.

Though the lyrics are taken from Leonard Cohen's novel *Beautiful Losers*, amid her strange synths that sound like condensation dripping in a cave, Buffy's voice seems supernatural, like the words came from a primordial source, rather than Cohen's writings. Her music is a timeless synthesis of past, present, and future. In a world where, only a few years earlier, Bob Dylan had shocked the world by playing GASP! an electric guitar, Buffy Sainte-Marie was making experimental goth punk. Her 1992 album, *Coincidence and Likely Stories*, holds the distinction of being the first major-label record to be made over the internet. Buffy and her producer used the then-new technology of MIDI files and the internet to send bits of music back and forth to create the album. "Starwalker" from her 1976 album *Sweet America* is considered the first powwow-style rock song.

Buffy pulls equally from the latest technology and the most ancient traditions to create her art, carving and discovering her own path along the way. She gives us permission to do the same.

Buffy was a recurring character on *Sesame Street* for five years starting in 1975, showcasing her musical combination of radical ideas and kind-heartedness. Sesame Street aimed to balance the scales of justice in education by providing early childhood education for parents who couldn't afford it. Buffy introduced real, abstract concepts and promoted an emotional maturity that some adults still struggle to grasp. In her albums, on television, she spread her message via song.

In 1983, Buffy Sainte-Marie became the first Indigenous person to win an Oscar when her song "Up Where We Belong" took home the Academy Award for Best Original Song, having appeared in the film *An Officer and a Gentleman*.

If you're wondering why she's not as famous as those whose careers she'd helped to inspire, like Bob Dylan or Joni, the answer is threefold.

One: Buffy's just not a fame monster. She tells a great story of going on tour with a then near-unknown, Paul Simon. Buffy had already had some success, so she was set to headline the shows. Paul Simon made a stink and insisted that Buffy should open for him. Buffy only learned about this when she read Paul Simon's autobiography, many years later. She said, laughing: "I didn't even know that was going on at the time. That's how unimportant it was to me."[30]

Two: Buffy was invited to be on the *Tonight Show* with Johnny Carson—a major pitstop on the road to celebrity—but producers told her she wasn't allowed to talk about Indigenous rights or pacifism . . . so Buffy refused to appear.

Three: Buffy knew that her activism may have cost her her career in some ways, but she believed it was a consequence of seeking justice. Many other Indigenous activists and friends, after all, had paid a price far worse. But in the late 80s, a bombshell of a story dropped into Sainte-Marie's lap. She was being interviewed on the radio when the interviewer apologized for having participated in a campaign to suppress her music in the 60s and 70s, when presidents Lydon Johnson and Richard Nixon were in power.[31]

In another interview, Buffy said, "I found out 10 years later, in the 1980s, that President Lyndon B. Johnson had been writing letters on White House stationery praising radio stations for suppressing my music," and "In the 1970s, not only was the protest movement put out of business, but the Native American movement was attacked."[32] Despite being blacklisted, Buffy continued her music and activism. She once said, "I don't like to despair. It's uncomfortable. It kind of hurts to despair. So instead of despairing, I try to do things about it."[33] Andrea Warner quotes Buffy saying something that my Aunt Bea used to say all the time, something which I, in turn, say *all* the time: "It's better to light a candle than to curse the darkness." Buffy believes that we are always evolving—mutating, ripening, becoming—and that idea is the foundation of her creative and persistent approach to her life and its rippling effect.

Buffy said, "I have two main prayers: one is 'thanks' and the other is 'wow.'"[34] When we think about music as a tool for Witchcraft, maybe our best bet is to just start with "thanks" and "wow" and see what rhythms and melodies are activated by these prayers.

Music is perhaps the most ethereal, nebulous form of occultural art. When you finish a painting or a sculpture or a poem, you have a tangible, material object. When you finish playing a song, all that is left is the echoing feeling. Vibration, resonance. The experience of a song. This is life.

We sing and play and clap our hands, and like Buffy, Wendy, Micheala, Brooklyn, Monefa, and Athena, we can channel our history, rage, and joy. We can materialize our emotions, affect the moods of those around us, heal our bodies and minds, connect to our ancestors and to the divine. Music is magic, it is part of our Witchcraft, and we join together in the infinite choir, nurturing the electrical soil in which the spirit lives. We hear the song in the distance and sing along.

Ritual

Make a cup of hot tea. I know it's Leo season, but your voice wants the lubrication of steamy liquid. Call in hot Leo.

Situate yourself in a comfortable space and position.

Think of your body filling with air like tea in a teacup—first fill the bottom, expand your stomach, then the middle, expand your diaphragm, then fill to the top, expand your lungs.

Go to Google or YouTube and search "Tanpura Drone."

Pick a result—these drones come in lots of tones and varying lengths, so just follow your instinct and your time budget and pick one.

Listen.

Hear the base note of the drone.

Find that note.

Listen.

Now, begin to vocalize that note: uhhhh, oooh, or ahhhh. "E," "A," and "I" feel too tight in the face for this, so keep it a soft vowel sound. Loosen your jaw. Relax your face, your brow, your lips.

Hear the note coming from you and from the tanpura.

Listen.

Breathe.

Conjure Leo's fearless bombast and sing.

Choose one sound, for now, and stick to it. The idea is to free some mind space. No lyrics. Not even shifting from oooh to ahhh. Like the drone itself, we stay in one place. One note, one sound. For now.

Keep this note going, pausing as often as you please to breathe; singing requires air, first and foremost. Don't hold the note until you're croaking.

Just sing your note and breathe and sing and breathe.

Hear how your voice blends with the drone.

Listen while singing. Sing while listening.

Hum.

Howl.

Roar.

Once you feel comfortable and centered in your note, the tanpura's note, once you are aware and at ease with it, allow your vocal to stray from that tone of origin.

Improvise. Create your own melody.

There are no bad notes. No wrong choices.

If you're having trouble freeing your mind, throat, and tongue to musical improv, start with your base note and Do-Re-Me from there like Julie Andrews in the *Sound of Music*.

We're not aiming for Beyoncé or Christina Aguilera here, though I do encourage you to bust out a couple runs if they come to you! Remember: you're not trying to impress anyone. You're not trying to be a great singer. You're trying to be a whole human, in line with your ancestral hum.

As we listen to our voices play with the tanpura drone, we are paying attention to how the different notes we sing interact with the base note

of the drone. How combined frequencies create harmonies. How differ-
ent combinations of notes tell different stories. How harmonies create
emotions. How we are connected to the great hum of the universe.
Notice. Hear. Listen. Music. Rhythm. Pulse. Magic.
　　Ear and Memory,
　　Gut and Feel.

Incantation

Clap your hands as you read the incantation and see if a melody emerges.
Slip, if you can, from speech into song.

　　Ear and Memory,
　　Gut and Feel.
　　Ear and Memory,
　　Gut and Feel.
　　Ear and Memory,
　　Gut and Feel.
　　Ear and Memory,
　　Gut and Feel.
　　Ehmmbadumbahedmbadumbadumbah
　　Ehmmbadumbahedmbadumbadumbah

6

New Moon in Virgo

Ritual and Ceremony

This circle is led by Amy
with expansions by Risa.

*The Virgo New Moon is an opportunity to self-actualize by
shaping the tangible world to enhance mental, physical
and spiritual health.*

—JASMINE RICHARDSON, ASTROLOGER

SPELLS. THEY ARE ALL THROUGH THIS BOOK. Words are spells, songs are spells, baking is spellwork. But what of the spells that don't come to natural, manifested, material conclusions like poems or loaves of bread? What of the spells that have no tangible product? These spells that value process over products are the rituals and ceremonies that inhabit and enchant our lives. We can cast our spells and we can *be* our spells. As author Veronica Varlow proclaims, "your life is the greatest spell you will ever cast."[1]

Regardless of whether those who choose to demean us Witches want to accept it or not, almost every aspect of all our lives is a *ritual*—a series of actions performed according to a prescribed order to achieve a certain result. Science calls this methodology; psychologists and philosophers are concerned with the study of habits. For Witches, rituals and ceremonies are a means of enchantment, bringing magic to the mundane, a means to short-circuit control.

We go to the gym after work with the expectation or hope that the set of actions we perform there will lead to a long and healthy life. We do this knowing that we have no real control of what will be. We are at the mercy of our genetics, at the mercy of chaos. And we beg for mercy by enacting steps, on repeat, to appease the hungry force of fate. Through this viewfinder, a monthly contribution to a savings account is a prosperity ritual. A skincare regime is a conjuration—herbs, oils, and tinctures transforming your bathroom faucet into a spigot pouring waters from the imagined fountain of youth. We are constantly navigating and negotiating the path between mind and body, cause and effect, the material and the divine.

We go about our lives repeating actions, so it seems to me that perhaps the first step in reclaiming our magic, our agency, our autonomy, our souls, the first step to enchanting our world, is to elevate these tasks, reframe them as ceremonial, transform them from tedious to extraordinary. Relinquish the mundane.

"When simple things are consecrated, by prayer and magical intention," suggests author Rae Beth, "they are imbued with the power of ritual and become spells."[2]

In *Advanced Magick for Beginners*, Alan Chapman underscores the simplicity of acts of magic:

1. Decide what you want to occur.

2. Ensure that what you want to occur has a means of manifestation.

3. Choose an experience.

4. Decide that the experience means the same thing as what you want to occur.

5. Perform the act/undergo the experience.

6. Result.[3]

In a world in which the weight of capitalism and climate change feels crushing, rituals give us an opportunity to focus, momentarily, on what we *can* control. When the lives we inhabit feel like airplanes flying through turbulence, we snatch back some self-governance by sanctifying any moment we can. We take back control of both journey and destination, we weather the storm.

House of Our Queer creator Bex Mui suggests that ritual has never been more important. Bex starts her days, not by diving into a digital inbox of To Dos, but instead by lighting incense for her ancestors and saying good morning to her plants and fish. "Clearing the energy to start my day has changed my relationship to work and my relationship to space," Bex claims. Rituals root and ground us in the unseen support that's all around us. Bex says "our true ancestors delight in us when we are living closest to our authentic truths."[4]

When I first moved to Montreal, I lived for a short time in a Sigma Chi fraternity house. I wasn't a member, of course, but they had a spare room, and it was cheap. The only catch was that one night a year, I had to leave the house and not return until the following day. On this night, they would perform their secret, sacred rites. No amount of charm on my part or alcohol on theirs would allow them to reveal the details of this ritual. Trust me, I tried. But it struck me that these boys, these future leaders of white-collar America, would keep and sanctify a mystical practice, guarding its secrecy like Knights Templar.

In Bohemian Grove, California, the Cremation of Care is an annual ceremonial production produced and performed by the Bohemian Club, whose members have included several former United States presidents, high-ranking politicians, bankers, and military officials. Rich, powerful, mostly white men gather to do magic in secret. It sounds like fiction, but it's real.[5]

If nothing else, the existence of the Cremation of Care ceremony is evidence that capitalist and hegemonic greed requires that those in power kill their Care. Capitalism and Care are mutually exclusive. Care must be destroyed.

We spoke to artist and therapist Edgar Fabián Frías about this phenomenon. Edgar said, "the reason they want to destroy care is because care gets in the way of profit." With The Golden Dome School collective, Edgar has performed a counter ritual every year for the past seven. The Resurrection of Care, which takes place just after Bohemian Grove's cremation, is an antidote to a poison. Golden Dome founder Eliza Swann "wanted to create something that would respond to this [Cremation of Care] ritual. It's the community coming together to resurrect care and to do some counter magic." Edgar said, "ritual, ceremony and community building are all practices that can transmute energy and change energy. Some of my powerful spells have come from exactly those moments when I feel disempowered, I feel angry, I feel like there's no hope. And I turn to my practice as a space to allow that energy to become something else."[6]

In frat house training grounds and in Bohemian Grove, the powers that be, world leaders, past, present, and future cultural architects, are harnessing the power of ritual and ceremony while simultaneously fostering a society that mocks and rejects Witches for doing the same. We resist by doing spells set up in opposition to that which would kill off our ability to care, ritualistically resurrecting care where it's been killed and burned to ash.

Risa: Writers about "Magick"—here I use the spelling from the Crowlian tradition—tend to use ritual *and* ceremony *interchangeably. But I think it's useful to tease out the differences.* Ceremony *is performed for an audience and the audience is part of the magic. Dion Fortune saw two main types of Ceremony:* initiation, *whereby a practitioner is introduced to magical forces, and* evocation, *where those forces are called upon to fulfill the practitioner's will. The audience is the fraternity and the ceremony makes a statement about the world that they affirm. The ceremony brings about a change of states, and—like particles—the behavior is influenced by the observers. Ceremony is not enough. A wedding is not enough. We need the rituals of love enacted every day.* Rituals *as in magical gestures that accumulate magical weight over time, that in and of themselves have the power to conjure the intangible profound, to pull on the threads of energy in this confluence of here and now to change the texture of the always-birthing world.* Ritual *as in a private communion with yourself and your ancestors and your body and all the small seeds you are calling forth. A daily watering, the magic words of seeing someone and loving them just as they are. Fresh flowers, spirit meals. All the consecrated minutia of care.*

Witchcraft is not a religion; it is not dogmatic or exclusionary. Rather, Witchcraft is a lens through which we perceive our surroundings, our inner and outer workings; it is a reframing device in our pursuit of defining ourselves *for* ourselves.[7] It is an acknowledgment of the Roshomonic reality that our perspective largely, if not entirely, informs our truth. We can make difficult things slightly less difficult by conjuring the sacred.

I hate cleaning. Hate it. I'm much happier making messes than I am tidying up their aftermath. But give me a hyssop floor wash (hyssop has been used for millennia to purify the body, spirit, and home, and is said to remove negative energy) with a splash of Florida Water (a beautifully scented cologne used in folk magic for offerings and cleansing), and I'll spend hours on my hands and knees, gladly and gratefully scrubbing circles as I wash away both the dirt and my own negativity.

Scientific American succinctly defines rituals as "the symbolic behaviors we perform before, during, and after meaningful events."

Researchers found that "rituals make a lot of sense and are surprisingly effective." They studied athletes and fishermen, people who had suffered loss, people in mourning, and found that

> *the superstitious rituals enhanced people's confidence in their abilities, motivated greater effort—and improved subsequent performance. These findings are consistent with research in sport psychology demonstrating the performance benefits of pre-performance routines, from improving attention and execution to increasing emotional stability and confidence.... Our results [also] suggest that engaging in rituals mitigates grief caused by both life-changing losses (such as the death of a loved one) and more mundane ones (losing a lottery).*[8]

Here's what Witches know that those who go searching outside themselves for the meaning of life do not know, or cannot see. The meaning of life is not prescribed; it is ascribed. We decide what is meaningful, what it means, why it means what it does, and how. We are in charge of what is meaningful in our lives.

I recently had some health issues that required blood tests, and the clinic booked my appointment for December 21, thoroughly interrupting my plans for Winter Solstice. At first I was annoyed, but when my inner Witch took over, this Winter Solstice bloodletting became a ceremony, a conjuration, a blood sacrifice and prayer for answers and for health.

In the early days of our first coven together, The Mystical Coven of Bosom Friends and Kindred Spirits, I, Risa, and a few others did a prosperity ritual.[9] We were all pretty broke at the time, students and artists trying to find our niche and still pay the bills. Prosperity was something that reality couldn't seem to provide, so, as is the case with billions of stories about the disenfranchised, we turned to magic.

We sat in circle, each offering an herb or a leaf and an honest prayer to the center. The spell resolved itself as they always did, with laughing, crying, singing . . . I returned home to find an email from a former client asking me to do some graphic design work. I was awestruck by the immediacy of our magic, empowered but also humbled by the fact that the universe had not dropped money on my doorstep. Instead, I had been given an opportunity to earn it.

Another time we did a spicy energy concoction spell—herbs mixed with ginger ale. We passed the chalice around the circle, each taking a sip and saying a prayer. Not one but two of our sisters found partners for steamy make-out sessions at the bar that night.

Skeptics will of course say that these are mere coincidences, or the tricking of our own mind to behave differently, more confidently. A placebo effect. But the startling thing about placebos, like magic itself, is that they work, or at least, they work more often or better than they should.

"The placebo effect is more than positive thinking—believing a treatment or procedure will work. It's about creating a stronger connection between the brain and body and how they work together," says Professor Ted Kaptchuk of Harvard. Placebos won't lower your cholesterol or shrink a tumor. Instead, placebos work on symptoms modulated by the brain, like the perception of pain. "Placebos may make you feel better, but they will not cure you," says Kaptchuk.[10]

And this is exactly the case with rituals and magic and Witchcraft. They change our perspective and create or open our eyes to opportunities, but the acting on, following up, being prepared for those opportunities, and being willing to put in the work, these things are up to the Witch. Depending on the beliefs, the practices, and the values of each individual Witch, rituals can connect us with our own divinity, with cosmic forces outside of ourselves, and/or with ancestors and deities, but for every Witch, the ceremonial must be entwined with the practical.

We do these rituals to enchant our lives and the lives of others, to conjure the opportunity, strength, and bravery to do the work, not to have the work done for us by supernatural beings. Even those who invoke gods to act as agents of justice, healers and hexers, don't petition the gods to work for free. This is why offerings are a large part of ritualistic practice, across time and place. In our world of cause and effect, reflection and ricochet, nothing is free, and nothing is without consequence.

Searching for ceremonial role models, we turn to two Witches whose paths could not have been more different, and yet both reached the same conclusions about the value of magic and ritual in our lives: Migene Gonzáles-Wippler and Genesis P-Orridge. Migene was born in Puerto Rico, where the Caribbean sea meets the Atlantic ocean, in 1936, the same year that Puerto Rico granted full suffrage to the island's women. Genesis was born into the bleak, dismal hegemony of 1950s post-war England. Migene was exposed to ancient spirituality in her youth and did a lifetime of study to legitimize that which she knew was true. Genesis was rejected by polite society and spent their life sneering at legitimacy.

A quick scan of self-described, New Age author, Migene González-Wippler's book titles—*Return of the Angels*, and *Dreams and What They Mean To You*, and if you're like me, you might be tempted to cry WooWoo. If it helps, know that she has a PhD in cultural anthropology, degrees in psychology and anthropology, has lectured at the American Museum of Natural History, Columbia University, NYU, and Princeton, was a science editor for the American Institute of Physics, worked for the United Nations, and has written dozens of books . . . and if it helps quell the desire to dismiss her, know that she said this: "I don't believe in the supernatural. I believe in nature and all things natural. Everything that happens in this world always happens through natural channels and in accordance with immutable cosmic laws. All things— both real and surreal—are part of the cosmos, where everything has a place and a reason for being."[11]

WooWoo is a relative term, right? I'm sure a lot of people I know personally would classify this book or *any* discussion of magic or even just the word *spirituality* as New Age baloney. And honestly, that's okay. Whether you feel cold, comforted, or cringey when the subject of, say, angels comes up, there is a place for you here. For me, as always, I find myself somewhere in the middle. I'll be honest, I'm hardwired for cynicism and a lot of contemporary mysticism sets off my bullshit detector, which drowns out anything even potentially useful that the guru or *spiritual life coach* has to say. I've been told my eye roll is audibly dismissive and judgmental, the vestigial tail of my former life as teenage know-it-all. As I've matured, I've come to think it's a slippery slope from skepticism into arrogance. As our friend, author and medicine woman Granddaughter Crow, once quipped, "A closed mind is a comfortable place but you don't grow there."[12]

So, dear Witches, as we move through this world of magic, through Migene's teachings, her claims that we can survive death or create a universe with a magic word, as we move through the power of ritual, world-altering ceremonies, let's unfurrow our brows, keep our bullshit detectors on as an act of critical thinking and self-preservation *always* ... but keep them set to low.

Just for today, let's suspend our disbelief, and believe. Because placebos work more often than they should. Because the connections between mind, body, universe, and spirit are not understood. Because Migene's approach to magic is so logical and matter of fact, she makes me believe her. In a condescending world, Migene González-Wippler helps me believe in magic.

Genesis P-Orridge spent their lifetime raging against academic notions of credibility. Genesis was an extremely prolific, variously pro-nouned, transmedia artist and philosopher who, by design, changed course at will; their projects expanded, contracted, and were abandoned when they got too popular. It's hard to boil down a life like Gen's, and I think that's what Gen would have wanted—to exit the "cheap flesh suitcase" of the material world and leave as legacy an undefinable life that defies catch-phrase-worthy descriptions, maintaining, in life and death, what Gen called a state of flux.

In 1976, though, Genesis P-Orridge was given a label that might stick forever. Conservative Member of Parliament Nicholas Fairbairn called Gen and the other members of their COUM Transmissions collective "wreckers of civilisation." Genesis was self-admittedly "a big mouth and fanatic by nature," so even at the time, without the benefit of the icon status that they would achieve later, Gen took this as a compliment.[13]

"We were so proud." Gen told the *Guardian* many years later. "We had a flyer with that on it the very next day. The irony of it was that Sir

Nicholas Fairbairn—the [Tory] MP who called us that—was involved in various sex scandals. And his mistress, a House of Commons secretary, tried to hang herself outside his office. It was classic British hypocrisy: everything we were against."[14]

For Genesis *everything* was a ritual, a ceremony, a vision quest, a psychic seeking, especially music and art. Gen said, "It has always been my belief that Creation, the making of 'art' in any medium or combination of mediums, is a holy act. To be an 'artist' is as much a calling from and to a divine service as becoming a physician, nurse, priest, shaman, or healer"[15] Gen also wrote: "If we don't end the idea of separation between every day life and magickal work, then we're going to be at the mercy of those who wish to control us. So for us, it's very much a political thing."[16]

In a condescending world, Genesis P-Orridge helps me believe in magic.

We Witches know, from our world of fake news and alternative facts, that believing something or believing *in* something doesn't make it true or real. Believing Earth is flat doesn't make it any less round. But believing that our lives have meaning and value, that we have control over something, that we have agency and power, a connection to our Earth and galaxy, believing that death is not an end but another arc in the spiraling circle of what it means to be alive? Believing that magic can and does or even *might* exist? These are world-changing beliefs, enchanting our lives and determining our trajectories, becoming reality. As Granddaughter Crow said, "What a person believes constitutes how they behave in the world."[17] These beliefs can be political, spiritual, or even the beliefs we carry about ourselves, about our worth.

"I don't believe in Witches," my father-in-law teased.

"That's okay," I replied. "We exist whether you believe in us or not."

The only requirement of belief for the Witch is that we believe in ourselves.

Placebos are not just about believing or flipping a simple switch to release brainpower.

You also need the ritual of treatment. "When you look at these studies that compare drugs with placebos, there is the entire environmental and ritual factor at work," says Kaptchuk. "You have to go to a clinic at certain times and be examined by medical professionals in white coats. You receive all kinds of exotic pills and undergo strange procedures. All this can have a profound impact on how the body perceives symptoms because you feel you are getting attention and care."[18]

When we move this notion from the medical to the magical, we see the same mechanisms at work. Our intentions, our fantasies, imaginations, needs, and the significant or insignificant moments in our lives require attention and care. Our silences and screams require attention and care. When we deliver this attention and care, it can have a transformative impact on how we see the world and perceive our place within it.

As our covenmate Sarah Snellman put it, "rituals are the manifestations of our emotions." Much like tears are our bodies' way of releasing stress hormones, symbolic actions can help us release fears or frustrations, break obstacles, or cut cords.

We humans, but especially we Witches, live and breathe by symbols.

When we do a binding spell, we are symbolically enacting our desired result—that the person or thing will be bound, contained. The equal yet opposite is true with a cord-cutting spell—we attach two candles with a string, then we light the candles to burn the string. We burn the symbol of attachment to help us achieve our desired goals of detachment or to process the detachments that happen in our lives. When we do a freezer spell, we are changing a liquid into a solid. When we burn things, they occupy that liminal space between material and ethereal. Chemical reactions make earth into fire into air. Herbs and words, ideas and intentions, turn to smoke, turn to wind and spread, and we pray, hoping these thoughts and molecules can scatter, adjust the atmosphere, change our world. When we freeze or burn, tie up or tie down, when we make something new out of bits of something else, we are creating a change of state, hoping this action will promote a change of state within ourselves. From sad to happy, bitter to grateful, anxious to inspired; as water turns to ice, we hope, oppression turns to freedom; as herbs turn to smoke, we hope, struggle turns into abundance. To transform is an opportunity to be transformed. Rituals provide this opportunity.

Rituals and ceremonies are, to me, like acts of performance art where the intended audience is both ourselves and Goddetc the divine, the unknown and unknowable, the great invisible web that connects and protects us all.[19] I leave room in this audience for ancestors, both chosen and unchosen, birds and squirrels, and mycelial networks.[20] We are pleading with our deities or begging into the void for change.

As WhiteFeather Hunter reminds us: you're never alone when you're in ritual.

WhiteFeather's BioArt coven is a communal enterprise with a manifesto that is a collaborative living document and rituals that are performed with what WhiteFeather describes as an Exquisite Corpse approach. *Exquisite Corpse* is an art/party game where each "player" adds another part, usually to a drawing, without seeing the work of the person before. So one person draws the head, folds the paper over, and hands it to the next person, who draws the shoulders and chest. And so on. In the BioArt coven, this practice turns into ritual creation, where each contributor is asked to come prepared with a step. Together they form rituals that none could have imagined on arrival.[21]

As we see in the confounding, spectral nature of magic, contradiction is a welcome inevitability. We do rituals to both disrupt *and* sanctify the ritualistic status quo. We create rituals to dismantle rituals. Because while we may not think about what we are doing, or why we are doing it, these tiny actions, moments, minutes, aggregate to become our lives, our life stories, our legacies.

Again somewhat paradoxically, we can also ritualize by de-ritualizing—consciously performing tasks differently, challenging ourselves to never do them the same way twice. And this becomes its own praxis, an anti-rule rulebook. A commandment of no commandments.

We Witches tend to like it both ways.

We study ancient traditions, read occult history and guidebooks, and then we take that knowledge and bend it to suit our needs or our will. Trained or experimental or both. Ludic or staid or both.

Again, in this space, we find the meeting of Migene and Genesis. I find myself vacillating between wanting "evidence" and following the intuition of the unknown, so I keep Migene and Gen as beacons at each end of the spectrum. I turn to Migene when I need logic and reason, an argument that will stand up to academic criticism. But sometimes I just don't care what anyone else thinks. I want to create new modes of thinking that aren't weighed down by human constraints of logic or manners. For these times I have Gen. Carrying these two Witches in my heart reminds me to hold space for every approach, to reserve my value judgments for my own actions. Equal yet opposite. Priceless difference.

I picked up Migene's *The Complete Book of Spells, Ceremonies and Magic* because it was one of the few books I found that took a more global approach to magic. And I was instantly charmed by her. Years in academia have done nothing to diminish her spritely sense of wonder. She claims that "there is enough scientific evidence to prove the existence of a Creative Intelligence at work in the universe and that 'magic' is nothing more than cosmic energies channeled by the human mind to achieve specific goals."[22] Isn't that wonderful? So simple. So unquestioning. Nothing more than cosmic energies. Of course, that begs our question: What are cosmic energies? We may never know for sure, but Migene has devoted her life to answering that question. She has written more than twenty books on religion and the occult with themes ranging from Kabbalah to Santeria, amulets and talismans to ritual magic and spellwork. Dreams and death.

I first met Gen through the decidedly uncharming music of Throbbing Gristle. Disquieting, disturbing noise that somehow comforts as it confronts. Gen and Throbbing-Gristle partner Cosey Fanni Tutti are credited with, through their ceaseless and ritualistic experimentation, inventing the genre of industrial music.

Genesis P-Orridge was proud to have been called a wrecker of civilization, but Gen didn't want to just wreck society. Gen wanted to cut it up, rearrange it, expand it, and evolve past post-war British civility to uncover the power of ritual and protest disguised as music and art. When approached in COUM's early days by an art critic, Gen told him "it's not art. It's just what we do."[23] When the critic told Gen that he might be able to get the COUM collective an arts grant, something like

200 pounds, Gen was like, okay it *is* performance art. This wasn't because Gen was a sellout. Quite the opposite. So compelled to fuck with the status quo, be self-expressive and confrontational, Gen had never had a straight job. Right up until death, Gen *never once* had a regular job. But this lack of straitlaced employment wasn't because Gen was lazy. Again. Quite the opposite. One of the tenets of Thee Temple ov Psychick Youth, a project that took place between 1981 and 1991, in their *Thee Psychick Bible* states, "Thee Temple strives to end personal laziness and engender Discipline. To focus the will on one's *true* desires."[24]

Gen picked up the question "How do we short-circuit control?" from William Burroughs when the two met; this would become a centerpiece of Gen's life. Gen had been a long-time fan of Burroughs and Brion Gysin's cut-up philosophy/technique of creating literature and applied it to visual art, music, daily life, and eventually, their own body.

Burroughs was a magician too, and I don't want to pass him by without retelling one of his spells. Burroughs had a problem with a local business, so he took his portable tape recorder and walked up and down the street in front of the business, recording the ambient sounds. He took those tape recordings home and ritually mixed them with violent noise. Then he returned to the street and continued his pacing while playing his sound hex creation. The rumor goes that the business closed, but even if it didn't, I just wanted you to have this idea of homemade spells and using what you're into—tape recorders or flowers, knitting or rocks—and implementing that in your conjuration. I can picture Burroughs grumbling angrily to himself as his heels scuffed the sidewalk, and I want it for all of us.

Another central praxis for Gen was one picked up in a communal-squat hippie collective called The Exploding Galaxy. The group's main focus was to disrupt the brain-washing of habits by unsettling every-day routines. Members weren't allowed to sleep in the same bed on consecutive nights or wear the same clothes on consecutive days—all the clothes were piled in a trunk and worn on a first come first dressed basis. Every action or proposal was met with the group persisting: Why? Why? Why?

Many people, likely myself included, couldn't handle this kind of constant scrutiny, but Gen thrived. It was the challenge that Gen was seeking and would inform much of their life. Almost inevitably, though, as we find with so many gurus, and why we have to question those who tell us what to do . . . Gen left the commune after a few months when it was discovered that the rules about sleeping arrangements and collective agreements regarding the community coffer applied to everyone *but* the Exploding Galaxy's leader and his girlfriend.

In *Thee Psychick Bible*, Gen wrote this:

> *If our self-image is primarily based on the faulty, biased, prejudiced and highly edited memory recordings of other people, with their own agenda of who we are intended to become, as defined by this percep-tual process of un-natural selection, then ways and tools that allow us to seize the means of perception become vital to our fight to con-struct a self, a character, an identity that is truly and independently our own.*[25]

I got stuck on this for a hot minute: seize the means of perception. We're familiar with Karl Marx encouraging the workers to seize the means of production, or Marxist-feminists applying this idea to bodily autonomy and proclaiming, "seize the means of Reproduction," but what does it mean to seize the means of perception? *Perception*—the ability to see, hear, or become aware of something through the senses. A way of regarding, understanding, or interpreting something. Per-ception is not just seeing or hearing, but also understanding . . . how we process and internalize what we sense. And *means* in this con-text? Facilities and resources. So if we reframe the question it might sound like this: How do we take control of the resources that inform our understanding of ourselves and the world? And I think the first step is critical awareness, an Exploding Galaxy of questions beginning with Why? Knowing that the answer we often get—"because this is how we've always done it"—is neither sufficient nor true. When we examine our Witches, we find that there have always been iconoclasts, people who transgressed against the mythical norm. In *Thee Psychick*

Bible, Gen wrote, "Accept nothing, assume nothing, always look further, be open-eyed as well as open-minded and don't kid yourself."[26] This has informed much of my approach to magic and to life: be open-minded, but don't kid yourself.

With Gen and Migene to guide me, I move back and forth and in spiraling fractals between doing my historical and scientific research and experimenting wildly, following what I have read, learned, and studied, and being guided by the illogical and intangible truths that I know in my heart and soul. I keep Gen in one pocket and Migene in the other to remind myself that every path to enchantment is valid—that if polar opposites Gen and Migene were to meet in a room as they met in my drawing that accompanies this chapter, they wouldn't argue, gatekeep, or nitpick each other's journeys. I like to think they would share philosophies, stories, and ideas. They would be inspired by each other, in awe and honor. They would laugh, their disparate paths having led them to the same circle, the same universe of infinite possibilities.

While we modern Witches can focus on the peer-reviewed benefits of rituals in our lives, we also have to recognize that thousands of years of accumulated wisdom were nearly erased by the crushing weight of colonial hegemony. We must consider the possibility that these are not metaphorical, psychological tricks, but real and genuine recipes for interaction with a force that we no longer understand. And perhaps too, among the flames and rising smoke of the burning of the library at Alexandria, the burning of Witches, Maafa, the burning of human history, match-lit by kyriarchal erasure, the knowledge contained within was not lost, but as with smoke, it filled the air with its particles, found its way into soil and clouds and ether to return to us in visions and dreams and rain. Ideas that seem to come from nowhere.

I look to the origins of humanity and find that *sacrifices*, the presentation of offerings to higher beings or the dead, appear as early as the Middle Paleolithic Period.[27] So every time I volunteer or make a donation, I frame it as a ritual sacrifice of my money and my time. I present the hours or dollars as offerings to a goal that is bigger and higher than my Self.

Genesis lived without running water for like *a lot* of their life. Comfort was a sacrifice made by choice. We all make sacrifices. The process of selection is also a process of negation. Time for money, money for stuff. So when we choose, when we sacrifice, let's do it willfully, consciously, ceremoniously.

"What would we do with more money?" our anti-capitalist hero once asked. "We'd just use it to make more art."[28]

But like many Witches, Genesis was also hunted by the great protectors of the status quo, and in 1975, was arrested and stood trial for obscenity. The crime involved collage-art postcards that Gen had made and mailed to some friends, part of a process that Gen and others call Correspondence Art. Genesis went to court and was found not guilty, due, in part, they say, to a voodoo doll that had been given to them by a practitioner friend who instructed Gen to place it under the jury box.

In 1992, Scotland Yard raided Gen's family home and seized two tons of archived material, claiming that Gen had participated in Satanic child abuse. For the record, there was no truth in this. No charges were actually laid. Amid the Satanic Panic, a friend of Gen's had made a film that was deemed Satanic, so that provided another great excuse to hunt a Witch. While Gen was in Kathmandu using their life savings to help Tibetan monks build a well (for real, that's what Gen was doing at the time), all of Gen's possessions, including their entire archive of personal and collected art, books, objects, was seized by Scotland Yard, never to be returned. It's worth noting that less than twenty years later, in 2009, Tate Britain acquired Gen's rebuilt archives. Less than twenty years passed between Gen's possessions being labeled criminal and them being labeled important art history.

And this is exactly why we need to question the status quo. Harriet Tubman, for example, went from Outlaw to American Hero. Genesis went from Obscene to Important. They did not change, their stories remain the same, but what did change is the means of perception. What changed is how polite society perceived Harriet and Gen and pretty much every single Witch we've found in our search for iconoclasts, resistors, and enchanters.

Archeology tells us that our human ancestors engaged in ritual practice seventy thousand years ago.[29] And, cross-culturally, we continue to do so with rituals for birth and death, coming of age, and marriage. We have the ancient Holi Festival of Colors in India, and the more contemporary invention, the Tomatina in Spain, each splatting us in the face with vibrance every year. We practice rituals and ceremonies constantly to celebrate, mourn, mark, dignify, or just short-circuit control.

"Conjure aims to control the oppressor. To flip the narrative. To give power to those who are powerless," says rootworker Beverly Smith. "So when I say resist magically, there's physical resistance, like when I and others go and protest in public, walk the streets, do sit-ins in front of the police department—and then there's magical resistance when I take effigies of the police and bind them with snake shed and go throw their ass in the graveyard."[30]

"Put a protection spell on battered women," she says, "on sex workers, on children in foster care. Light a candle for them. Write a prayer for them. A ritual of binding for those who are violent. Do blessings. Draw attention and raise awareness. That is potent social justice magic. To be aware of the need for change. Magical people are helping to manifest progress." Our symbolic acts are magic echoes in reality. "Ritual is an act of making something sacred. What uplifts you, uplifts me. We are young gods in the making."[31]

One of the most ubiquitous occult practices of our time is the traditional blowing out of birthday candles. From our first year on Earth, we are indoctrinated into this practice. A cake is made or purchased, the birthday babe's name is written in sugar across the top, candles are placed according to age and lit. The crowd gathers to present the flaming cake while singing the traditional birthday hymn and the birthday babe is invited to blow out the candles as they make a secret wish. To reveal the wish is to doom its materialization.

The number of layers, the quality of the fondant, the penmanship of the icing script, none of these have any bearing on whether or not our wishes will come true.

The effigies we burn can be made by anyone, with materials gathered from bogs and bins.

In her memoir, *Initiated*, Amanda Yates Garcia conjures memories of her mother chanting, singing incantations over a pot of mac 'n' cheese. And I have done this myself, drawing a red ketchup pentagram over the neon-orange cheesy glow, a prayer that my next meal will be healthier. I slow down. Think about the steps. Appreciate each moment. This moment. This one right here that I might have otherwise ignored. I sanctify moments in any way I can with the words of Maya Angelou echoing in my spirit. "Try to live your life in a way that you will not regret years of useless virtue and inertia and timidity. Take up the battle, take it up! It's yours, this is your life, this is your world."[32]

Take up the battle.

This is our world.

We often call our spiritual activities our "practice," and there's something important there about the notion of *practicing*. When we practice, we try to get better at something. We repeat an action over and over in order to master it, but perhaps there is no mastery here in our world of magic. No full explanation. *Occult* is defined as "of, involving, or relating to supernatural, mystical, or magical powers or phenomena … beyond the range of ordinary knowledge or experience; mysterious."[33] Our second definition comes from *medicine* "(of a disease or process) not accompanied by readily discernible signs or symptoms."[34] Magic and the occult are, by definition, unknowable, forever mysterious, and that's why we call what we do a practice. We are in constant conversation with the cosmos and some questions will forever go unanswered. We keep practicing.

We go to band practice or basketball practice so we know what to do when the big game or big show comes along. Similarly, we create a foundation when we practice our craft, a place we can go back to when fortunes or misfortunes arise. One of the most helpless feelings is not knowing what to do, or what to do next. We keep practicing.

On the British side of my family, the first reaction to bad news is to stick the kettle on and make a pot of tea. Obviously the tea itself is warm and comforting, it can be tailored with or viewed as magical herbalism, but this automated act functions in the same way as, for example, the tree pose in yoga. The physical action requires just enough focus to calm the frazzled mind. The physical action makes a tiny bit of space for clearer thoughts. Step one: stick kettle on. Step two: drink tea and figure out step three.

Risa and I formalized our coven around the death of a friend. There was nothing we could do to bring her back, so we lit candles of black, white, and red and blessed her journey, grateful for having known her. Perhaps as the candles burn down, as Veronica Varlow told us her grandmother suggested, they burn upward on the other side, creating a signal fire to alert the spirit world that its presence is needed.[35] Perhaps the lighting of candles was just an excuse to gather, a mundane action, the mystical equivalent of turning on a kettle. Perhaps something is at work that we will never understand in which the energies of colored candles burning creates quantum wavelengths in our universe. Science tells us that everything has a wavelength, as difficult to observe as they may be. Whatever the case, we felt better, more connected afterward. We practice our craft so that when these times fall upon us and knock us down, we know how to get back up. We know, if nothing else, what to do next. We keep practicing.

Take up the battle.

This is our world.

Once again we encounter Migene González-Wippler and Genesis P-Orridge, both finding a way through death, despite taking dissimilar paths. Migene's was an academic approach. Pulling from laws of thermodynamics, fields of neurology and psychology, theories of evolution, Migene concluded that "based on what science has to tell us, we can postulate that our personality does survive the trauma of physical death and continue to live in another world or on another spiritual or astral plane."[36]

When Genesis lost their soulmate Lady Jaye, they went to Benin to participate in a twin ceremony that would reunite them. And in this ritual, Gen confirmed that for now, they would be the half that existed in the material world, while Jaye carried on into the immaterial—two halves of a whole—until they could be together with Lady Jaye again in another realm.

Edgar Fabián Frías told us that there comes a point when you have to decide whether or not you believe in magic.[37] Another artist, Emmie Tsumura, had this decision thrust upon her. In her battle with cancer, in confronting her own mortality, she met an Indigenous healer who told her, in no uncertain terms, "You have to believe in magic. You have to."[38]

"My humbling and enriching experiences in Santeria have taught me how great are my limitations and also how infinite my possibilities, all possible through the ashe, the power of the saints," Migene wrote. She went on to say, "Many of the experiences that I have had in Santeria may seem difficult to believe, but they pale in comparison to the ones I purposely did *not* cite—because they are completely unbelievable! The orishas have given me love, success, money, protection, and above all, greater self-understanding and a sense of inner peace.... There is no way one can explain these things; they just happened."[39]

We become Witches because of our desire to explore, understand, explain. We become Witches when we surrender. Risa and I have chatted with dozens and dozens of Witches, all of whom, ourselves included, have a story that ends something like this: "I can't explain it, but it happened. I know because it happened to me."

Our intuition, our knowing, our emotions, our dreams, our fantasies, our goals, our experiments, our moments ... our vision of a different world. They deserve our attention and care. They deserve reverence and ceremony, sanctity and space. Under this Virgo New Moon, let's give it to them.

One of Gen's final shows was 2016's "Try to Altar Everything." That's *Altar* like a ceremonial sacred space. A L T *A* R. Altar Everything. Gen told *Dazed* magazine: "It really does sum up a lot of what we do, taking things that are already around and reassembling them to inject them with something special, an energy or resonance that speaks to you in a way you wouldn't expect."[40]

This is the way we Witches, I think, can seize the means of perception, by trying to altar everything. Recognize the ideas behind objects and behaviors. Create nonconformist habits and networks that recognize the sacred energy of all things.

Gen dropped their cheap suitcase and rejoined Lady Jaye in 2020.

As we Witches head into autumn, with the Virgo Moon begging us to create order out of chaos, let's ritualize and borrow a mission statement from Genesis P-Orridge to ponder as the leaves and empires fall around us:

> *Our mission is to fall through the cracks of stale tradition every hour of life. To find the places and sounds no one has dared to think of. To have real faith in oneself in an age when the white noise of conformity has never been turned up higher is no easy task. But everyone has the potential to do it. . . . discard all inherited value systems [and] social conditioning. End gender. Break sex. Destroy the control of DNA and the expected. . . . Our daily mission is to subvert, seeking and fighting to answer Burrough's challenge: How do we short-circuit control? Please go out and try to change the fucking world. Try to Altar Everything.*[41]

Ritual

For the Virgo New Moon, cut up a habit—switch hands. So, if you are right-handed, use your left. If you are left-handed, use your right. Eat a meal this way. Stick your dominant hand in your pocket if you have to. Notice how your new approach to the task has tremendously affected the task itself.

Brush your teeth with your wrong hand, and use your new awareness to slow down. Make your toothbrush the first magic wand you encounter every day. Try to avoid that auto-pilot mode we all sink into during our daily, repetitive tasks. As you continue to brush your teeth, count them like mala beads and enchant the job with another incantation:

North
South
East
West
I bless my teeth as I bless my loved ones.
I bless them with my attention.
I bless them with my efforts.
I brush

to the North and South
To the East and West.

Rinse and spit away that which no longer serves you.

Notice how bringing a ceremonial approach to mundane tasks removes the mundanity, and bring this heightened awareness with you as you analyze and reshape your habits into rituals.

When the full moon comes, concretize a ritual for yourself. Whether it is a weekly cup of chamomile tea, a ritual bath, or the singing of hymns, make space for magic and let it be sacred.

In a condescending world, make space to believe.

Incantation

I believe.
I believe in my magic.
I believe in my agency.
I believe in my power to change the world.
I take control.
I short-circuit control.
I altar everything.
Everything is sacred.
Nothing is mundane.
Everything has a reason.
I have a reason.
I have a reason.
A reason for being.
I am symbolic
And
Very
Very
Real.
I take up the battle.
This is my world.
How infinite my possibilities.

7

New Moon in Libra

Geometry

This circle is led by Risa
with expansions by Amy.

The Libra New Moon strives for balance. Sometimes that manifests as sacrificing everything for folks to get along. Other times, it looks more like the poker-faced Queen of Swords, unafraid to wield its blade. Ruled by Venus, the Libra New Moon values beauty, art, and connection with other souls. It is the art critic, the socialite, the diplomat, the lawyer, the activist, and the advocate—as motley as these roles may appear.

—ELIZA ROBERTSON, ASTROLOGER

THE SMALL YELLOW BIRDS ARE BACK IN THE BRANCHES OUTSIDE
my window as I sit down to start this chapter on geometry. The leaves
are ready with their colors for the fall. They are the fires to light the dark,
and they are dissolving into darkness. The woods are wild with mushrooms, the vines of my fat squash tangle down the hill, and the beans
have formed a giant floppy Witch hat on the triangle of branches we
made out on the lawn. This is the Libra New Moon, and it loves balance
and beauty, the extreme pleasure and comfort of putting things where
they belong, and the rhizomatic layering that, in these parts, comes right
before everything crystalizes into snowflakes.

It turns out that the small yellow birds are goldfinches. They were
with me at the beginning of this book, in the bright balance of Spring,
and here they are again as I try to trace out the resonant magic of geometry. And I'm glad to have their company because I've struggled with
this chapter.

Vanessa Oliver-Lloyd, artist, forensic anthropologist, and cofounder
of the now-defunct Art Witch Academy, helped me put this struggle
into words when she said it was the idea of math as a universal language
that pushed her to connect with geometry in a magical way, and not in
the "super triggering, traumatizing mathematical way that I learned in
school."[1] You might relate to this experience of math or sciences as part
of high school trauma. I think, for a lot of us, a giant chasm opens up
between the arts and sciences around that age because of the way those
concepts are taught.

*Amy: I spent my time in high school assuming that math was full of only
right and wrong answers, without room for imagination, emotion, or specu-
lation. When a teacher wrote a complex equation on the chalkboard, one that
couldn't be easily, materially demonstrated with an apple pie cut in triangles, I asked—my young mind curious about the humans behind the numbers,
the paths toward ideas—"How do they know?" And she replied, "They just
know." And, sadly, I never really studied math again. Because I didn't know
that she was wrong. They didn't just know. They guessed and imagined and
calculated and theorized and calculated some more in an effort to explain and
connect with our universe.*

Poet Jarod K. Anderson wrote:

Dear Science,
   Humans conceptualize complex ideas through metaphor not jargon.
   You don't start with the jargon and move toward meaning.
   Start with meaning and move toward jargon.
   You need communicators who understand how to capture imagination.
   In short, you should hire poets. "[2]

I have been stubborn about keeping geometry in the book. I wanted to claim the power and poetry of this symbolic language for myself and all of us, though I wasn't sure exactly why. I kept picking away at this and other chapters, and meanwhile, the lake froze. And then, while skating in circles on the lake under a brilliant sky, I dropped suddenly into a mathematical memory.

When I was seven my mother, my new step-dad, and I moved from snowy Waterloo, Ontario, where they had finished their grad school programs, out to Los Angeles, where my step-dad got his first teaching job at UCLA. I mention that Waterloo was snowy because that's the main thing I remember about it—being pulled to school in a red sleigh by my mother through the snow—but actually, we moved in the summer. My childhood memories of California are all disjointed, sense memories. Especially the quality of light: moving from Ontario to California was like stepping from a world drawn in pencil crayons into a stained glass window. There were flowers everywhere and the classroom had wide-open windows and the air smelled like pink jasmine and honeysuckle. And when we got there, they put me in some summer program, and it was about geometry. It was about making art with geometry. I learned how to use a compass for the first time and how to move the compass point along the circumference of a circle to make intersecting spheres, unfolding waves, a bright and steady blossoming. I learned this and then everything disappeared.

The memory is so clear: there's no one in the room but me, and I can't fathom why that would be the case, but there I am, and the scene is palpitating with colored light and jasmine. I am alone for hours in this cool adobe room, with the hot sun breathing in and out on a breeze through a wild, unfurling jungle outside the windows. I sit in a calm euphoria as I draw swooping spheres in bright, sharp colors. I see the meeting points opening like flowers into an infinity that spirals gently back. This memory hovers like a hummingbird, strange and inexplicable. That moment stained my memory. It's a kaleidoscopic dream that changed forever how I saw the world around me. I was very far from home, I was at the edge, and also in the center. And where I was, the spheres were singing.

And so I want to sketch out an understanding for myself, and for all us Witches, about geometry in magic, and the magic possibilities inherent in taking up geometry.

To begin, draw a circle around yourself in your mind. Ancient Mesopotamians would draw zisurrû, a magical circle drawn with flour, around the bed of one who needed protecting, or around the bull whose skin would become a sacred drum. Once, I went to a therapist who sat on the floor with me, gave me a rope, and invited me to use it to make a circle around myself while we spoke. Whether you feel comfortable with ancient Sumerians or modern therapists, the circle makes a space that's just for you and what you allow.

Within this sacred, ancient protection, orient yourself within the cardinal points. Place something small to mark north, east, south, west a token each for earth, air, fire, and water. Use anything that works for you—stone, incense, candle, and a glass of water will work—and now you'll notice that you are in a square within a circle. Now and always, your breathing life force is at the meeting point of a living axis of dynamic possibility.

The goldfinches are here to remind us that all our circles are spirals. We are always fluttering forward in that other dimension of time. All our geometries are partial, our best impressions of what we can imagine as we peer through our tiny bright viewfinders, lit in the dark of our electrical minds. "The task of the right eye is to peer into the telescope, while the left eye peers into the microscope," wrote artist, novelist, magic-maker Leonora Carrington.[3] We can draw on geometry to help us orient ourselves in the vastness, both minute and massive. To see the birds, as well as the patterns they trace, in flocks across millennia.

By flying in a logarithmic spiral, falcons take advantage of the curve's unique properties to maintain a fixed gaze on their prey while retaining body alignment . . . Nature loves the logarithmic spiral. From sunflowers, seashells and whirlpools to hurricanes and spiral galaxies we discover this extraordinary form at all scales from the microscopic to the cosmological.[4]

I want to consider geometry as a tool for seeing the vastness, for keeping our gaze fixed, and for retaining our alignment.

Looking at the natural world through geometric abstraction reveals a background pattern of simple forms. This method of abstraction was invented by looking at shadows and playing with strings and straight-edges, and it opened up new kinds of symbolic thinking in human minds, so much so that early geometers saw in these abstractions direct evidence and language of the sublime.[5]

Geometry emerged out of the need to demarcate land, map spiritual ideas onto space in the form of altars and art, and lift up architectures around us that would hold. The builders who learned these lessons—about pyramids that could rely on massive cantilevered stone and leave spaces inside for holy secrets; about how to make a vaulted, arching ceiling resting on the weight of a perfect keystone; about hollowed wombs of glorious resonance where secrets echoed—these people transmitted their knowledge carefully across generations. For a while, they had more power than princes or popes, and so they were driven underground. The original guilds of stonemasons preserved a branch of knowledge that was occulted—hidden—throughout the middle ages and beyond, and it was, at least in part, knowledge about the taking shape of the built world.

The rationalization and abstraction of the world allowed the sciences to emerge. It allowed us to build libraries and subways, but it also drew property lines around fluid, common spaces. Sometimes when I feel overwhelmed and claustrophobic in the built world—in the city or the suburbs or on the long highways that cut across the North—in those moments, it's helpful for me to think that geometry is called the *mother* of all mathematics. Sacred abstraction gave birth to construction. Simple symbols hold incredible, fertile power.

The origin story I was taught about geometry was about a single famous man, Pythagoras. But widen that perspective to see the circle: men and women who studied and philosophized together over 2,500 years ago. The Pythagoreans were a spiritual cult that believed you could strip away everything else and the universe would still sing in numbers, and in that circle, women were teachers and philosophers. They were right at the heart of investigating this mystery. And at the heart of the circle was a woman called Theano. Theano might have been Pythagoras's wife, or his daughter, or neither, but whatever her angles of relation, we know she was there—a leader, a philosopher, an innovator, and a teacher of geometry in its most spiritual form. After Pythagoras died, the group fractured and some followers wanted to worship at the altar of the math they had already discovered. But some historians suspect Theano was the leader of those Pythagoreans who wanted to keep asking new questions.[6]

I picture Theano and Pythagoras drawing circles around and through triangles and squares. From within my own circle squared, I add a triangle in my mind. It's a cone, actually, one of the possibilities for a triangle in three dimensions. It's a Witch's hat covered in vines reaching up to the stars that sing of the past they knew. I spread out; I connect to dimensions. And in this mind-geometry, I draw myself into the histories unwritten. And I call out to the stars, water, and dust that are the records of Theano's true contribution.

I mourn and am furious at the violence repeated against marginalized lives and stories. Ideas were brutalized and burned, like so many possible identities sent into hiding. And in that mourning, it's helpful to me to remember that we all exist within this invisible geometry that spins out to constellations in motion.

In Babylon, some bright minds charted trapezoids over hundreds of years to map Jupiter—that shining benefic—across both velocity and time.[7] This math wouldn't be "invented" in the West until hundreds of years later. The rediscovery of these ancient Babylonian trapezoids is recent; it dates to 2016, and it changes the story of geometry. It tilts the kaleidoscope, and the past and the present intersect in a new way.

The Venus tablet of Ammi-Saduqa, which dates from the first millennium BCE and depicts Venus's motion, is one of the earliest examples of Babylonian planetary omens.[8] These charts of planetary omens helped spiritual leaders tell stories about the unseen world, predict changes in weather and movements of water, build bonds of community and safety, and exert political control. Priests and Priestesses in ancient Mesopotamia held stations equal to the King.[9] Being able to read shifting geometries to predict future movement was a power then, and it is now.

Mesopotamian spirituality held reverence for transition, and for living beyond the gender binary. Innana's priests and priestesses could change their gender with her power, and they charted her course through the sky in the body we call Venus. And as they charted her course on the zodiac, tracking each superior conjunction, they saw that every eight years she traced a pentagram. And so that five-sided star became part of the geometry of the divine. Following your path across binaries is sacred geometry.

Constellations were drawn by storytellers, have been redrawn, and will be drawn again. And so taking up this tool, geometry—this progenitor of maps and star charts and architecture—and using it to meditate on and conjure for all that is missing, hidden, occulted, and unseen might be a praxis that can help keep the future open. Doreen Massey introduced the idea of "Geometries of Power":

Imagine for a moment that you are on a satellite, further out and beyond all satellites; you can see "planet earth" from a distance and, rare for someone with only peaceful intentions, you are equipped with the kind of technology that allows you to see the colours of people's eyes and the number on their number-plates . . . Look in closer and there are ships and trains, steam trains slogging laboriously up hills somewhere in Asia. Look in closer still and there are lorries and cars and buses and on down further and somewhere in sub-Saharan Africa there's a woman on foot who still spends hours a day collecting water. Different social groups and different individuals are placed in very distinct ways in relation to these flows and interconnections.[10]

Once introduced, this idea shakes academic foundations. Massey becomes "the geographer of space and power," and as she evolves her thinking about power geometries, they don't collapse her into despair.[11] They give her belief in the possibilities of activism and politics. A foundation, a whole architecture of hope.

> *"Identities,' in this formulation, are temporary constellations, always interrelationally hybrid . . . It is the fact of their plurality and interrelation which keeps the future open for politics."*[12]

Identities are temporary constellations that keep the future open. They are not fixed; they are bent by the gravity of emerging networks of ideas, of stories, of politics; and they are affected by velocity—the stickiness of memes, the catchiness of songs, the degrees of interconnection—and time. Change is possible.

For a while when I was in grad school, I would relax by drawing intricate maps. I mapped everyone I knew with lines showing how I'd met them, and who they were connected to. I mapped every place I went in a day, a week, a month. I mapped all the ideas I had around the history of open source as a communications system, and that map eventually became my thesis.

Using geometry to guide our research opens avenues for discovery and for resistance: a history of maps shows the shrinking of public spaces, the gerrymandering of voting districts, the violent carving of Indigenous land.

Draw your own maps of the spaces you move through, both physically and energetically. Use your geometry to triangulate your identity, and to see your power to nudge the systems you touch toward more just evolutions.

Metaphysically speaking, use the lesser banishing ritual of the pentagram—as Pixie Coleman Smith and other members of the Golden Dawn would have—to draw the planetary movement of Venus around you in pentagrams. Call out your names for the divine, sing to the elements, orient yourself within the cardinal points. Draw a square for spells of material success, and a circle for protection. Call upward with a triangle for the divine perception of time. Use your geometry to center your power at the cross-section of these forces and to be interpenetrated by them, woven up with them, to ride and to direct them.

This future-opening, future-believing-in, future-ever-crafting is the praxis of the re-enchantment. It requires constant readjustment, new learnings, and new understandings of power geometries, but it's doable. This opening can happen in the mathematics of the present, moment by moment, when we triangulate ourselves and our networks, not just in relation to each other or in relation to huge, seemingly immovable entities, but in relation to those entities as they have been built. With what velocity, and across how much time? How immovable do they seem when compared to the enormity of what came before and what lies beneath? Current power structures seem inevitable, but we can decide to design and incant and act for the sake of other possibilities.

Lady Frieda Harris, in her 60s, as bombs rained down on London, studied a new geometry in order to encode secret spiritual teachings into her art. She dyed her hair red and navigated the night streets between the Lord's of London, the world's most famous occultist, and a couple of mathematicians drawing a new understanding of the world. She walked this crooked path to summon the knowledge she needed to bring a bright new divination deck to light. And then she retired to India to live on a houseboat.

Lady Frieda Harris was perhaps the best friend Aleister Crowley ever had, and she used her own art, financial resources, and strength of character to convince him to collaborate with her. A project they thought would last months turned into years and resulted in the luminous Thoth tarot deck.

Crowley was a person who thought a lot about the power of shapes and symbols.

During World War II, at the request of friend and Naval Intelligence officer Ian Fleming, Crowley provided Winston Churchill with valuable insights into the superstitions and magical mind-set of the Third Reich. He also suggested to the prime minister, if reports can be believed, that he exploit the enemy's magical paranoia by being photographed as much as possible giving the two-fingered

"V-for-Victory" gesture. The sign is the manual version of the Apophis-Typhon, a powerful symbol of destruction and annihilation which, according to magical tradition, is capable of defeating the solar energies represented by the swastika.[13]

The Crowley who Lady Frieda knew was a brilliant, sardonic teacher. He was also a desperate heroin addict, at times a wonderful poet in the visionary style, and an unavoidable character in the history of magic. He was certainly an unavoidable character in the life of Lady Frieda Harris, who, despite the rollercoaster of arrogance, neediness, insight, and hilarity that was their friendship, remained a good friend to him to the end of his life. She was inspired by the ideas he brought into harmony for her, from the Qabalah's sacred cross unfolding from the cubic stone, the seed of all creation, to astrology, numerology, Egyptian history, spirituality, and more. She charted her way between these ideas to create the divination deck and to find her way to a life outside the circumscribed world she was born and married into. She is not an icon of activism or resistance: she is an artist who found a way to be happy. And that's a start. To find a route to a life we deserve, knowing that growth is very rarely a straight line.

Their Thoth tarot deck glows. It is alien and art deco and mathematical-hallucinogenic. Like Pixie Coleman Smith's deck, every single card is a complete work of art.[14]

Lady Frieda was a spiritual seeker.[15] Frieda studied Anthroposophy and projective geometry at Rudolf Steiner House with George Adams Kaufmann and Olive Whicher, and continued to study privately with Olive. Frieda was also a Co-Mason. Co-Masonry was a radical feminist branch of Freemasonry that not only accepted all people equally but also did away with the provision requiring belief in a God, at least for a while. She created a powerful set of Masonic Tracing boards drawing on projective geometry.[16]

Lady Frieda became a member of O.T.O. in 1938 after befriending Crowley. "Crowley's diaries first mention Frieda Harris in August 1937. Presumably unknown to her, the artist became the subject of sex magic workings by Crowley, probably to secure his influence over her."[17]

Crowley said of Lady Frieda: "Her vision's quite remarkably good."[18] He recognized her Co-Masonic degrees, and they began to collaborate. She created the art for several of Crowley's books, and then Crowley borrowed a copy of a secret publication containing "A Description of the Cards of the Tarot" for her. Lady Frieda suggested that she and Crowley create a deck according to these old Golden Dawn specifications.

Lady Frieda Harris lived from 1877–1962. She was the wife of British Parliament Member, Liberal Chief Whip and Deputy Leader of the Liberal Party Percy Harris. "In her later years, after doing set design for Ram Gopal's ballet *The Legend of the Taj Mahal* (1956), she moved into a houseboat in Srinagar and studied Hinduism."[19]

Her husband Percy was liberal (for the time) and passionate about social housing. We can posit that they loved each other and had shared values (because why not assume love?), but still, we get a glimpse of how she felt balancing political life and her own longing for art, spirit, and magic when she writes to Crowley:

> *My spiritual state has been sadly neglected, perhaps because I have been trying to paint & live Percy's life at the same time. Now these circumstances are giving me a chance. I have had 3 days rest, the first in 2 years & I've even had time to read a bit of Magic & try to assimilate yr. book. How satisfying to ones inside hunger.*[20]

Lady Frieda was sixty when she began to collaborate with Crowley. Crowley was deep into addiction by this time. He was broke, feared, hated, and had been run out of Italy. Perpetually short on cash and desperate to pass on the framework of his philosophy, he let Frieda convince him—and pay him—to collaborate on the deck, and they begin their work.

The collaboration was largely long-distance, so we have piles of letters with insight into their process. Based on the letters, the two were great friends with huge mutual respect who sometimes made each other crazy. Frieda worked much of the time in a small caravan in the complete darkness of wartime blackout at night, bombs falling around her. She writes: "I have done the 10 of Swords & promptly Russia takes up arms. Where are we going!" And later: "we are driven mad with soldiers here."[21]

The deck was deeply important to both of them. Crowley wrote, "It is the vindication of my life's work for the last 44 years; and will be the Compass and Power of the good ship Magick for the next 2,000 years."[22]

Harris struggled with the work and struggled to manage Crowley who repeatedly asked her for more money—more than the monthly stipend she was already paying him to work on the cards.

Nevertheless, she loved the work and, like every seeker, the struggle to see the patterns in the violence and beauty of life consumed her. She writes:

Shall I never get on a bit? Yoga practices I never seem to advance in. I cannot live more quietly, but even then the business of living takes time. I am positively alarmed at the prospect of the end of this work, as if I do not get any more handed to me, I shall have to return to the awful life I have escaped from in my conscience during the last 2 years, and I doubt if I can. I do not think the ritual of Magic is much good to me, I seem to have to draw everything I want to understand . . . I am bored by occult people, loathe commercialism, do not want fame or notoriety, do not want money, but yearn, long, desire for solitude. Any financial success will be yours. I have had my reward in the work. I wish I could paint in crystals.[23]

When the deck was complete, Frieda set up and funded a series of shows of her works as well as a limited edition of two hundred decks of the cards. That was the only time the Thoth deck would be published in either her or Crowley's lifetimes. He was furious, claiming that she devalued the work. He seemed to always want more from her, and she was disappointed by the way he always seemed to want more from everybody.

Crowley could be a difficult person to like, and Frieda was a strong enough character to step away from his tantrums (and to throw a few of her own.) Over the years, however, she continued to assist Crowley financially and in the end was one of two executors of his will.[24]

Though Crowley's ideas are interesting and helpful to some of my own instincts about magic, as usual, I find myself more interested in her: in her cards, and in the worldview of a person who has to draw things to understand them, for whom that worldview could be best painted in crystals, and who, to approach a means of communicating what she saw, decided to study new forms of geometry.

> *Higher math is, by its nature, an esoteric pursuit plumbed by a relatively small group of scholars and specialists. Projective geometry, after its nineteenth-century zenith, found a new incarnation in a different kind of esotericism: the world of mysticism and magic(k). While the specifics may remain obscure even to many of the faithful, their significance has been preserved in the seminal writings of Kaufmann and Whicher. And courtesy of the imaginative hand and eye of artist executant Frieda Lady Harris, projective geometry has also been disseminated surreptitiously in Aleister Crowley's immensely popular Thoth Tarot, whose beautiful and mysterious images beckon viewers to explore the depths of its secrets.[25]*

Projective geometry was lost and found again many times over the centuries, but by the 1930s, this strange branch of mathematics was seen as a way of looking at the world that could help ask and answer major questions about space and time, because in projective geometry even parallel lines meet. In fact, in projective geometry, as opposed to other forms of non-Euclidean geometry, there are *no* lines that do not meet, eventually. Olive Whicher and George Kaufmann delved into the philosophical implications of projective geometry to map out answers to life's most elusive questions. "Here, the concepts of duality and of shapes without measure are understood to demonstrate that scientific principles governed growth and beauty in nature; furthermore, these principles apparently exert their generative influence on the world from an ideal, creative space (or counterspace) that is knowable to the trained mind."[26]

George Adams Kaufmann had become interested in projective geometry as a path from which he could explore theoretical physics that didn't chase the discovery of the atom. Instead of looking for the units that were presumed to build the universe—and that ended up building world-ending weapons—Kaufmann went looking for something else. Maybe something world-building instead.

Paul Dirac, who formulated the Dirac equation that predicted the existence of antimatter, said that when he was developing quantum mechanics, he used his favorite branch of mathematics—projective geometry.[27] When pressed, he could never give answers about how projective geometry had guided him to his quantum discoveries. And perhaps that was because he was neurodivergent, or because of the abuse he had suffered at his father's hands when he had struggled to speak as a child.[28] Or maybe it was both those things, and how they led to a way of seeing shapes bending in the curving universe, all lines meeting, matter and antimatter together filling up the most minute of spaces with beings that are both particle and wave, binaries twisting together at infinity, drawing life from the counter-space.

Projective geometry looks at lines and shapes and curves when they are hit by light and casting shadows or when they are reflected in a curved mirror, and asks, "What truths remain?" Throw most rules out the window—things we thought impossible are true in this bending way of looking at the world, but when we look at images drawn with this curved perspective, we still recognize them immediately. Something remains. This way of looking is as true as the ways of looking that are not bent or sidelong; they are part of the universe.

For some, projective geometry gives shape to the idea that the material world is a projection of the spiritual world, for others it led to the insight that the universe can be seen from the perspective of energy in motion. Adams and Whicher used projective geometry to argue that the infinite midpoint of non-Euclidean space was to be found in the plant world, in every single bud. Not in any one place, but in every growing place. This idea was connected with that of the lemniscatory correlation—a figure eight or infinite shape—between space and counter-space.[29]

Olive tells a story of walking with George by a flowering hedge, when he

described in geometric terms how the germinating impulse—the united group of small flat leaves or an individual leaf, how it emerges as a cone from a point of growth and as it grows it loses ever more of its vitality—actually the living substance is a physical manifestation of an etheric space. This growth process is found, instead of in an ethereal space, in the space and with the powers of the "point of growth", which contains an infinity on the inside. So a seed or a germinating embryo is physically small but ethereally large. It was an exact analog to the concept from higher mathematics.[30]

This is a geometry of infinities on the inside, a mathematics of flowering. In her art, Lady Frieda attempted to illustrate these mathematical visions of the very nature of the universe; a vision about things that are profoundly separate actually meeting somewhere, maybe way out there, or maybe way in here.

Olive and George loved Lady Frieda. Even in her nineties Olive remembered how Lady Frieda dyed her hair red and invited Olive to her flat to teach her new geometries in exchange for drawing lessons. However brief and circumscribed the alchemy of their friendship, Lady Frieda's art inspired the mathematicians in their work, and they in hers, and in that brief moment, the figure-eight path of influence between art and science was lovingly fulfilled.

Lady Frieda Harris wrote:

Contrary to everybody's impression, the Tarot Cards were not intended for the purposes of divination. They are a Map of the Universe and they might quite easily be compared with the symbols of mathematics. Regarded as such they represent a convenient means of stating cosmic problems . . . I have tried to introduce among the cards an element of Time . . . This really means that you can look at any of the pictures, thinking in what I may describe as four dimensions. This requires great concentration and is an incentive to meditation.[31]

You are here. At a point on your unique orbit that intersects with this line of text. You are, like Lady Frieda Harris, like Crowley, and Amy and I, and all the Witches we've been missing, a seeker. Both particle, alive in this moment, and wave, stretching across time. Infinite on the inside.

Maybe ceremonial sex magic makes sense for you, maybe you are a nature Witch, or a city Witch, lab Witch, activist Witch, healer or gardener, solitary or community organizer. Art Witch or math Witch. Either way, all ways, you are like Frieda's figure of Art in the Thoth Deck, which Crowley and Frieda chose to replace Temperance. Art is drawn as that figure of alchemical combination, that Queer Intersex Goddetc Diana who combines fire and water to bring new life from the dark, new kinds of connection and kindness to light.

Olive called Frieda Diana, she said it suited her better, and there she is in the deck, crafting her magic, just like you. Endlessly combining your light and dark matter at the center point of infinity.

Hilma af Klint was a sacred painter who channeled geometric visions of the universe. In her Atom Series, Hilma wrote: "Every atom has its own midpoint, but each midpoint is directly connected to the midpoint of the universe."[32]

Hilma's works were channeled within a pentagram of women (De Fem, the Five) who met religiously to listen to each other and to the universe. Her works address these curving new forms of geometry and the relatedness of all things that are growing and living and dying across great speeding arcs of space and time. They were so powerful for her, touched such knowledge, and—despite her education in the art world— were so completely removed from what was happening in art at the time that she insisted her work not be shared for twenty years. She archived them meticulously though. She knew what she had made.

For Hilma, the discovery of electromagnetic waves unlocked new ways of understanding the universe. The messages in her paintings became dedicated to the atom—the atom absorbing energy, moving electrons, making waves.

Heinrich Hertz, who discovered electromagnetic waves and exploded how Hilma and many artists and philosophers thought about the universe and time, was also the first physicist to use projective geometry in mechanics. For mechanics and particle physicists, occultists and theosophists, a new way of doing geometry opened doors.

Brooklynn, Sonic Witch, said to us: "I think that science will slowly be able to explain the magic in the world."[33]

Our covenmate Vanessa of the Art Witch Academy called from Shanghai to talk about geometry.

My previous experience of Geometry was comprised of using Pythagorean theorem on my dig sites. Because I'm an archeologist, that's the extent of using geometry in my archeological practice . . . but this is something I thought you should know: The human skin has stripes on it like tigers, only you can't see them, they are the remnants of our cells forming while in embryo, and they trace how some cells become organs and others become skin. You can only see these lines using UV, though some people have a condition that makes them visible to the naked eye. These are lines that bring us all together."[34]

We are all invisibly marked by the geometry of our cells expanding. We wear this on our skin.

Amy and I developed the refrain "Please Expand!" between us, a throwback to those notes teachers would write in the margins of our essays when they wanted more, because we always wanted more from each other when we spoke. So we started calling this out to each other, and to our interview guests, and to our covenmates. No need to apologize for our wandering ideas. We want to uphold each other in our wandering. We want to say this over and over until it sinks into a groove: Please, Expand! Let us into the spaces in your wild thoughts. Resolution is not required. When Vanessa pointed me toward Blaschko's lines, I heard it again: Please, like your cells, Expand. Show us the marks you leave as you go.

Let us participate in pattern-making. Veronica Varlow told us: "you are a reflection of the best parts of people."[35] What is the geometry of your ideas reflected through another's dendrites and neurons, through their Blaschko's lines and cell walls?

Veronica told us that her grandmother, who taught her Bohemian Witchcraft, believed that when a candle burns down in this world, it slowly appears in the Spirit World. And on that other side, your guides see a new altar rising and they come to see what your working is for. Among those ancestors and animals and books and rock stars and places—all the guides that have shaped you—the most powerful is *you.*

Because *that* place exists outside of nonlinear time, and so it includes the you that has crossed over.

This is a Witch philosophy of space-time: continuous and curved, a ride along leminiscatory space, a Mobius strip, an ouroboros where parallel lines meet and the infinity on the horizon is also the infinity within.

Maryam Mirzakhani won the Field's Medal just a few years before she died of breast cancer at age 40. She was the first woman to win what is known as the "Nobel for mathematics," and she won it for her solution to the Magic Wand Theorem with Alex Eskin.

> *"Imagine a room made out of perfect mirrors," Eskin said. "It doesn't have to be a rectangle; any weird polygon will do . . . Now place a candle in the middle of the room, one that shines light in every direction. As the light bounces around the different corners, will it always illuminate the whole room? Or will it miss some spots? . . . There are no dark spots," he said. "Every point in the room is illuminated."[36]*

Geometry today is a practice of revealing unknowable spaces. Of mapping diffusion and imagining movement through the vast and expanding universe. Maryam found a way to show that, within our circles, within our strangely shaped communities, light eventually comes to all dark places.

Even when it feels like systems are spiraling backward, and brutality and injustice are winning, remember the magic wand. Hold on to this metaphor as you cast your circles, and draw the people in your life into new shapes and relations: within all our weird polygons, your light eventually touches every place.

Ritual

Light a candle when you take up this mapping, and invite your mind to open. Draw yourself first in a circle, and then within a square inside the circle. Envision a cone reaching up from you to a star above you that has seen long into the past and awaits your future.

Use a compass, straightedge, and bright colors. Dedicate a section of your grimoire to this.

Map everything you care about, and who you know—or know of—that is connected to those passions. The places where circles overlap and names get dense can tell you about who you are. Where you have open spaces, you have new possibilities.

Map your privilege. Look at a timeline of your life; ask at each step, what dynamics were at play? What came to you a little more easily because of something in your skin or class? What power does your privilege give you? What doors can you open, what levers can you pull to change the world for another?

Map your ancestors. Include every book that marked you, every animal you've loved, every great recipe, every place, plant, and event that constitutes your kin. Research the patterns of your kin and draw them in until your cells feel their resonance.

Play with this in the dark of the new moon time. Let these geometries play on your subconscious mind. Let yourself play. Play with pentagrams, looping petals like the ones Venus draws in the sky over years.

While you draw and chart by candlelight, sing to yourself. Your light and your voice fill all the space.

Incantation

I draw new maps,
I am the light and shadow cast
I keep the future open.

The universe still sings in numbers.
In every growing place.

I draw new maps,
I am the light and shadow cast
I keep the future open.

The universe still sings
I keep the future open.

8

New Moon in Scorpio

The Circle

This circle is led by Amy
with expansions by Risa.

*The New Moon in Scorpio is ... allowing part of yourself to die,
death is in our wealth and the rebirth centres our power in this world.*

—MONEFA WALKER, ASTROLOGER

MY FIRST CIRCLE WAS AROUND THE KITCHEN TABLE AT MY GREAT
Aunt B's house, and it took the form of a near decade-long Euchre
tournament. *Euchre* is a card game with four players, two teams of two.
Witchily, you and your partner score points (treats?) by winning tricks.
So around this table, with my mother, Aunt B, and a fourth, sometimes
my grandmother, sometimes Aunt Dorothy or Aunt Janet, I learned to
play Euchre and so much more. Over the shuffling deck, I picked up
family history, family jokes, and my Aunt B's words of wisdom about the
game. As I matured, I discovered that these lessons were always translat-
able, transferable to every aspect of my daily life.

I learned that Fate deals your hand, but how you play the game is
up to you.

Scorpio is an idealist, so let's take that energy and use it to imagine
a functional, balanced, and harmonious society. Then let's make those
spaces real.

In Euchre you can score 0, 1, 2, or 4 points per round. If I was disappointed to only get 1, Aunt B would say, "One at a time's good fishing!"
I now understand this outside the game as her advice to appreciate
small steps, not to be impatient—to catch and appreciate fish one at
a time.

If I was staring at my hand too long, agonizing over which card to
play, she'd say, "Play one, look at the rest." Outside the game, this became
a motto. If I have several things I'm mulling over, I take action on one
and mull over the rest. I can get stuck in my head, so I try to make sure
I don't miss my turn because I'm not able to choose which card to play.

Aunt B had a million idioms that I absorbed through my skin like
the steam rising from a bowl of Campbell's soup. When I want to stop
complaining and do something, I tell myself in Aunt B's voice, "Better to
light a candle than to curse the darkness." To this day, I understand concepts best when they are presented in metaphor, or better yet, in rhyme.

"Turn down a bower, lose for an hour." Don't squander opportunities
that arise.

Once, after a particularly trumpetous fart, she proclaimed, "Better
to bear the shame than to bear the pain." It is better to be honest than

perfect. We may feel judged for the metaphorical stench of our truth, but to hold it in cramps our whole system. And this is the aim of the circle: to create a place to safely release gas without having to bear the shame of not living up to society's toxic and impossible standards. In circle, we do not cause ourselves pain by holding it in. We don't judge others for releasing. Telling the truth is a spell.

Aunt B died when I was sixteen, but she lived on as my friends and I invoked her name in our own circles, around our own card games. We played Euchre and Cribbage, Rummy and Canasta, but all of these games were just an excuse to sit in a circle and chat. In the TV show *The Golden Girls*, and if you're a fanatic like me, you might be thinking of this already, Dorothy and her mother Sophia had their best talks over a game of Gin. As a group, The Golden Girls encircled the kitchen table to eat cheesecake and talk through their joys and sorrows, each bringing their differing personal perspectives to conjure celebration, commiseration and, more often than not, solutions to their problems. When Sophia instructs us to "picture it!" she is invoking the knowledge that, as psychologist Pamela Rutledge wrote:

> *Stories are how we think. They are how we make meaning of life. Call them schemas, scripts, cognitive maps, mental models, metaphors, or narratives. Stories are how we explain how things work, how we make decisions, how we justify our decisions, how we persuade others, how we understand our place in the world, create our identities, and define and teach social values.*[1]

A circle doesn't require a card game, or even a cheesecake. Nor does it require goddesses, chanting, bonfires, calling the corners, or drawing down the moon (though these things can certainly heighten the atmosphere). A *circle* is any place, in any form, wherein Witches, women, and/ or other marginalized people gather to safely exist, to listen, and to be seen. Hear stories. Tell stories. Share our gifts and burdens. Bear witness to trauma and steal its power. Bear witness to joy and watch it multiply.

A circle can be a quilting bee or sewing circle, a book club or group therapy.

Risa: A circle can be a grid on a laptop screen of loving faces in various states of pixelation, like our coven's new moon zooms. Totally healing and delightful.

A Sunday brunch with your pals at which you piece together the hazy adventures of the previous night can be a circle. And this circle is perhaps Witches' most powerful tool. It doesn't have to be framed as magical because it *is* inherently magical. It's how we change the world, bit by bit: together. It is gathering in honesty, vulnerability, cooperation, and collaboration, the halving of problems and the doubling of dreams. The solving of some mysteries and the discovery of others. A perpetual motion machine in which we both produce and absorb energy, an infinite ouroboros, a ring of power *and* protection, a warm embrace, arms looped around and around each other.

We, both as Missing Witches and in our personal lives, have held several circles—some with close friends to celebrate, or mourn, or to conjure prosperity, others with groups of strangers to venerate our ancestors or gather perspectives, seeking clarity on a certain issue or theme.

Though they take many forms, the only integral quality of circles is that when we enter, we release judgment.

Scorpio energy may feel controlling, but we can channel that drive into controlling our narrative, willfully leaving our egos outside.

The fear that others will judge or rank us is so powerful it is often paralyzing. The circle allows us to slowly stretch out of our atrophied mindsets.

The compulsion to judge and rank others is so powerful that it must be constantly, consciously resisted. The circle is that resistance.

As author Judy Grahn told me, "our bonding is what makes a revolution happen."[2]

A circle is a training ground where we are free to brag and boast, knowing that our self-praise will elicit encouragement and agreement rather than a competitive glare or dismissive one-upmanship. In circle we are free to weep and grieve without worrying we'll come off as weak. In circle we are free to rage, to vent our anger without being labeled "bitch." In circle we are free to express our needs and desires, knowing the circle won't paint us as needy or desperate.

In circle, there is room for disagreement. Correction. It's how we learn to question our self-perception and worldview. When I inevitably made rookie mistakes at the Euchre table, Aunt B would explain what I'd done and what made it a bad move. I was allowed to make mistakes because the score didn't really matter. I honed my strategy with loving guidance. But I also knew that Aunt Dorothy never wanted to be my partner. For her, the score mattered. Keep this in mind as you form your own circles. For many, compassion is blocked by a sense of competition.

It takes practice to stop keeping score.

It takes practice to recognize that it's not up to us to determine the value of other people's choices, or worse, the things about themselves they can't control. It takes practice not only to speak, but also to be silent. Neither avoid nor solve, but simply bear witness.

I remember silently holding my grandmother's hand at my grandfather's funeral, staring at my feet as they dangled from the pew. The attendees lined up to deliver their brief condolences and platitudes, and one by one, shuffled off. She squeezed my hand. "I'm glad you're here," she whispered, "everyone else keeps running away." I kept those words and remembered them years later when a friend's mother died in high school. We all gathered for the funeral, but my friend was standing alone. No one was talking to him because no one knew what to say. And no one wanted to say the wrong thing, so they said nothing. I felt my grandmother squeeze my hand as I walked over to my friend. I made a stupid joke, he laughed, and the whole room exhaled.

That exhale is the circle and what the circle conjures. A collective sigh of relief that is also a howl, a giggle, a roar, and a moan.

Most people do not have a place they can call circle, and to be honest, many wouldn't want it. The idea of admitting to personal vulnerability, ignorance, difference, need, or desire is abhorrent. To remove the mask is unthinkable, akin to the nightmare of showing up for school stark naked. Hot Take: These people are not Witches. As Witches, we must accept that being afraid is no excuse to avoid the darkness. It's natural, and in some cases healthy, to be afraid, but we Witches do not allow this fear to control our lives. The more afraid we are to share some part of ourselves with (trusted) others, the more likely it is that this is a truth that must be told. The less afraid we are to admit when we don't know, the more we can discover, and Witches live their lives learning to get comfortable with the great unknown. We cannot be blackmailed because we have no shame.

With the help of Sylvia Federici, we can connect fear and competition to our Witch history and destabilize them. She wrote, "Witch-hunting in all its different forms is also a powerful means to destroy communal relations, injecting the suspicion that underneath the neighbor, the friend, the lover hides another person, lusting for power, sex, wealth, or simply wanting to commit evil deeds."[3]

It isn't easy to craft trusting relationships in this suspicious world under these contentious conditions, is it? These circular spaces are hard to find. That's why we Witches must do what Witches do. If we can't or don't find what we're looking for, we make it ourselves. Iconoclasts, ancient, *and* ahead of our time, Witches are ice-breakers, and our diving in gives others permission to jump in and feel the waters for themselves. We conjure the world we want to see and invite others to join us in the vision. We start shit.

Maggie Kuhn founded The Gray Panthers after being forced to retire at age sixty-five. In a world that had set an expiration date on her value, Maggie assembled a gray-haired gang who advocated for nursing-home reform and against ageism, as well as becoming a part of the anti-war movement of the 1970s. Maggie is the voice behind a (mis)quote we often see memed on Pinterest or when scrolling our social media feeds, "Speak the truth, even if your voice shakes." But the full quote holds us even more accountable. "Leave safety behind. Put your body on the line. Stand before the people you fear and speak your mind—even if your voice shakes. When you least expect it, someone may actually listen to what you have to say. Well-aimed slingshots can topple giants. And do your homework."[4]

We do some of that homework in circle. Although there is no doubt of our individual power as Witches, it is alchemy, chemistry, the air we breathe, all life that comes from combining things to create other, more complex inventions.

Caitlin Libera wrote, "Whether you wish to reclaim terms like Witch and Coven or not, the spiritual needs that can be met by a group along with the need for support and community will more than likely send every Pagan in search of a Circle at some point along the way."[5]

But I want to make a quick distinction here between a circle and a coven. A circle is pretty much just actually sitting in a circle (or in a grid if you're online) and talking. It's a moment. An opening and closing of a portal. The term *coven*, as used to describe a group of Witches, can be traced back to archeologist and scholar Margaret Murry, who was the first to use this word in this way. For our purposes, a *circle* (think family reunion) is a shared place, moment, and intention, while a *coven* (think family) is, as one of the most influential Witches of our time, Starhawk wrote, "a Witch's support group, consciousness raising group, psychic study centre, clergy-training program, College of Mysteries, surrogate clan, and religious congregation rolled in one. In a strong Coven, the bond is, by tradition, closer than family: a sharing of spirits, emotions, imagination. 'Perfect love and perfect trust' are the goals."[6]

"Perfect love and perfect trust" is a phrase that gets tossed around by neopagans and it certainly is a wonderful thought. But as with every tool, it can be manipulated and used to harm. Take it from Patti Wigington who wrote:

> *I was once challenged by a community member when I pointed out that a popular book was full of shoddy scholarship, blanket statements, and just plain awful ideas. Her response was "But Author X is a respected member of the community! Where's your perfect love and perfect trust?" Well, as far as I was concerned, it didn't apply to encouraging people to throw basic critical thinking out the window, nor did it mean that someone was automatically immune from criticism.[7]*

In every situation, we must be wary of those who ask us to obey without questioning or believe without considering something critically. That's how Witches get burned. But we can imagine a utopia where love and trust are perfect, unconditional, and ubiquitous, and we can begin to form that place for ourselves, within ourselves. To move toward a perfect love and perfect trust of oneself can be antianxiety medicine. Say, "I love myself and trust myself to make good decisions, to be okay, to make others feel safe around me."

In "Powerful Women Work Together" Christine Page said:

> Our conversations might sound pretty superficial, "I like your shoes, are you enjoying the show, do you have children?" But this allows us to share feelings, to share stories, and we innately know, this is our strength, our bonding is our power . . . when women work together, we can truly move mountains with our power.[8]

We form a circle because it has no beginning and no end, a constant process of going around. Equality. In it, there is no hierarchy, no center stage, no guru or preacher, no star of the show, no finish line. In a circle, both literally and metaphorically, everyone can see and be seen. The circle is drawn round, plump with compassion, with curiosity, and with care. In our attendance we are superficial and deep, playful and productive, loud and silent, scholarly and sentimental. Healer and healed.

The circle is also a symbol of protection and safety. Many practitioners of magic create a circle of salt, chalk, or ash around a spell on a table top, or around a clearing where they gather.

But the circle offers another layer of a somewhat less symbolic, more practical protection, and that is the confidence and validation that comes from knowing that you have support.

Founder of Black Witch University Lakeesha Harris has expanded her vision of the Radical Healing Circle, shifting her vocabulary from calling it a "safe space" to describing the circle as a "Brave Space." She wrote, "We must cease to suffer trauma in silence and alone. We must call out and call in and gather in truth and stand in our magic."[9]

When we spoke, Lakeesha said, "There is no safe space for us, especially as Witches, but we can be brave together."[10]

As author and host of the now iconic 1980s cable access series, *The Goddess in Art*, Starr Goode told me, "We are waking up . . . popping the bubble of patriarchy's spell."[11] Because of a combination of revolutionary thinking, bravery, and protest, and the new accessibility of technology, marginalized people are *un*silencing themselves, gaining voice. The zeitgeist is changing because the voices that inform it are changing, adding harmonies and dissonance to the choir. Starr told me about her own coven, Nemesis, which began in the 1980s. "I think one of the wondrous things about Nemesis is that we've endured—to be together through the tinctures of time, births, deaths, marriages, art projects, all kinds of ceremonies that mark the passage of our lives." I could sense the real love and tenderness that Starr has for her coven. She said, "If you're in a circle, there's a power in the circle. It's really fundamentally changed my life to have a circle that I can draw on. The love and power of that circle. It's a very stabilizing and empowering force." This circle is how Starr draws her power, even though she says much of it boils down to just sitting and talking. But she assures us, "there's nothing more powerful than that— that's all you need is to sit in a circle and talk. . . . That is one of the missing values of patriarchy. . . . the web of life in the sense of connectedness."[12]

This connectedness is something that I think all Witches seek and have sought, through all time, in every culture.

Amanda Amour-Lynx is a queer, Two-Spirit, Mi'kmaq artist and social worker living in Tkaronto (Toronto), Ontario. We spoke about the healing nature of connection, conversation, and storytelling. Amanda believes there is a conjunction between disconnection and disease. She says her projects "focus on Indigenous storywork to explore healing trauma and unearthing collective truths" claiming that "spirituality, connection, and community are at the root of wellness." We discussed the link she's found between personal healing and structural healing— healing one's self and healing one's space. She said:

I like to think about what happens in a talking circle, where everybody takes turns to facilitate active listening and compassion for one

another, and to withhold our judgement. Within that turn-taking,
it helps us to understand different perspectives, or we can see differ-
ent ways to identify with someone's else's story. I like story-telling as
a tool for working through your own personal shit, or hubris, and
the ways that can be a transmutation of the energy that needs to be
worked through or wounds that need to be healed. There's always this
ambition that telling my story can potentially allow somebody to feel
more okay with having that experience themselves or feel less alone.[13]

In that same conversation, Michelle Beausejour—an ancestral
Michif, L'nu and Celtic artist, entrepreneur, and community organizer
from Tkaronto, now living in Tiohtià:ke (Montreal)—reminds us that
although every Nation has its own interpretation and representation of
the Medicine Wheel, what they share is that "there is no hierarchy in
a Medicine Wheel." Interconnectivity, alignment. Holistic and whole.
"We are all responsible for each other. We need to take care of each
other."[14]

Amanda directed me to Kathleen Absolon, who wrote:

I have heard over and over how Indigenous people have been helped
through our own cultural mechanisms such as sweat lodge ceremonies,
healing ceremonies, sharing and talking circles, dances, songs and
other cultural pathways to wellness. Indigenous ways of health and
recovery remind people of the beauty of who we are, where we come
from and what we know. It builds healthy esteem and confidence in
our identity. It instills good feelings about being Indigenous again
and reconnects people to the power of their identity. We must respect
who we are, what we know and where we come from. Our recovery
and rediscovery is imperative to our healing as a peoples.[15]

When we go looking for a role-model Witch to teach us about the
world-altering beauty and power of difference and authenticity, talking
and sharing, holding brave and sacred space, recovery, rediscovery, and
rejoicing, one star leaps out of the galaxy in our dark Scorpio New Moon
sky: Audre Lorde.

"Moon marked and touched by sun," she wrote, "my magic is unwritten but when the sea turns back it will leave my shape behind."[16] When self-described "Black, lesbian, mother, warrior, poet," Audre Lorde wrote those words in her poem "A Woman Speaks," she was only partly correct—some, though definitely not all, of her magic is most assuredly *written*.

Audre is a posthumous mentor to me. As I navigate my life, I often take direction from her words. My first Twitter account still shows one of her quotes as my pinned tweet. I put a clip of her reading "A Woman Speaks" in an episode of the first season of the *Missing Witches* podcast, but it took years for me to gain the confidence to write about her myself. I'll be honest, writing about Audre scares me—smarter people than me have written theses and diatribes, even earned PhDs in the study of her work. She's the ultimate sister outsider who led a complex life from inside an even more complex identity; the ultimate sister outsider whose primary message was that we can look, *act*, think, **be** different, and still be unified in pursuit of common goals. The ultimate sister outsider who shouts in my ear that *I am not free while any woman is unfree, even though her shackles are different than my own.* . . . How can I express the debt of gratitude I owe to the person who taught me the lesson from that pinned tweet: "If I didn't define myself for myself, I would be crunched into other people's fantasies for me and eaten alive."[17]

The best way I know how to show my gratitude is to gather in this circle, in this book, in this moment, and raise the voice of Audre Lorde, a Black, lesbian, warrior poet who had the courage to speak out, though she often felt that speaking to white women about racism was "wasted energy because of destructive guilt and defensiveness."[18] Because being in circle is not just about speaking your truth or getting something off your chest; there is also healing and growth in the listening. Other perspectives expand our knowledge and our wisdom as we go toward our collective future.

My loftier hope is to inspire our coven members who don't know Audre to seek her out, read her books, and fall in love. Watch YouTube clips of her speeches. Be part of her circle. (Tip: start with her collection of essays, *Sister Outsider*, be forever changed and better prepared to change the world. The essays included bear such titles as: "Poetry Is Not a Luxury," "Uses of the Erotic: The Erotic as Power," "The Uses of Anger: Women Responding to Racism," and "The Master's Tools Will Never Dismantle the Master's House.")

As the *New York Times* pull quote on the back cover of *Sister Outsider* (at least, the edition I have) states: "Lorde's work will be important to those truly interested in growing up sensitive, intelligent and aware."[19]

Audre guides us to unlearn and work against our own destructive guilt and defensiveness, and part of that work is done in circle. Actively listening. Laying down our defenses and rejoicing in our differences, coming to collective agreements on a best course of action.

She said a poetry reading is "a ritual of shared emotional experience. There is a touching, a strengthening of what I'm trying to do with my poetry and a connection between people which I believe is what Poetry is all about."[20] This is true of every circle.

The incomparable Angela Davis, in a speech about Audre at Medgar Evers College, boiled much of Audre's philosophy down to a single, chantable, catchphrase of a message: *Unity does not require that we be identical.* Audre spoke of the influence of homophobia in conversations about race, and the influence of race on conversations about sex and gender, opening up conversations to become a kind of patron saint of Intersectional Feminism. Angela says Audre

> worked hard to pull apart the assumption that Sameness was a pre-
> requisite for Unity. . . . We continue to rely on her insights whenever
> we attempt to imagine and organize radical movements that bring
> together people across racial, gender, sexual, national borders.[21]

Audre's work speaks to the ideas of both community and individualism. She demands that we live authentically and speak our truths, but also, as importantly, that we shut up and listen to the truths of others, insisting that we must "develop tools for using difference as a springboard for creative change within our lives."[22] For Audre, difference is not a barrier, but a creative resource with limitless potential that requires our voices and our ears, our minds and our souls in equal measure.

Audre didn't believe in the imposed binary of life and saw no distinction between her poetry and her academic critical theory. In the introduction to *Sister Outsider*, Nancy K. Berano wrote:

> *Audre Lorde's writing is an impulse toward wholeness.*[23]

In circle there is room for sharing what we know, what we've studied and learned, but we also make space for how we feel, what our guts say, our inklings and intuitions. Our wholeness.

In a conversation we had about the link between Witchcraft and activism, druid and root worker Beverly Smith said, "everything we do to help each other is an act of resistance."[24] In this world, care is a revolutionary act. Honesty and vulnerability are transgressive traits that we use to push back at our collective capitalist brainwash that shoves us toward desperation or greed, viewing others as competitors instead of collaborators, threatened by differences instead of being enriched by them. Circle and community building is an act of resistance, specifically to counter the divisive goals of Witch hunts in all their forms.

In our quest we invoke Audre, "If I didn't define myself for myself, I would be crunched into other people's fantasies for me and eaten alive."[25] And Aunt B, "Better to bear the shame than to bear the pain."

Because our society has falsely equated *normal* with *healthy*, and *normal* with *good*, we feel ashamed of those bits of ourselves that fall outside of what Audre describes as a

> *mythical norm, which each of us within our hearts knows "that's not me." In America, this norm is usually defined as white, thin, male, young, heterosexual, Christian and financially secure. It is with this mythical norm that the trappings of power reside within this society. . . . By and large within the women's movement today, white women focus upon their oppression as women and ignore differences of race, sexual preference, class and age. There is a pretense to a homogeneity of experience covered by the word Sisterhood that does not, in fact, exist.*[26]

It is a relief to have the myth of normality busted to make space for your authentic self as you enter a circle, but having that space has the following cost: you must also hold that space for others. There are many aspects to authenticity, dear coven, and one is to practice what we preach—to back up our hashtags with real listening, real learning, and real action. We must carry the circle mentality with us as we go about our daily lives, extending it out past our boundaries.

Our covenmate Jasper Joy lives in a house full of Queer single parents supporting each other. This is the circle mentality taken to its highest power.

In circle, there is space for excellence and trauma, plus everything else that is revealed in between as we slowly expand our understanding of personal responsibility. The circle is where the learning and listening starts. It is where the work begins, but certainly not where it ends.

Brené Brown said, *"If you trade your authenticity for safety, you may experience the following: anxiety, depression, eating disorders, addiction, rage, blame, resentment, and inexplicable grief."*[27]

Maybe in addition to our various definitions of authenticity there are also two different definitions of safety here: the safety of security—normal family, normal friends, a normal job, a retirement fund, a suburban home—and a self that fits into the status quo, an unrocked boat. I think this is the kind of safety Brené means here with her Eat Pray Love journey of discovery and self-actualization. But there's another kind of safety that lives on the flipside of authenticity. Actual physical, psychologically life-threatening, life-ending danger.

So before we carry on with this Audre Lorde–inspired sermon on Being Yourself and Sharing Your Truth in a circle of perfect love and perfect trust, let me just acknowledge that there are spaces where you can be killed (legally or illegally), or driven by bullies to suicidal thoughts, for being yourself, if that self is Witchy, Queer, slutty, loud, Trans, or just in any way *different*. If this applies to you, know that you owe your true self only to your self. It's okay to keep your secret safe until you can get to a place where you and your secret *are* safe. Look for that place. Whether it's in a different country or a different coven. Create that place. Save yourself for the circle.

We know that growth lives outside of our comfort zone, in taking chances and being vulnerable. But once again—safe from being killed: important; safe from people looking at you funny on the street: not as important. "Better to bear the shame than to bear the pain" doesn't apply if your honesty attracts the attention of a monster looking for its next victim.

In her poem "Coal," Audre reminds us that the price for speaking out is much higher for some than others, "who pays what for speaking."[28] For some, speaking out could mean death.

So, because in this nonbinary universe there are no either-ors, only ands and in-betweens, we must paradoxically strive to be safe *and* brave. In her essay "The Transformation of Silence into Language and Action," Audre gives us a push. "I have come to believe over and over again that what is most important to me must be spoken, made verbal and shared, even at the risk of having it bruised or misunderstood."[29]

Because visibility matters, Witches have to live in the nonbinary space between safe and brave; we have to make sacrifices to make things easier for the next generation, protecting them from future harm, while still protecting ourselves as best we can.

Audre's book *Zami* is what she calls a mytho-biography, chronicling her early life. And in it we find DeLois.

DeLois lived up the block on 142nd Street and never had her hair done, and all the neighborhood women sucked their teeth as she walked by. Her crispy hair twinkled in the summer sun as her big proud stomach moved her on down the block while I watched, not caring whether or not she was a poem. Even though I tied my shoes and tried to peep under her blouse as she passed by, I never spoke to DeLois, because my mother didn't. But I loved her because she moved like she felt she was somebody I'd like to know someday. She moved like how I thought god's mother must have moved, and my mother, once upon a time, and someday maybe me."[30]

Who is your DeLois? Do you remember? In your childhood, did you see someone who, by behaving as if they were someone special, inspired you to express your true self?

I have a few: documentary clips of Haight Ashbury in 1967, Grace Jones in a Philip Treacy hat, John Waters's *Hairspray* . . . , but the most visceral DeLois-style memory I have is seeing the Club Kids on *Geraldo*. I was twelve years old, and even though they were set up as punchlines for audience mockery and disdain (no one knew then that Michael Alig would murder Angel Melendez six years later—the Party Monster himself died not long after being released from prison, so needless to say, the idolatry began and ended in the early 90s, but the spark! The spark only grew.) . . . So, even though they were set up for scorn, all I saw was art and freedom embodied, superficial as it may have been.

I want this book, this circle, to be a DeLois. I want you to read about these Witches and walk taller, prouder, though they make suck their teeth as you pass. Know that you are somebody special—an insider to a rich and powerful lineage. A part of a circle. A DeLois.

In *Zami*, Audre wrote about finding a niche at school, a group of weirdos, a "sisterhood of rebels" who called themselves The Branded.

> We were The Branded, the Lunatic Fringe, proud of our outrageousness
> and our madness, our bizarre-colored inks and quill pens. We learned how
> to mock the straight set, and how to cultivate our group paranoia into an
> instinct for self-protection that always stopped our shenanigans just short
> of expulsion. We wrote obscure poetry and cherished our strangeness as
> the spoils of default, and in the process we learned that pain and rejection
> hurt, but that they weren't fatal, and that they could be useful since they
> couldn't be avoided. We learned that not feeling at all was worse than
> hurting. At that time, suffering was clearly what we did best. We became
> The Branded because we learned how to make a virtue out of it.[31]

But even among the different, Audre was *more* different. As she wonders why she wasn't invited to her fellow rebels' houses, we begin to understand that her quest for intersectionality has deep roots.

*It was in high school that I came to believe that I was different
from my white classmates, not because I was Black, but because
I was me.*[32]

Audre describes that "as a forty-nine-year-old Black lesbian feminist
socialist mother of two, including one boy, and a member of an inter-
racial couple, . . . I usually find myself a part of some group defined as
other, deviant, inferior or just plain wrong."[33]

"Just plain wrong" was Audre from the jump. Born in New York
City in 1934, she was the youngest of three sisters. Her two older sisters formed a pair of placid perfection while Audre was, according to
her biographer Alexis De Veaux, "recalcitrant." In *Warrior Poet*, Alexis
wrote:

*Her memories of childhood became almost mythic constructions of an
ugly duckling who was legally blind before age 5, clumsy, inarticu-
late, born left-handed, a stutterer (who got whipped repeatedly), fat
and black . . . By her own accounts, she was lonely, unwanted and
unloved.*[34]

Audre's sisters, Phyllis and Helen, in addition to being closer in
humor, were also closer in age, so they became a duo, leaving Audre to
find her way as a third wheel without an axel.

"Helen and Phyliss were obedient catholic girls," wrote Alexis. "They
learned their catechisms inside out, never questioned the nuns, and did
what they were told. Audre was, on the other hand, recalcitrant, refusing
to fit into the mold."[35]

She argued and reasoned and questioned. Her grades for conduct
were consistently lower than her grades for academics.

Audre wrote her first poem at thirteen and had one published at
fifteen in *Seventeen* magazine. Before her death at age fifty-eight, she
lived in Germany and Grenada; worked as a librarian, professor, poet,
world-class world-changing public speaker, and activist; and created a
legacy that I hope will inform our collective future.

There's a video on YouTube where Audre reads her poem, "A Woman Speaks," the poem that I invoked when introducing Audre in this chapter: "Moon marked and touched by sun, my magic is unwritten, but when the seas turn back they will leave my shape behind . . . I have been woman for a long time, beware my smile. I am treacherous with old magic."[36]

But before she goes into her reading, Audre makes this statement:

I've just returned from a feminist conference and book fair in
London where, for a week, over and over again, I was brought
or made very very conscious of the ways in which Black women
and white women do not hear each other, so yet again, this is an
attempt.[37]

Her "An Open Letter to Mary Daly" is a crash-course master-class in calling in before you call out (Another Tip: you can find the full text for free online. Seek it out because we are, by necessity, more enlightened Witches for having read it.) In a preamble to the publication of this letter Audre wrote: "The following letter was written to Mary Daly, author of *Gyn/Ecology*, on May 6, 1979. Four months later, having received no reply, I open it to the community of women."[38]

Here's some quick background before we get into the letter. So, in 1978's *Gyn/Ecology*, "Daly claimed that male culture was the direct, evil opposite of female nature, and that the ultimate purpose of men was death of both women and nature. Daly contrasted women's life-giving powers with men's death-dealing powers."[39] I admit, I haven't read *Gyn/Ecology*, and I'm not remotely as in to gender essentialism as some of the radical feminists I've read about with their all-female Utopias, but damn, there's something to that thesis. Let's replace the reductive "men" with "white supremacist capitalist patriarchy" and read it again: "the ultimate purpose of white supremacist capitalist patriarchy is death of both women and nature." That feels real.

Audre had some issues with the book, and so she wrote Mary a letter.

DEAR MARY,

This letter has been delayed because of my grave reluctance to reach out to you, for what I want us to chew upon here is neither easy nor simple. The history of white women who are unable to hear Black women's words, or to maintain dialogue with us, is long and discouraging. But for me to assume that you will not hear me represents not only history, perhaps, but an old pattern of relating, sometimes protective and sometimes dysfunctional, which we, as women shaping our future, are in the process of shattering and passing beyond, I hope.[40]

Reading *Gyn/Ecology*, Audre wondered:

Why are [Mary's] goddess images only white, western european, judea-christian? Where was Afrekete, Y emanje, Oyo, and Mawulisa? Where were the warrior goddesses of the Vodun, the Dahomeian Amazons and the warrior-women of Dan? Well, I thought, Mary has made a conscious decision to narrow her scope and to deal only with the ecology of western european women.

Then I came to the first three chapters of your Second Passage, and it was obvious that you were dealing with non european women, but only as victims and preyers—upon each other. I began to feel my history and my mythic background distorted by the absence of any images of my foremothers in power.[41]

Audre ends the letter thusly:

I had decided never again to speak to white women about racism. I felt it was wasted energy because of destructive guilt and defensiveness, and because whatever I had to say might better be said by white women to one another at far less emotional cost to the speaker, and probably with a better hearing. But I would like not to destroy you in my consciousness, not to have to. So as a sister Hag, I ask you to speak to my perceptions. Whether or not you do, Mary, again again I thank you for what I have learned from you. This letter is in repayment.

In the hands of Afrekete,

Audre Lorde[42]

Oh Audre! "I learned something from you. Now I'm going to repay you by teaching you something" is an excellent approach to disagreement, criticism, and communal understanding. It turns out that Mary did write back; her response was found among Audre's papers after she died. I won't reprint the response because it felt to me like a lot of excuses (the caliber of which includes but is not limited to: "I didn't have your address"), but I will note one thing. Audre's letter was dated May 6, 1979. Mary Daly's response was dated September 22, 1979. *Four and a half months later.* You'll recall that Audre said she had waited four months for a response. So I can't help but wonder if Mary got wind of Audre taking the letter public, and only then wrote back . . . you know . . . for the optics.[43]

We know that Audre is a role model, a vocal advocate of the power of difference and unity, but does that make her a Witch? Maybe, but we're here to be specifically sacred, so let's focus for a minute on the spiritual path of our sister outsider. Her poetry speaks of a soul, Black and proud, seeking and finding the gods of her ancestors, while lamenting a history that tried to erase them.

Poems "The Winds of Orisha" and "From the House of Yemanjá" ring out with lines like, "I will become myself an incantation" and "I am the sun and moon and forever hungry."[44]

For me, since our first book *Missing Witches*, and to be honest, much of my life is structured around the Wheel of the Year, Audre's poems "Solstice" and "Equinox" are of particular interest. She describes her poem "Solstice" as "A Call To Power" insisting we need to feed our spirits lest they abandon us.[45]

In "Equinox," she wrote about her children coming home from school in the spring, and she wonders if her children will ever know the kind of peace she sees in them in this moment. She laments the burning of her kin and the earth, but concludes with the idea that in order to go on living, we must be very strong and love each other.[46]

Nature is real and tangible, the environment we live in, the topography of parks, window-sill gardens and forests, the movement of the earth and sun, but we Witches also live inside the metaphor of nature—the solstice when we are decided, clear and full; the equinox when we are mailable and admire the transitional times. The spring equinox brings the promise of growth, but that growth depends on the seeds we plant. It is the same for farmers as it is for activists and poets, and it all depends on our communication. We must be very strong and love each other in order to go on living.

Audre was diagnosed with breast cancer in 1978 and had a mastectomy. In her battle, she wrote *The Cancer Journals*, viewing her cancer as another difference on which she would not be silent or rendered invisible. She wrote:

> *Prosthesis offers the empty comfort of "Nobody will know the difference." But it is that very difference which I wish to affirm, because I have lived it, and survived it, and wish to share that strength with other women. If we are to translate the silence surrounding breast cancer into language and action against this scourge, then the first step is that women with mastectomies must become visible to each other.*[47]

This is what the circle is for. It's the way we make a space for truth and spiral outward from there with our real bodies, our real selves. Unwillingness to bear our pain silently is a core tool in our re-enchantment of the world because it renders us visible to one another, and in that visibility, we share our strength with those who are afraid. Our circles are concentric, radiating out from our centers into the world.

She is, in her poetry, the sun and moon, and moon-marked and touched by sun."[48]

Audre returns again and again to these celestial circles, a part of them as they are part of her. Circular. They are individual celestial objects, the moon is an independent being and yet, what we perceive of it is largely dictated by the reflected light of the sun. We must look beyond what we are told to find the truth, knowing we are affected by both. Marked by speech and touched by silence, we are the sun and moon; we rely on each other to reflect and be reflected.

So, too, our very existence relies equally on light and darkness, in all its beautiful difference.

Audre declared herself *both* the sun and moon and proved we need not be identical to be unified in the dance of our reality.

Here, in this circle, in this Missing Witches coven, I want us all to feel like we belong, not because we are all the same, but because we appreciate and admire each other's differences. That here, if nowhere else, we are insiders, each bringing our own strengths and vulnerabilities, our gifts, powers, our variant and atypical strands forming a web overlaid in delicate protection of our unity. That as you see my words, Risa's words, and the words of the Witches we've found, that you also feel seen. We outsiders tend to each other's battle wounds and emotional scars. Wailing sympathetically together, like a less creepy *Midsommar* Hårga cult, and using that collective strength of difference and unity to carry on the fight. We must be very strong and love each other in order to go on living.

For Scorpio's New Moon, take Audre with you to your circle, invite her as a friend and introduce her with this:

> *Change means growth, and growth can be painful. But we sharpen self-definition by exposing the self in work and struggle together with those whom we define as different from ourselves, although sharing the same goals. For Black and white, old and young, lesbian and heterosexual women alike, this can mean new paths to our survival.*
>
> *We have chosen each other. And the edge of each other's battles [...] We seek beyond history. For a new and more possible meeting.[49]*

Incantation

We gather
and
I have a valuable contribution to make,
Holding space for myself
And others
As a speaker

As a listener.

I

Define myself for myself

And will not be tempted by defensiveness

Or judgment.

The Circle is Unbroken

But never closed

And so it is

For my Soul and Mind.

I seek beyond history

For a new and more possible meeting.

I must be very strong and love the other

in order to go on living.

My silence will not protect me.

Ritual

Your ritual for the Scorpio New Moon is to a) form a circle, or b) attend a circle.

As the year-end holidays gear up, and the sunlight gears down, it is especially important to affirm or reaffirm the importance of our connection to others, before the traditional, annual stress makes us wonder if we might be better off alone.

According to the *Old Farmer's Almanac*, November's full moon is called the Beaver Moon, when beavers usually go into their lodges for winter. And whether or not our new moon falls in November, we too can create that lodge, that safe, brave space.

Audre Lorde said, "Your silence will not protect you." So let's talk.

Option A: Form a Circle

This circle can be online or in person with three or more people (including you).

I know some of you solitary practitioners will be scared or skeptical, but new moons are for new things. Just try it. If you don't like it, that's okay. Bibliomancy is also great, and you can return to your silent stacks of magic books tomorrow.

And don't be discouraged. The moon in Scorpio reminds us, gently yet sternly, that relationships can be hard. I met two strangers who became great friends at a circle. It was a public event held in a public park. There were dozens of invitees, but only we three showed up. The right three. Not everyone you ask will say yes and that's okay. The right ones will.

But I want you to take a chance. I want you to encourage others to be vulnerable by first being vulnerable yourself. Reach out.

You don't have to frame it as a coven meeting if your friends or family don't get the whole *Witch thing*. Call it whatever you want or whatever you're comfortable with—add an element of craft if you like. As an example, in the leadup to Christmas 2020, with us all in pandemic lockdown, a gang of us Witches got together on Zoom and made decorations as we chatted. As I said before, your circle can be a card game, a book club, a crafternoon party. All this is just an excuse to get your circle in place.

Honestly, a lot of people are just waiting for a safe/brave space to be vulnerable and to be asked, How *are* you? What do you need? What are your dreams?

And *you* can provide that place.

Don't expect an immediate catharsis or instant epiphany. A real bounty of a circle takes time. Finding the rhythm and flow takes time. Confidence and trust are built slowly, one conversation, one action at a time. And one at a time's good fishing.

Here is a kind of script you can use as a jumping-off point.

> They say, "A problem shared is a problem halved," so I wanted us all to get together to check in, share, and help me figure out if the reverse is also true: is a dream shared a dream doubled? What are your crazy pipe dreams or pipe goals that seem too farfetched to say out loud? I want to hear about them. This is like brainstorming, so there are no wrong answers or bad ideas. No judgment! I'll go first! (Yes, you must go first. You are brave and strong and safe and you can pull open this gate.)

Option B: Attend a Circle

If forming a circle of your own is just all too much this month, maybe attending a circle is just the confidence boost you need to try creating one next year, and maybe it'll be the energy boost you'll need for upcoming yuletide.

Risa and I host circles online, so you can watch for those on our website and socials. We also love Amanda Yates Garcia, aka The Oracle of LA, who (as of this printing) hosts monthly rituals with tenderness of heart.

One of the silver linings in a (post) pandemic cloud is that online events have become the standard. It has never been easier to find each other, set an intention, and make a connection.

If you can't conjure the confidence for Option B, I'll give you an Option C. Hold a circle for yourself. Create a ritual of opening that space for you and you alone. Ask yourself about yourself. Ask about your crazy pipe dreams and your irrational fears.

Start from your very center and expand.

9

New Moon in Sagittarius

Potions and Poisons

This circle is led by Risa
with expansions by Amy.

*Luna renews in Sagittarius, and everything is possible.
Revel, dance, and be merry that you are here, now. The wisdom is
in knowing that you've already embarked on your most perfect quest.*

—THEA ANDERSON, ASTROLOGER

IN THE DARK OF THE SAGITTARIAN NEW MOON, I invite you to become your most fully realized kitchen Witch. Light a single candle before each meal, stir maple syrup into coffee clockwise while you call forward what you need, map your desires onto every water glass and gulp it down. Plan the coming days and weeks like a recipe. How will you nourish yourself and your community? What will you invite into your system?

Over the years, as I've moved deeper into this woods life and evolved out of my former shapes, I've been slowing down. I feel older, and sometimes calmer. I feel my identity shifting into something participatory, an ingredient in the lake system that moves through me and my family. I have become an ingredient in something larger than my potions, and I have become a potion-maker.

And so on the Sagittarian New Moon, I invite you to join me. Let's use food and drink to cast spells of gathering, of love and hope, of family weaving, of transubstantiation and renewal. Let's make potions that speak to our skins, our shells, our flora; the nerve fibers that hum from taste buds, sense receptors, emotions; the electrical linings of our digestive systems. Potions for our outsides whispering in and our insides singing out. Let's make a magic that is material, commingling with our sweat, our stomach acids, our blood, our biome. Because this is core to what a Witch is.

> Pharmakeia, *such arts are called, for they deal in pharmaka, those herbs with the power to work changes upon the world, both those sprung from the blood of gods, as well as those which grow common upon the earth. It is a gift to be able to draw out their powers, and I am not alone in them.* "Pharmakis," *I said.* Witch.[1]

Sagittarius is the seeker time, and this new moon is a time of vision quests and working with herbs to work your changes.

This is crone time, cozy and boney and candlelit. Potions are weapons and medicines that we learn to craft over time, and we learn them from ancestors reaching across time. This is about the knowledge of life and death forces in plants; it's about following life's path through death and fermentation, through transformation, the alchemical marriage to utterly new life shapes on the other side. This is Cerridwen time, that goddess whose cauldron is all cauldrons, the Cauldron of Transformation, the Cauldron of Rebirth, and the Cauldron of Inspiration.

Cerridwen "represents the womb of the Goddess from which all life manifests into this world. She labors continually at Her cauldron, stirring up the forces of inspiration, divine knowledge and the eternal cycle of birth, death and rebirth. She is the Wheel of Life."[2] Potions and potion-makers concoct the very stuff of life and death, and so this is the origin story of poetry.

This is the season of the cauldron and the leather pouch. Of containers and companions. Because to make a potion, we first need seed bags, our mason jars of dried herbs, a cauldron. We need to take our eyes off the hero's journey and turn to more humble questions.

> *How did a sling, a pot, a bottle suddenly get into the story? How do such lowly things keep the story going? Or maybe even worse for the hero, how do those concave, hollowed-out things, those holes in Being, from the get-go generate richer, quirkier, fuller, unfitting, ongoing stories, stories with room for the hunter but which weren't and aren't about him, the self-making Human, the human-making machine of history? The slight curve of a shell that holds just a little water, just a few seeds to give away and to receive, suggests stories of becoming-with, of reciprocal induction, of companion species whose job in living and dying is not to end the storying, the worlding. With a shell and a net, becoming humans, becoming humus, becoming terran, has another shape—the side-winding, snaky shape of becoming-with.[3]*

Our crafting in this dark moon draws us closer into the leaky, spiraling circle of becoming-with; to the juicy apple of the knowledge of good and evil, and to stories that include the human, the hunter, but aren't about him; to a pouch, a net, a soup pot that holds both light and dark, theft and inspiration, crone and mother, seed and stone, nourishment and poison, patient and poet. If we are to dedicate ourselves to resisting the total consumption and destruction of all biodiversity, and to re-enchanting the world with seeds, storying, and worlding that becomes-with the more-than-human world, then we do well to take up that cauldron of possibilities that we call kitchen magic.

The experience of crafting food is a time-traveling, shape-shifting potion. It allows us to step into another dimension. We cross time, we taste for a little while another culture, we travel into the home of the recipe writer. There are always memories with us when we cook. Who ground the flour? Who knew to heat the pan before you crack the egg? Who taught you? Who is here?

Spirits like spices were brought from their homes, ecosystems, and sociopolitical systems across the world to be in our cupboards, to speak to parts of our tongues, our muscles, our dreams. We follow the recipe makers' choices and reenact their journey, and when we do, it can be an act of care for ourselves and for those we feed. It is also an act of translation. The potion-maker, cook, kitchen Witch interacts with the possibilities—delicious, noxious, healing, deadly—in each ingredient and in their chemical reactions together. This branch of magical praxis involves communication with the more-than-human world, and so it can call for a shift away from a perspective that dominates our thinking and keeps us separate.

Throw a small pinch of cinnamon on a hot element and it will sparkle; you will breathe in fiery sweet lightning bugs of passion in the air. Cinnamon was used to embalm bodies in ancient Egypt and China, and it has been central to life-preserving mysteries for thousands of years. Once, years ago, when I was waking up from a kind of zombie life, I grabbed almost a fistful and threw it, and the stove went up like firecrackers. It was part of a spell that helped me to wake up and come into my own skin again, and that let me bring my whole heart to Marc. These days, our daughter May makes the coffee with me every morning. We grind the beans from independently owned farms and send love to the farmers. She stirs the grains slowly counterclockwise and whispers to it things she wants to go away: "take all sickness from this house, take the ice from the lake, take all the worries." And then she stirs it clockwise and we whisper, "fill us up with love and laughter, bring on the good times." And when she's inspired, she sprinkles in a little nutmeg, cardamom, or cinnamon. Each morning I savor my awe for the incredible sweetness of being together.

Rebecca Beyer, ethnobotanist, plant folklorist, and author of *Wild Witchcraft* told us:

> *The first time I felt really called to eat a plant, I didn't know what it was at all, and it turned out to be Datura, which is deadly under certain dosages . . . There's a trickster spirit to a lot of things. The medicine of the land is beyond human in its sense of humor. So sometimes it feels very cruel or unfair . . . It's important to look at the ways the plant world calls for us to interact with them and never assume it's from this human perspective.[4]*

In the potion, as in the seed bag, the focus shifts from the hunter or the hero or the chef. It widens our perspective to the more-than-human sense of humor that bubbles and shakes and sparkles and calls out to us: Eat Me.

The first time I made the simple, ancient mead recipe in Julia Skinner's *The Hidden Cosmos: A Fermentation Oracle Deck with Recipes*, I lovingly tended and tweaked it for days, adding mugwort flowers and lemon, turning it in the sunlight, and sipping tiny portions.[5] But then one night, during a new moon circle with our coven, like the datura calling Eat Me, I felt suddenly called to finish the jar. I drank three glasses of the yellow, fizzy, bright and bitter mead that Julia calls a Mead of Inspiration. I never felt dizzy or tipsy, but I got lit up in another way. The days I sampled that mead as it fermented glow bright in my memory, and that night was a crescendo.

The next day I felt off, as if I was next door to myself. I felt busy. I felt accompanied. I felt overwhelmed. I felt very clearly that my mind-body was having to make shifts and make room as it welcomed a host of new microbial agents. I felt their trickster spirit in me, bubbling everywhere, gut and brain. I felt changed and ill, a little in love and a little afraid.

Potion-making can be overwhelming because the ingredients do want, in some way, to overwhelm you. And because the world of it is vast; to know the stories and properties of just the ingredients in your cupboard right now could take a lifetime. Increase this exponentially as you feel the call of the plants in your area, the bacteria, and the fungi quietly implicating themselves in your life, wondering if you will notice, working their spells with you whether you notice or not. Rebecca offers us this: "It's a colonized mindset to think you have to know all or nothing ... You can know 10 plants deeply and be a wonderful healer."[6] Our potions are a language we speak, a way of listening to the natural world and of being changed by it. To begin to use this most powerful, magical tool, we can choose a single ingredient and learn its story. Follow its history back through colonialism and genetics, through species migration, and through evolutionary histories. All the way back to the point of mutual ancestry. Rebecca invites us to begin simply. Go into your cupboard, or out into the land, and ask: Who is here? Anyone want to come for tea? Then listen. You could use a pendulum, a simple necklace, and ask Yes/No questions. You could make a simple board with Yes on the vertical axis and No on the horizontal, or add the alphabet. You could just turn your ears inward. Ask questions, take small tastes of plants you are getting to know and listen for the answers, and if answers aren't clear, come back and ask again. "I find my ears are rusty after a long time of not listening."[7]

Take your time getting to know these spirits. Go small, go slow. Listen with your nose, your tongue. Paracelsus wrote, "What is there that is not poison? All things are poison and nothing is without poison. Solely the dose determines that a thing is not a poison." All things are poison. There is a trickster spirit in everything.

Author Sophie Strand told us:

> (T)he idea of poison is a relatively modern idea that's more reflective of our inability to dose anything, we always do things in extremes. Any substance, when not taken seriously, when not understood as being sacred and animate and different than you, can be used ineffectively even if it's a medicine ... I think of everything as being pharmakon which is that older Greek term for something that can be either a poison or a potion or a medicine.[8]

If the materia of this world—materia as in *Materia Medica*, all materials with healing properties, and as in the alchemical *Prima Materia*, the primary matter akin to chaos from which all matter comes—if these can all become poison when they are not understood as sacred, then, Witches, potion-makers, maybe the reverse is also true. Any materia when understood as sacred and animate and different from you can be a medicine. The primary matter is always here; its sacredness is always present.

> *Progressive doses of poison are ever-wider gates unto the spirit-realm, the last of which is death. Not all gates are pleasurable, and many bring great pain. Yet within the ambit of the Art Magical we may posit a schemata of Gnostic Poisoning, a continuum whose polarities are benefic and Malefic, healing and harming.*[9]

The Witch sees the shades of color along the binary of poison and potion. Restoring a reverence, assuming animacy, can help us to see the medicine in everything. Medicine for the web, medicine for the story of life on this holobiont that we breathe with around the sun.[10] We will need to walk with the tricksters along the poison edge to do so, but the path is there for us all.

> *Let me say what sorcery is not: it is not divine power, which comes with a thought and a blink. It must be made and worked, planned and searched out, dug up, dried, chopped and ground, cooked, spoken over, and sung.*[11]

As we approach this craft, this tool of the re-enchantment, this labor and long work of wills and sacred relationship, we can take with us Donna Haraway's plea to "make the relay."

> *We must somehow make the relay, inherit the trouble, and reinvent the conditions for multispecies flourishing, not just in a time of ceaseless human wars and genocides, but in a time of human-propelled mass extinction and multispecies genocides that sweep people and critters into the vortex. We must dare "to make" the relay; that is to create, to fabulate, in order not to despair.*[12]

Dare to make the relay—to re-enchant our commingling—in order not to despair. To feed the world, to be fed, to be fed upon. There's transgressive magic here that's been intentionally marginalized.

Potion-makers became poisoners when it became necessary to divide and terrorize to grab land.[13] Public lands that people shared and fed their families from were enclosed, and part of that spiraling death of the commons was the loss of common knowledge—folk knowledge of what the land knew and provided.

When medicine started to be regulated around 1200, women were barred from formal medical training at universities, and those that continued as physicians or midwives were sometimes labeled Witches.[14]

Witches were hunted while pieces of what they knew were incorporated into modern medicine.

*In 1775, a patient with 'dropsy'—a term for swelling probably caused by heart disease—came to Withering's Birmingham practice. (Witherington is the Scottish doctor credited with the discovery of the cardio-active drug digitalis.) No treatment seemed to work, so the patient sought a second opinion from a local Gypsy woman. She prescribed a potion containing an estimated 20 different plant ingredients, and he was cured. Keen to learn its properties, Withering tracked down the healer and figured out that the active ingredient in her potion was purple foxglove (*Digitalis purpurea*). He then performed a clinical trial of sorts, testing different doses and formulations on 163 patients. Withering ultimately determined that drying and grinding up the leaves produced the best results in small doses. Digitalis plants gave us the modern heart failure drugs digoxin and digitoxin.[15]*

Foxglove is a beautiful plant cultivated in many flowering gardens and, as all good gardeners know, all parts of the plant are poisonous. But the traveler women, liminal women, and people with oral histories of our relationships with plants have kept knowledge of how to walk that line between poison and potion.

When I started working on this chapter, it had been two years since May went into anaphylactic shock. And then it happened again, the day after we increased her dose of baked milk with the immunotherapists at the Montreal Children's Hospital. This was always part of the possibilities around doing the work to slowly increase her tolerance of bovine proteins. But still, there is the slow-motion terror of watching it happen again.

The EpiPen is miraculously quick. This medicine, which was derived from the adrenal glands of sheep, animals whose milk she is deathly allergic to, brings her back from the brink in seconds. She returns to herself, furious and terrified, but amazed at how much better she feels. The EMTs arriving in full PPE were scary, but then very funny and very kind. She had them turn off all the lights in the ambulance so she could ride in the dark and watch the "shooting stars" of cars going by.

The hospital in Covid times was like a horror movie—all paneled and taped off everywhere, halls empty, like a ghost town—to try and keep a few rooms separate from the pandemic raging through the rest of the building. We go into this place to be safe, knowing death is everywhere in the air.

May slept for twelve hours and we watched movies in bed all the next day. And afterward, we looked around with the eyes of people who've been violently shaken into remembering how brilliantly precious every fucking second is. And, in some way, of course this whole experience makes me want to stop the immunotherapy, jump the fuck off this daily train of feeding her small poisons, which are potions at this dose, conjuring her immune system's resilience.

I want to never subject her to any of this again and just stay home, forever eating vegan food we've grown and prepared ourselves, safe from everything in the world—Covid, heartbreak, everything. But she has me tell her the story of Rapunzel every night as she falls asleep for weeks after it happens, and I think she's telling us both: there is no life kept away from danger. I can't go from poisoner to prisoner-keeper. So we go back a step, a smaller dose, but we keep going down this road, walking with our companions: milk, courage, death.

Every medicine, every potion, is a choice to defy death. You take a dose, carefully measured, to change the pattern of your genetics and assert your own desires on the map of your life. We look at the endless spirals of our DNA, watch the dance of viruses moving through the walls of our cells, and see that at no moment are we fixed, and we never are alone. We are an unfolding relation and our choices matter in that dance.

Our choices matter and so do our lives. We have a right to health and autonomy, a right to the pursuit of happiness, which means having a right to choose the potions that shape our fate. Including modern versions of that ancient essential remedy: potions to end a pregnancy.

Sarah Diehl, director of Abortion Democracy, said:

> *The hypocrisy around abortion is unbelievable. The criminalization of abortion doesn't have any impact on the numbers of women who have abortions, just on how dangerous it is for women. 60–80,000 women die every year because of illegal unsafe abortions worldwide. Five million women become very sick from it . . . And it's not talked about at all. Every third woman worldwide has an abortion in her lifetime. I think it has to be accepted as a part of human sexuality, not a tragedy.*[16]

Abortion is and has always been a fact of life, a piece of the magic of life that comes as pregnant people dance with our choices, our companions, our futures. And it has been at the heart of why women are persecuted and witches are burned. We mapped our fertility; we tested medicines until we found ways to protect ourselves against the determination of our lives by forces outside of us.

Here in the egg basket of our own bodies, we crafted in order to choose when to carry seeds and let new lives sprout, and that power is undeniably divine. Bringing new life into the world, and feeding that life from our bodies put us directly into a place of power that Dr. Phyllis Rippey sees as central to the construction of gender.

> *If chest-feeding people can have these little beings who see them as all providing and all knowing, it's almost as though only those people*

can experience what it's like to be a God . . . and so there's a kind of
jealousy there . . . and so we start to see a control of women's bodies . . .
Historically there's just tons and tons of rules that men have created
for how babies should be breastfed.[17]

And there are tons of rules about sex and abortion. And about who can work, who can inherit, who can own land or get educated. Control over women and marginalized people's experience of Godliness becomes a stand-in for the experience of Godliness itself in the power-hungry ego. Not life-giver but cage-keeper. And that control becomes addicting, because it is a mask. Control rages and consumes bodies.

When bodies have been broken down, stripped of their rights, subject to violence, when no other routes are available, they turn to poison. Like it or not, this deadly edge of what the plant world knows has always been in our toolkit for resistance.

In seventeenth-century Italy, divorce was illegal. A woman who had been raped would be pressured to marry her rapist, and rape or physical abuse within marriage was legally nonexistent. Women had no rights to their lives, to their pursuit of happiness. And so, a woman emerged who had a way with plants. Giulia Tofana mixed arsenic and belladonna to make her Aqua Tofana. Women hid it in plain sight with their perfumes and cosmetics, and when they couldn't take it anymore, they slipped a few drops into their husbands' wine or food. Once and he might become weak, apologetic even. Twice and he'd be sick. A third time and he'd die. And in this way, Giulia was indirectly responsible for the deaths of over six hundred men.

Across the world in revolutionary Haiti, under the leadership of Vodou priestesses and priests, poisonings evolved into organized revolts.[18] It came to be known among colonists that midwives were using abortion as a means of resistance. Women sought help to end pregnancies resulting from rape and to keep their children from an enslaved life, and to save their own strength. They chose to protect what, in them, was a tool against oppression, to increase their own chances of survival, and to give themselves the right to choose to bring their beloved children into the world when they would be free and safe. The ability to safely end a pregnancy let more people escape to join the Maroons in the woods, to add their skill and knowledge to the growing communities there, to become tactical and spiritual leaders and organizers, to tip the scales and turn the tide. Abortion can be a potion for freedom from oppression.

Even the sainted have mixed this potion. Hildegard of Bingen was a healer who also knew that to heal the living person, sometimes the doorway to possibility inside them that had been opened by one kind of seed needed to be closed by another.

> She describes the use of several botanical emmenagogues (menstruation stimulators) and abortifacients: asarum, white hellebore, feverfew, tansy, oleaster, farn ... she explains: "A pregnant woman will eat it, either on account she languishes or she aborts an infant which is a danger to her body, or if she has not had a menstrual period for a time period so that it hurts.[19]

Hildegard, in her book *Causae et Curae*, examined both the material and metaphysical causes of illness and offered plant-, animal-, and ritual-based remedies.

> For a weak heart, she proposes a daily teaspoon of "wine for the heart," consisting of boiled parsley, honey, and wine. For stomach pain, a nightcap of wine mixed with powdered ginger, galingale (a ginger relative from Southeast Asia), and zedoary (another ginger cousin, from India). And for matters of melancholy, she offers her "cookies of joy" (or "nerve cookies"), wielding the key ingredients of spelt flour, nutmeg, cinnamon, and cloves to "calm all bitterness of the heart and mind, open your heart and impaired senses, and make your mind cheerful.[20]

Hildegard is also responsible for the earliest surviving writings on the use of hops in beer. Hildegard wrote in the *Physica*, circa 1150, "[hops] stops putrification when put in [beer] and it may be added so that it lasts so much longer."[21] Hildegard brewed beer in a time when fermentation wasn't well known or understood, and it was considered a divine act. For hundreds of years, it had been women tending to these kitchen miracles. And those potion-makers, it turns out, are at the very crux of Witch history.

Julia Skinner, author of *Our Fermented Lives* and creator of the *Hidden Cosmos Oracle Deck*, told me about the history of women and brewing. While we spoke, two carboys of hoppy beer sat brewing behind me, making their presence known.

> *One source I looked at said that it was the most dominant profession of women in medieval court records . . . And then at some point, men decided that they wanted to do brewing and they wanted to make it something that they could control. And so, as often happens, rather than being able to continue to exist in their spaces of expertise, women were pushed out and their histories largely erased and their professional work actually vilified . . . Perceptions of witchcraft became a very central part of the narratives around getting women out of those spaces. . . our modern image of a witch, pointy hat, bubbling cauldron, cats, broom, all of this stuff originates from the alewives. Women who sold ale on street corners in England . . . The pointy hats, those were their costume. Like: "I'm the beer person. Here's my hat." And they would keep cats because they had stores of grain that mice would get in. They had a broom to sweep up fallen grain off of the floor. And of course, the bubbling beer.[22]*

Hildegard fermented with the women in the abbey kitchen. Unusual for the time, she was trained to read and write, and so she transcribed their recipes as well as her own visions. She lived and worked at this small opening of time before the university system overtook the dominance of the abbeys, excluding women from the pursuit of knowledge even more completely.

> *Though the time of the witch burnings were a few hundred years in the future, Hildegard herself could have stood in their flames for she committed many of the "crimes" of the Medieval witch. She was a healer, she received visions from God, and she was independent, and she invented her own language for mystical purposes. She also healed people through herbal folk magic.[23]*

Behind a wall, she let down her hair and listened to women, laborers, and herself. And she began to say the burning things she heard inside her own mind. This flourished into compendiums of sicknesses and cures, recipes, and remarkably accurate ideas about healing with plants.

In "Are the Correct Herbal Claims by Hildegard von Bingen Only Lucky Strikes?" a team of German and Swiss scientists focused on Hildegard's references to eighty-five specific plants, ones still being used today for medical purposes.[24] They found 212 health claims by Hildegard from this group of plants. Thirty of them have been cross-referenced as correct in their claims according to contemporary standards.

If she had been making the claims up randomly, only between 6 and 7 of her cures would have been accurate. The study finds the probability of this happening just by chance is 1 in 10,000,000 . . . The finding from this approach that medieval medical claims are significantly correlated with modern herbal indications supports the importance of traditional medicinal systems as an empirical source.[25]

She wasn't making it up. She was reading everything available at the time, including new translations from other cultures, and she was working in the monastery clinic and kitchen, testing plants and combinations, and listening carefully to the people around her.[26]

I think Hildegard was seeing with more than one eye, trying to see the vastness in the heavens and under the microscope. She was following threads of connection beyond the dominant narrative.

Sophie Strand told us:

I've been thinking a lot of capitalism and patriarchy as being narrative dysbiosis. Which is when you take too many antibiotics and you kill off your gut biome. There's too much open real estate so that a pathogen can take over and bloom, like a yeast or something really terrible, and the issue is if you take fungicides to kill the yeast it takes the same problem again and again and again . . . So the way I've been thinking about tackling patriarchal capitalism is being a bad story. As being a monologuing pathogen . . . how do I overwhelm it with a

*probiotic of other stories? How can I go back and see if there are other
healthier modes of the masculine in mythologies, fairy tales, folktales,
herbal lore and how can I compost them with modern science?*[27]

As Witches, we are called to craft in ways that overwhelm the monologuing pathogen, to nourish each other with potions and probiotics
and stories and songs.

Julia Skinner introduced me to the work of Maya Hey, who wrote
about her experience apprenticing at Terada Honke, one of only two
natural sake breweries out of the approximately nine hundred sake
breweries in Japan.

*Natural, here, means that laboratory-optimized microbes are not
added to the fermentation process; instead, the brewery relies on
the work of endogenous bacteria and yeasts that have inhabited the
open-air brewhouse since the brewery's inception in the 1670s.*[28]

This is similar to Julia's approach to fermentation as a democratic and
meditative practice. You do not need to buy special yeasts or containers:
the bacteria is with us everywhere and all your jars will work, Julia says.
"Fermentation can be seen as a process that is contingent, emergent,
and predicated on intimate relations between interconnected species."[29]
This is the potion-making I am interested in as part of a practice of
resistance and re-enchantment. One that requires that I bring myself
into relationships with interconnected species, one that slows me down
and calls out to my animal/plant/bacterial/fungal body to pay attention
as I engage with the animacy around me.

*When preparing the shubo starters, Terada Honke uses song to keep
the time and mashing rhythm consistent from batch to batch, year to
year. Huddling over barrels, the brewers mash rice with wooden poles
to the tune of a call-and-response work song with lyrics that give
thanks to the rice harvest, the gods for providing abundant blessings,
and the well water that springs up in fervor. The song is a gathering,
an invitation to come together through rhythm, concord, and the collective well-wishing for good sake.*[30]

The ways we engage with food, drink, medicine, potions can tune us—on a cellular and bacterial level—to each other. Our recipes are songs and our songs can be recipes for keeping in time with other species, with our ancestors. "The latest microbiome research points to the fact that there are as many microbial cells in a human body as there are human ones.[31] This means that the notion of "We" already encompasses multiple species. So, how do we practice being humans, let alone healthy and sustainable ones, given that our ontological status is, and has never been, solely human?"[32] Potion-making is a practice of making-with, becoming-with other species to build relationships along tension lines from healing to poison.

Witches consider every interaction with "ingredients" as a moment open to relationship building. This can mean everything from whispering your wishes and secrets and love into the yeast as you pour it into the warm water and add sugar, waking it up before you make your daily bread; stirring passion clockwise into your lover's coffee; making cookies for the neighbors; making hot honey mint tea to bring to the protest. These are all memories of my own potions that live in a different way inside of me because they emerged from a collaboration with "ingredients." These are potions that have enchanted my life and fed my sense that magic and resistance and connection are possible. They have been like cinnamon on the fire, burning into my skin a world that I claim as possible.

Maybe the most obvious and profound example of contemporary potion magic for healing is the legalization of marijuana alongside the increasing normalization of psilocybin and LSD therapy. For so many, that guided interaction with the plant world feels profoundly related to an awakening about the connectedness of the universe, an easing of the terror of death, a rewiring of lost memory and mind function after Covid, a respite against the mental onslaught of depression. Adding folk knowledge and plant relationships to medical frameworks to expand our healing resources feels like a wave that is coming to offer solace to so many.

But for Sophie Strand, who is chronically ill and writing directly in the face of her own death, there can be a slippage here back into our isolating ego minds. Back into the logic of that monologuing pathogen.

Maybe the model of being always in need of a medicine isn't what I should be thinking about. I should reframe it and say, how can I be a medicine? We're so extractive. Part of why psychedelic culture, for me, feels a little problematic right now, is it's like, I just need a heroic dose to have my equal awakening. And then I will act better. How can you be a medicine? Where in the landscape needs you? How could you act medicinal? Why do you always need to be taking, and eating? I don't land on any solid answer about what medicine is to me or what a potion is to me. I just know that I have to be in an interrogative relationship . . . I'm intimately metabolically looping with my landscape. I'm not different than my landscape . . . I am entangled with it.[33]

While we enter into these relationships with heroic ingredients, let's stay rooted here and ask: How can I *be* a medicine? Where in the landscape needs *me*?

Amy: We spoke to Indigenous Medicine Woman Asha Frost whose book You Are the Medicine *integrates the notion of healing a body with the idea of healing a society. As readers enter the book, Asha confronts them with a conversation around the harm of appropriation. A conversation that is "vital for true reconciliation, equity and healing." She says, "I understand why folks want to learn about our Medicine ways. They are so beautiful and filled with so much depth and connection. Our heritage is filled with richness, tradition and teachings that continue to connect us to Earth and Spirit." She uses the word* extraction *to refer to both what is ripped from Earth as well as what is ripped from a culture, but rather than turning people away, she asks that we "come closer and really see Indigenous people and the issues that we deal with in the present day." This too is a medicine.*[34]

Rebecca Beyer reminds us that before Cerridwen or Hera, before deities that anthropomorphized the spirits of the sea and wind, our first impulse was to honor the water, wind, land, and flame themselves. "I don't work with a lot of deities because I like to think back to our first animistic inclination: to not give an offering to Poseidon but to leave an offering to the ocean, not to the god of the winds but to the wind itself . . . I think it's a kind of coming home as we rebuild our animistic connections."[35]

When drawing on the kitchen craft of potions and poisons, let's bring our offerings to the land. And in doing so, let us feed relationships that re-enchant the world.

Rituals

- Inspired by Rebecca Beyer: Take a glass of milk, alcohol, or meat into the woods. Bring a pendulum. Make the offering and ask, "Is anyone here? What do you want me to know? How can I be of medicine to you?"

- Inspired by one of our family potions: Our daily broth. We keep a container in the freezer and add to it all our vegetable scraps suitable for broth: onion skins, garlic ends, celery tops, bits of beets, potatoes, and carrots. When the container is full, May empties it piece by piece into the slow cooker. She examines the ends of all our cooking, she tastes them—frozen and bitter— she digs her hands into the pile. She helps us fill the slow cooker with water and we talk about the water circle, pumping up from the lake, pouring through us and our food, the septic tanks that need to be emptied to protect our water source. The broth simmers for a day, and then it cools, and she helps push the soggy veggie material through a sieve and pour it into jars. Make your own daily broth a ritual. Use it to cook rice, make soups, sauces, and spreads and as you do, taste and thank every ingredient.

- Feed a protest. Follow the community work foundation laid down by the Black Panthers in the 1960s and find a mutual aid society in your community. "Feeding people is a form of activism."[36]

- Sagittarius New Moon holiday ritual for a coven (Inspired by Zoe Flowers's ritual for the Missing Witches coven)

    1. Walk in a circle singing and burning something that grows where you live. Imagine a circle of safety and light. Only that which is in resonance with your highest good may enter.

    2. Decorate an altar together. Invite each person to explore the space and choose one item to symbolize their guides for this cycle.

    3. Pour wine into a cauldron, turn it on low, and take turns adding deliciousness to it; e.g., oranges, cloves, ginger, maple syrup, pomegranate, cinnamon sticks, apple cider, and chamomile tea. Each time you add something, call in what you want for yourself and each other for this new moon and new year.

    4. Let it simmer, but not boil, and light five candles.

    5. With the first candle, envision your outdated beliefs being absorbed.

    6. With the second candle, release ways you have withheld love from yourself and others.

    7. With the third candle, release blocks to your abundance— energetic, material, emotional, and psychological.

    8. Ask the fourth candle to take all the sadness of the last twelve months.

    9. Ask the fifth candle to absorb any residue of people, places, or things that shook your confidence in the last eighteen months.

    10. Once they are all lit, breathe and meditate.

    11. Then pour a cup for each and one for your altar. Drink and reflect on what needs to be released and write it down.

    12. Burn the papers.

    13. Pour the dregs of your potion onto the ashes.

    14. Take this mixture outside and throw it in handfuls into the dark, somewhere where it can become soil, chanting.

Incantation

For releasing loneliness
For releasing separateness
For releasing powerlessness
For releasing control

I release, I release, go now, I am at peace.
I release, I release, go now, I am at peace.
I release, I release, go now, I am at peace.
I release, I release, go now, I am at peace.

Where can I be a medicine?

10

New Moon in Capricorn

Divination

This circle is led by Amy
with expansions by Risa.

*Because Capricorn is opposite the Moon's home of Cancer, the ancients con-
sidered this sign to be the Moon's place of detriment. Traditionally speaking, the Moon has fewer resources in Capricorn. This New Moon prefers to
"work through it"—to process emotion through toil, striving, and a facade of
imperturbable calm. The work of this Moon is to apprentice vulnerability as
a sign of their strength, not a limit of it.*

—ELIZA ROBERTSON, ASTROLOGER

JOANNA MARTINE WOOLFOLK SUGGESTS THAT THOSE BORN UNDER
the sign of Capricorn "are marked by a purposeful pursuit of their destiny."[1] The dark of our Capricorn New Moon, it seems, will be an auspicious time to examine the tool that is perhaps most associated with Witches, seers, soothsayers, Vodou queens and fortunetellers. The art of divination. Here we examine our destinies, our notions of fate, psychology, imagination, and the nonlinear nature of time, where the spirits of the past might somehow advise us on our futures.

We Witches find ways of noticing patterns—patterns in the past and present that might help us predict the future. In true anti-consumptive, anti-capitalist form, we use what we have around us, what we make and what we find. When we were kids, we pulled petals from wild daisies, chanting to determine if he loved me or loved me not. In one incarnation of diviners' prolific use of pendulums of all varieties, old wives would hang a needle or pencil on a thread above a pregnant woman's belly to determine the baby's sex by the motion of the dangling object. In Cameroon, the workings of spiders and their webs and the actions of crabs are subject to diviners' translation in a practice known as Nggàm.

Visionary artist Leonardo da Vinci wrote in one of his many notebooks:

> I cannot forbear to mention . . . a new device for study which, although it may seem trivial and almost ludicrous, is nevertheless extremely useful in arousing the mind to various inventions. And this is, when you look at a wall spotted with stains . . . you may discover a resemblance to various landscapes, beautified with mountains, rivers, rocks, trees, and an endless variety of objects.

We find messages in shapes formed by the tea leaf remnants of a comforting cuppa, in clouds, in tree bark. Illumination can be wrung from stains on a wall if we allow it.

I have witnessed water so clear, I thought I could see tomorrow, but I do my best scrying in my mirror. Scrying requires only a reflective surface. The shiny epidermis of a creek or a looking glass confronts us with ourselves and mirrors a new way of seeing. It allows us "to be shaken out of the ruts of ordinary perception, to be shown for a few timeless hours the outer and inner world."[2]

As is so often the case in our magical workings, we see the metaphorical made literal—we are reflecting, pondering, full with the secret knowledge that taking a good hard look at ourselves is always prophetic.

Lest we spiral out into the tangle of what it is to divine, to be divine, to access the divine, to do divination, let us turn to anthropologist Philip M. Peek for a definition we can ground ourselves in:

> *A divination system is a standardized process deriving from a learned discipline based on an extensive body of knowledge. This knowledge may or may not be literally expressed during the interpretation of the oracular message. The diviner may utilize a fixed corpus, such as the Yoruba Ifa Odu verses, or a more diffuse body of esoteric knowledge. Divining processes are diverse, but all follow set routines by which otherwise inaccessible information is obtained.[3]*

Diviners use their chosen tools to access otherwise inaccessible information and help inform their choices. Whether or not we believe in spirit realms, Witches can apply the art of divination to the world-changing practice of thinking in new ways. Even my most nonspiritual friends won't turn down a card pull when they're in a quandary. If nothing else, it's a jumping-off point to talk about a problem.

Long ago, I was struggling with an either/or decision and a friend suggested I flip a coin. "I'm not leaving my life choices up to a coin toss," I scoffed. She assured me that heads or tails couldn't tell me what the right path was, but it could definitely show me how I really felt. "Gauge your reaction," she said. "Flip the coin and notice how the result makes you feel. Are you excited? Disappointed? Relieved?"

Professors give out essay questions and writing prompts in an effort to give their students new ways of thinking about the material they present. Teasing out new ways of understanding the work at hand, teachers expand our comprehension by way of theme and form and content and context with questions for us to ponder.

For our purposes, in the cynical modern world, we can enchant and resist by giving ourselves questions for consideration in our own lives. Divination, in this sense, becomes a way out of capitalist patriarchal notions of singular, unquestioning systematic thinking—of societal brainwashing—and allows us to examine any given situation from the point of view of a third party: the cards, the bones, the tea leaves. Of course, as with all life, what we find in our fortunetelling is still up for our own interpretation.

Even Brigit Esselmont, founder of go-to card-meaning website Biddy Tarot says, "reading Tarot is NOT about memorizing the cards and following the book. It's about trusting your intuition—and letting the cards guide you to the answers you need."[4]

Many of us reject dogma. It has been used against us. To hurt us. It feels contrary to the creative nature of our fundamental humanity. We live on the outskirts of socially acceptable, and have turned our backs on the rules we were taught. We face forward and find something else, something older, less gate-keepy or more compelling. Bex Mui, founder of a new kind of church she calls House Of Our Queer, expressed the welcoming otherness of astrology and tarot, calling them tools of queer spirituality.

> For the queer community astrology and tarot have become really
> common and appealing and even mainstream tools within the
> LGBTQ community for spiritual access. It's a common language that
> you can use to talk about spirituality, which is something our commu-
> nity hasn't really had before. I think one of the reasons it's so popular is
> because queer and trans folks, like everyone else, want to have spiritual
> centers, we want that connection, that community, and that type of
> guidance. Astrology and tarot are some of the only practices that hav-
> en't been institutionalized in this country in a way that has forcefully
> disconnected us or told us that we're not a part of it, or that many of us
> in the community are holding pain and rejection and shame around.[5]

We are all seeking guidance without shame, without rejection. We look to our tools of divination for answers to questions we are afraid to ask out loud, or for answers beyond human knowledge. For otherwise inaccessible information.

Renee Sills told us: "I think one of the gifts of astrology is the echo in it. There are so many narratives in the world telling us who we should be, and what can come through with an astrology chart and understanding your own aspects is affirmation and integration. When you get to see and feel yourself coming back to you."[6] Renee's mother used astrology as a parenting tool. She was able to see things in Renee's chart that allowed her to take a step back from parental pressures and see her daughter's choices as being in alignment with Renee's true self.

When astrologer Jasmine Richardson adopted her nine-year-old niece, the two had been estranged for seven years, and Jasmine "wanted a window, a way into knowing her personality and what might be the best way to parent her and also understand myself as a parent. . . . Her chart has really helped me parent her."[7]

Kestrel Neathawk is an astrologer and therapist who lives in utter awe of the beguiling beauty of enchantment. "I'm into appreciating the mystery and asking these questions without having the need to know." Even with her clients, Kestrel realizes she doesn't have all the answers, but they ask the questions together in collaborative dialogue.[8]

Eliza Robertson shimmers between schools of thought saying, "maybe the planets do not affect our personalities, but they reflect us and we reflect them, and that's part of the magic . . . It can be a struggle to have a rational argument about why astrology is real or why astrology is worth studying or worth understanding because it precedes reason and transcends reason—it's a form of magical thinking." She asks, "Why couldn't we be a reflection of things that are much vaster than us and also things that are much punier than us? There's the macrocosmos, there's the microcosmos, there's the very famous quote—the principle behind astrology is also the principle behind magic. It's beyond argument—the rational syllogism isn't really the point —it's something intuitive and something felt. There's so much synchronicity and there's a magic in discovering that yourself."[9]

Eliza compared the chart of an event Risa and I did as Missing Witches, taking over the pulpit of a church, inspired by the activism of Monica Sjöö, and a chart of Monica's inspirational event. She found lots of overlap, and her reading was validating; it put our work inside the framework of historical magical feminist activism. A story told and retold again and again.

Astrology can be understood as cellular, a rotating, traveling system, moving particles, tides, and time in rhythm with the dance. If we can open ourselves to new ways of being and thinking, we can give ourselves permission to change like the seasons.

Alice Sparkly Kat suggests that history itself is a collective memory. They said, "astrology is a language, and when we use it, we are also tearing it apart." They wrote:

> Bad astrology reproduces capital, power and labour, even when it
> is technically precise. You can track every mid-point, declination or
> zodiacal release period and still do bad astrology when you do not
> challenge the conditions of capital, power and labour that capitalist
> racial patriarchy accepts to be true, real or inevitable. Good astrolo-
> gers are story-tellers. Good astrology acknowledges and resists cap-
> ital, power and labour. Good astrology shrinks the west. There is no
> one way to practice good astrology. The west is a story, it is a dream
> within a dream, an anachronistic archive. Our job as astrologers
> is not to tell the story of the west better or to tell more stories using
> the west's vocabulary, but to acknowledge that the story of the west
> was built by real histories of pain. The west may be a story, but your
> trauma is real.[10]

Eliza mentioned as above, so below, but Alice reminds us that the next part of this adage is "as below, so above. The meaning of the sky comes directly from us. You are the thing that animates heaven."[11]

Since I don't know what time I was born, I focus my personal relationship with astrology on the phases of the moon, the turning of the wheel of the year, and on looking up on a clear, cold, winter night to be comforted by the sight of Orion above, comforted by the knowledge that it has always been there, connecting me to humanity's visionary history.

Tarot, unlike stars, is a human manifestation of this visionary history, created by us and for us with our symbols, art, words, and magic. The cards can be utilized without the benefit of any other information, just signs and instinct and guts. With a creative and metaphorical mind, one capable of transforming flashcard messages into life lessons.

Inspired by Pixie Colman Smith and Edward Waite, I created my own seventy-eight cards, four suits, and a major and minor arcana. I made my tarot deck by way of collage. The images were tiny cut-up bits of magazines and old, ratty picture books. The meanings were pasted together the same way, from different sources, pulling bits of definitions to inform my divinations. Another of my favorite decks, also based on the Smith-Waite is the Golden Girls Tarot. Because I grew up with the sitcom gang teaching me about companionship, compassion, cooperation, progressive values, teachable moments, and the value of an occasional comedy roast to keep us grounded and self-aware, I have found this deck to give readings with specific and pointed results. Many Witches believe that our tools are inhabited by bits of the spirit or energy that created them, that symbols have power beyond our understanding. My Golden Girls deck has kitchen table cheesecake energy that always serves the truth with a mug of kindness and a side of respect.

Bone-throwing is a practice of both African and Norse lineages, in which bones are tossed to the ground or onto a cloth, and meaning is interpreted based on how they land. Angela Alberto is a death midwife, so it feels right that she would choose these skeletal symbols to be the primary tools of her divination practice. Nonetheless, I asked her: "Why bones?"

"They speak," she said. "They hold the energy of who they supported, which we can call on. They hold wisdom we can glean. I imagine bones to be the most ancient form of divination next to rocks (which I also use). They remind us of what's inside us, of death and our mortality. They remind me of the Earth. They are divine."[12]

I learned a similar, more accessible (i.e., no bones required) method from Reeta, a gifted diviner and tarot reader by trade. She called it *desha* and told me she picked up the practice from her relatives in Kuwait. The process is like the throwing of bones, but instead of bones, the diviner creates their own collection of bits and bobs, each with its own ascribed meaning. These can be anything from beads and charms to buttons and bread tabs—trust me when I tell you it's good fun to go searching around your home for the desha-appropriate, microparticles of your life. We spill the collection forth and take note—is a coin covering up a heart-shaped candy? Maybe your work is interfering with your relationships. My desha started with a dozen or so pieces and continues to grow as I add more little symbols to my tiny universe of otherwise inaccessible answers wrapped in cloth.

We can bring our skeptical, nonmagical friends along for the ride by reminding them that many therapists and psychologists use tarot, astrology, and other divination methods in their healing practices. Not because these doctors rely on spirit messages for diagnoses, but because they have found them to be effective in provoking dialogue. Similar to the Rorschach inkblot test, oracle cards can be used to tease out someone's preoccupations; to present an abstract, interpretable image or scenario; or to harness the power of metaphor to expose reality.

But it seems like the cards, leaves, and bones are often eerily direct in their answers to questions.

Again, many Witches from across cultures believe that we *are* channeling ancestors or spirits who guide us and our divination tools as we work our magic. Many Witches *do* rely on spirit messages to inform their prognostications. So as we straddle the real and the surreal, the material and the ethereal, we have to leave the door open to this unknown country of possibility, this notion that we are portals for other energies not yet understood. Perhaps ancient knowledge crunched under colonizer feet is digging its way back into our consciousness.

Most tools and practices of divination are specifically designed to contact the spirit world for specific answers or instruction, primordial pleas to the Goddetc. Stones, animal entrails, shells—humans have utilized anything and everything that might give us clues to our fate, to access otherwise inaccessible information.

Migene González-Wippler wrote, "Twenty-one cowrie shells make up the sea-shell divination known as the caracoles . . . The cowries are mouthpieces of the orishas."[13]

A more contemporary example, the Ouija board, has been *debunked* by science as the users' unconscious pushing of planchettes, and it has been dismissed by modern-day occultists when word spread that Ouija was a Hasbro toy company trademark. Just one more thing to sell to wannabe Witches. But the history of this magic predates the mass-market version, and when we look inside, we find a real Witch.

Pearl Lenore Curran was coaxed by a friend to try a Ouija board in 1913. A spirit, who said her name was Patience Worth, made herself known through the board and planchette. Together, Pearl and Patience produced prose, poetry, and novels, channeled from the spiritual to the material world with a parlor toy.

In 2011, the psychologist Richard Wiseman wrote: "Eventually even the most ardent believer was forced to conclude that Pearl Curran's remarkable outpourings were more likely to have a natural, not supernatural, explanation."[14]

Experts agree that Pearl made the whole thing up. Or she was crazy.

Because that's the easiest way for our hyper-normative society to function.

And although even we Witches might balk at the notion of Ouija ghost novellas, something happened to Pearl that made her start writing books. Ghost or none, real or imagined, Patience Worth inspired Pearl to think differently. To seek, to imagine, to create.

The North Star of our pantheon, Harriet Tubman, had visions, received messages. She has had these powers erased, forgotten, or dismissed by science and history. She sought. She imagined. She created. She was a Witch. See, the "Missing" part of the Missing Witches project comes in many forms. In American history, Harriet Tubman's story is often told; in it, she is a hero of civil rights, a literal trailblazer, a railroad conductor, a freedom fighter. Monuments, schools, museums, and libraries, even a US military ship, bear her name, so obviously I had heard of Harriet Tubman. What I had not heard was that she was a Witch. The Missing part, for me, in Harriet's story was the Witch part.

Born Araminta Ross, Harriet went by the nickname Minty. I'll be using this nickname from time to time because Minty was often the name that appeared on wanted posters. It reminds me that Harriet was an outlaw. She is, of course, considered a hero now, but then, she had a bounty on her head. To calibrate our moral compass, we must question the status quo and the ulterior motives behind what we are told. Witches are outlaws.

It's said that Minty had visions, prophetic dreams, and nightmares that came true. Some will argue that these were mere hallucinations, brought on by a traumatic brain injury she incurred at age twelve or thirteen when a slaveholder cracked her skull with a pot. The story goes further: the pot hit her because she stepped between the projectile and its intended victim. Even before the injury, she was willing to stick her neck out to protect others.

So I'll ask you, dear Witches, did this braining make her crazy or did it open her mind to her gift?[15] We could ask this question of many strong, powerful, determined female leaders who were painted as hysterical or burned at the stake, whose visions were chalked up to psychosis, a bump on the head, or the Devil. Joan of Arc comes to mind. Harriet Tubman had well-documented prophetic visions and changed the world: Was she insane, or gifted?

Harriet is often called a Conjure woman, which is great for the purposes of this book, but was she? And what does that mean?

Walter Rucker wrote:

Among slaves at least, conjurers were respected not solely because of the apprehension their powers inspired. In the words of W.E.B. Du Bois (1982), these spiritualists had multifaceted and multidimensional functions in the slave community; at any given time, the conjurer could be "the healer of the sick, the interpreter of the Unknown, the comforter of the sorrowing, the supernatural avenger of the wrong." It would be through many of these roles that

African conjurers helped to encourage slave resistance throughout the Americas."[16]

So let's go through the checklist: Healer of the sick. Check. Harriet was a civil war nurse who used her knowledge of plants to cure or ease discomfort. Interpreter of the Unknown. Check. Harriet spoke to God and had absolute faith in the messages she received. Comforter of the sorrowing. Check. Supernatural avenger of the wrong. Check check check check check.

In his book *Conjuring Harriet "Mama Moses" Tubman and the Spirits of the Underground Railroad*, Witchdoctor Utu wrote:

> *Her seemingly supernatural powers, psychic visions, incantations and unique cures were the stuff of a conjure woman. . . . She continued to be an almost ghostlike entity to those in the slave states, who feared her and her supernatural ways. She was known to come out of her trances and dreams with knowledge of an ambush that lay in wait, and change course. And they would come to find out later that there had indeed been an ambush waiting . . . Divining by animal activity, clouds, rocks, and bones as well as her dreams and visions, she reputedly carried a gourd as a container, housing roots and herbs that she would shake in certain times of need.*[17]

In these strange times, these times of need, we can conjure Minty, who just did what her gut told her was right, who helped people, who was brave and never gave up hope or the fight. She used the North Star as a literal and metaphorical guide, so when we Witches need to snatch some hope from the baffling despair of this newish millennium, we can look there too.

There, in the sky, Witches, the North Star acknowledges pain and still encourages us to move forward. It was there before gender-reveal party wildfires or Covid-19, before police, before racism, sexism, before fear. It was there before industry, war, money, or even greed. It is that self-same star that shone on Minty as she won the freedom of her brethren that shines on us today. It's still there—if we look up, past the settler faces dynamited into sacred ground to get to the missing history of real

American heroes. Real Witches whose names aren't told in school, but whose magic has shifted the culture we inhabit, who are hidden, moving in shadows and behind the scenes.

Thea Anderson looks at how astrology can help us tell the lost or silenced stories of marginalized people. She has a relationship with Harriet and her journey to freedom. Thea told us, "We are all on a journey to freedom."[18]

"Harriet knew the pathways to freedom by sight and feel," she wrote.

She crawled over forest and waded through black rivers. No matter how treacherous the journey, she kept her eye to the North Star—the gleaming tip of Ursa Minor that lit the way to freedom. Polaris is the anchor around which the rest of the sky rotates, as it never rises and sets. It has been used for centuries as a guiding torch, and it lit the way in utter, choking darkness.

She used trickery, divination, and cunning to rescue her people. She is best seen as chthonic Mercury who guides souls through the Underworld.

Our culture today requires that stories be evidenced, so that they can be taught. That has its place. But, as I've come to learn through astrology, magic, and ritual, there are other ways to know something. Reality can be embodied, performed, and orated across generations through the tradition of storytelling. It becomes a truth that is whole because it is lived. I think astrological analysis can restore the magic to where it belongs.[19]

Thea told us:

The past is enchanted. Moving into a space of enchantment puts me in the resistance. It puts me in a place of power. The system is very interested in educating us in falsehoods, eliminating imagination from curriculum, rewriting the past to suit capitalist agendas . . . the moment I can look at something from an astrological lens or magical lens or imaginative lens, when I move into a place of enchantment I feel like there is action there, and I can align my action from a place of love. Because I'm scared, I have children, brothers, black men in the world—it's scary, I'm scared every day, but I love this world. In my investigations and opening up, there is an uncovering. I can add newness to the archives, and that, to me, is a form of resistance.[20]

Loli Moon is an astrologer who believes we can heal by tides. She told us:

I think that when it comes to resistance and working together to overcome these systems and build a better, bigger world, it starts with understanding our position in the revolution. Not everyone's position is the same. Through astrology we can understand our strengths, our opportunities, our shadow aspects, and understanding ourselves in that way can help us use those strengths and elevate those opportunities for resistance.[21]

Gazing up at the same stars that Minty beheld, we meet another prophet who used her divination powers to free her people, to find her place in the revolution. Lozen was a warrior, healer, and hero of the Chihenne Chiricahua Apache, who, when the Indian Removal Act was passed in the US in 1830, was a ten-year-old girl whose power and difference was already beginning to show.

Lozen, too, is said to have had a psychic ability; she was "gifted." But when we work very, very hard, when we learn, commit, and sacrifice, do we call a return on that energetic investment a gift, or did we earn it? In my thinking, Lozen was not gifted. She earned her power in ways we'll see, but keep in mind, as we ride our horses alongside her, your Witch power is not a gift that you either receive or don't. We don't wake up on Christmas morning to find it under a festive tree; it isn't in an envelope delivered by an owl.

Our power is a wage we earn when we put in the work. It is a birthright, but it is activated by our yearning, our learning, and our labor.

Much of the information I gathered on Lozen's life comes from *Warrior Woman* by Peter Aleshire. As one reviewer on Goodreads noted:

The book is written by White Eyes but it's better than nothing at all.[22]

And that's, I think, how Risa and I feel when we tell these stories. We go looking, with, admittedly, white eyes, for the lives we didn't know about, the names we hadn't heard in school, the Witches we've been missing—not to become authorities, but to learn for ourselves and pass these tidbits on to you, our Missing Witches coven. We are trying to know better because like Maya Angelou said, "when you know better, you do better," and that, for us, like the Goodreads reviewer wrote, is better than nothing at all.

Nikki Sanchez suggests, for those descendants of colonizers "paralyzed by guilt and shame" that "this history is not your fault, but it absolutely is your responsibility . . . ." And even this, Nikki claims, can be tied back to divination. "The Mayan prophecy," she says,

> teaches us that this is the time, for the first time in all of human history, that our consciousnesses have come to a level of evolution where we can actually see from one another's eyes. The way that it's explained is that the eyes of the serpent can see through the eyes of the eagle, and so the eyes of the North and the Eyes of the South can actually see through one another's eyes, and begin to work together and understand each other's world views. And the secondary part of that prophecy is that absolutely every person who came to be alive on Earth at this time came for a specific reason and came with specific gifts that are needed to do this work that we have laid out in front of us . . . We need you.[23]

Risa: We can turn to divinatory tools and practices to see with other eyes, to move our subjectivity around.

Some of the oldest writing about divination appears in the Roman Empire and centers around augery—interpreting the acts of birds. I picture patriarchs telling the Emperor to fight or flee based on the appearance of a vulture or the behavior of chickens, and I have to think—was this another instance of colonizers mistaking a traditional practice? We're slowly catching up to what Indigenous people have been able to learn from birds. Veery birds, for example, are better at predicting hurricane seasons than contemporary meteorologists. I picture Tin Hinan watching the ants, Dihya al-Kahina *studying the movements and migrations of birds. Was divination a grounded knowledge, a wildcraft, a practice of seeing through the eyes of the more-than-human world, before patriarchy detached its power from Earth and put it into the realm of the White Sky God?[24] And if this is so, how can I bring my practices back into the soil around me? I ask the trees and listen to the lake.*

Once with a friend I followed an untraceable set of instincts, hours off the route we'd planned to take, a wild road in the night. We set up tents and woke up in Chiricahua National Monument. Steps away from where we slept, a wild architecture of balancing rocks and stone hoodoos rose like a megalith forest of stone bones. Stones shaped like faces, carved by wind and rain, perched in utterly impossible formations in the desert. A fire had whipped through just days before and, in the way of wild things, the entire place glowed green with moss and lichen. In the cracks, another world is growing. I walked through silently. I knew, in my own stone bones, that this place had a story I was missing. But it would be another year before Amy would introduce me to Lozen.

Lozen was born in late 1840 within sight of the Sacred Mountain near Ojo Caliente—Spanish for Hot Eyes, one of the oldest natural health resources in the United States. The area is home to hallowed hot springs where legend states that a Tewa hero once accessed the underworld via the warm water.[25] Their varying temperatures and mineral contents mean that these pools are not just holy, but healing.

So of course, this spot is now a resort and spa, created around a bathhouse built in the 1800s by a territorial representative to Congress. In 2020 a fire at the Spa destroyed the historic bathhouse, but it has been rebuilt and reopened now for a soak to, as the ad states, "Heal yourself body and soul with a retreat to Ojo" . . . if you can afford it.

Colonial Capitalism is like tinnitus—a constant ringing in our ears, a ceaseless high-pitched frequency that demands to be heard above all else. Miasmic. We go looking for sacred stories and find a holy spot where our connection to nature, our bodies and souls, and to the spirits of the land is bought and sold. Holy places with ticket prices.

Regarding Mt Rushmore: In the Treaty of 1868, the US government promised the Sioux territory that included its site the sacred Black

Hills *in perpetuity*. "Perpetuity" lasted only until gold was found in the mountains.[26]

The more we learn, the clearer it becomes: our treatment of Witches, of women, is echoed in our treatment of the land.

These links are perhaps most clearly visible when we note what Eryn Wise calls the frightening way fossil fuels and violence against native women are connected. She writes in an article by that name:

> *A boom in the oil industry had introduced many small towns to an influx of non-Native male pipeline workers. This caused the ratio of men to women in said communities to change drastically. On average the ratio is around 10 to one, and in some places it can be as high as 20 to one. As Christine Nobiss of Seeding Sovereignty has previously written, the rise of violent crime is directly coincident with the oil boom: "It may not be obvious to non-Native people, but the health and safety of Native American people is directly linked to the health and safety of our land.*
>
> *A catastrophic web has been woven between extractive industries and Native communities, and we are each called upon to observe issues of broader concern. It is evident, now more than ever, that extractive industries are having disproportionate adverse effects on Indigenous peoples, particularly on the wellbeing of Native women. The continued desecration of unceded Indigenous territories and sacred resources resulting from extraction projects have contributed to disease, birth defects, reproductive health issues, and delayed early childhood development among community members. More atten-tion needs to be given to Indigenous women living near points of extraction. This is the land we inherited from our ancestors. We are still here, intrepid and Indigenous; and we are moving forward."[27]*

Lozen learned her divination from the land itself.

The universe operates in patterns, webs, connections. You can think of it literally or metaphorically, but we are Earth. Lozen's power, in my view, wasn't so much that she was psychic, but that she was listening, connected to Earth to such a degree that it sent her messages. Once again, whether we search for the patterns in oracle decks or spider webs, we give pause. To think. To notice. To imagine other ways of being. To access otherwise inaccessible information.

The Apache did not refer to themselves as *Apache*; this was a word that translated to "enemy" in Zuni and was later adopted by the Spanish. Apache instead referred to themselves with variants of *Nde*, meaning "the people."[28] The name *Lozen* was an Nde war title meaning "one who has stolen horses in a raid." This reminded me of a German turn of phrase, a compliment: *Jemand, mit dem man Pferde stehlen kann.*

It refers to someone who is reliable, trustworthy, a friend with whom you can do something extraordinary, difficult, or crazy. Somebody who is game for everything.

Literally translated: Somebody with whom you can steal horses.

And Lozen was all that. Strong, loyal, and trustworthy; someone you could steal horses with.

Her brother Victorio called her his "right hand in battle" saying she was "strong as a man but braver than most . . . and cunning in strategy . . . Lozen is a shield to her people."[29]

Of course it helped that she, like Harriet Tubman, had the ability to detect the movement of her enemies. According to legend, Lozen would stretch out her arms, with her palms facing the sky. Then, she would follow the sun, praying to Ussen, the Nde Creator of Life. When she felt a tingling in her hands, and when her palms darkened, Lozen would know the direction from which her enemies were coming.[30]

But before she came into her power, Lozen came of age. By seven she had demonstrated her proficiency with horses, and her ability to win footraces and keep up with not only the boys but with her tribal leaders. She learned the land and the stories that the land tells.

Soon it was time for Lozen's Sunrise Ceremony. For over seventy years the Sunrise Ceremony was banned by the US government (as were most native spiritual practices and rituals). With embattled demands from Indigenous activists, the American Indian Religious Freedom Act came in 1978, and the Sunrise Ceremony could openly be practiced on reservations again.

The four-day ceremony that Lozen passed through marked a girl's transition into womanhood, acknowledging the power of her blood. Each of the ninety-six hours is filled with specific prayers, songs, dances, face painting, and the testing of resolve. These four days were followed by four more days of meditation. After, Lozen went up to the sacred mountain and found a place to sit alone.

She sat for days and nights. Alone. Listening. Passing through emotions like weather—storms of despair, the calm of dew. She sat until the power of Ussen responded to her silent pleas. A horse appeared and taught Lozen a song. The song would give her Horse Power, to heal the sick and injured, to communicate with stallions and nags, to hear voices, inaudible voices in the wind and land.

Peter Aleshire wrote:

> She told Victorio and Nana she had been given a ceremony to locate the enemy. . . . She sang the song thus: Upon this earth, on which we live, Ussen has power. This power is mine. For locating the enemy. I search for the enemy, which only Ussen The Great can show me.[31]

Lozen's people needed her. The White Eyes were coming, with greed and guns and perhaps their most powerful weapon of all: the Indian Removal Act. Some trivia: Davy Crockett, who I didn't even know was a congressman and not just "King Of The Wild Frontier," voted *against* the Indian Removal Act (IRA), stating that this decision would "not make me ashamed in the Day of Judgment."[32]

The IRA was signed into law on May 28, 1830, by United States President Andrew Jackson who appears on the American $20 bill. Quick reminder: he was set to be replaced by Harriet Tubman, but . . . nope . . .

So the IRA mandated the forced displacement of thousands and thousands of Indigenous people, removing them from the land that they had inhabited for thousands and thousands of years. So the colonizer settlers could extract resources. Get paid. We call part of this story the Trail of Tears, but we could equally call it the Trail of Blood, The Trail of Oil, The Trail of Gold. The Trail of Greed.

Many tribes fought back, and Lozen's was one of them; she rode alongside her brother Victorio. Lozen was an expert strategist and military leader, but she also had a determination and courage that inspired the people around her. James Kaywaykla remembers riding behind his grandmother as the band fled and fought American forces. Coming up against the Rio Grande, they were frozen, terrified to cross the torrent. "I saw a magnificent woman on a beautiful horse," he said. "Lozen, sister of Victorio. Lozen the woman warrior! High above her head she held her rifle. There was a glitter as her right foot lifted and struck the shoulder of her horse. He reared, then plunged into the torrent. She turned his head upstream, and he began swimming."[33] Once Lozen had led the people across the river, she returned to battle. A nurturer *and* defender. And because she was deeply connected to the earth, she possessed a wealth of knowledge about the medicinal properties of plants and minerals, making her a renowned medicine woman and healer as well.

Some have speculated that part of the reason that Lozen isn't as well-known as names like Geronimo or Crazy Horse is that she was an actual secret weapon, and her comrades feared that to speak of her power would be to make her a target.

Faced with arrest and forcible relocation Victorio led a guerrilla war, fought many battles and skirmishes with the United States Army, and raided several settlements until the Mexican Army killed him and most of his warriors in October 1880 in the Battle of Tres Castillos.[34] After her brother was killed in battle, a distraught Lozen rejoined Geronimo to exact her revenge in true warrior fashion: she returned to the warpath quickly, purposefully, and often with deadly results.

Lozen had epic power and courage, fought longer than Crazy Horse or Geronimo, and, as Aleshire wrote, she fought "more effectively than Custer...evaded a full one quarter of the United States Army...Lozen, the war shaman of the Apache represents one of the most successful, respected and influential woman warriors in history. Yet historians have almost entirely overlooked her remarkable life story."[35]

And there is the thread that weaves in and out of every Witch we've found. We may be overlooked, but we will not be forgotten. Whether or not they know our names or acknowledge our contributions, they will live inside the world that we Witches help to create. Most of our names won't appear in history books, but we can be secret weapons, changing the world from the shadows *and* the light.

Geronimo went on the run with 140 followers including Lozen after rumors began circulating that their leaders were to be imprisoned at Alcatraz Island. Lozen and another woman Dahteste began negotiating peace treaties. Self-described "queer indigenous activist" Eryn Wise claims that "Lozen and Dahteste were two-spirits who were in love before being violently separated by colonization."[36] And I applaud this take. Lozen never married, so it's comforting to think of her finding true love within a lifetime of war.

The American leaders dismissed them, but Lozen and Dahteste carried on with their attempts to negotiate. The rebels believed they could triumph until it was revealed that all the Chiricahuas had been rounded up and sent to Florida. If they wanted to rejoin their kin, the Nde needed to head east toward captivity. The warriors agreed to surrender and laid down their arms. Five days later they were on a train bound for Florida.

Lozen was separated from Dahteste, taken into US military custody as a prisoner of war, and sent to Mount Vernon Barracks in Alabama. She never returned to her home and died in confinement of tuberculosis on June 17, 1889. At forty-nine years old, she had been fighting for almost her entire life.

Sometimes I wonder about the high road . . . about negotiation and respectful discourse, agreements, concessions, compromises. And of course these things are very good, but only when there is mutual trust and respect between the two parties. Lozen spent her final active years negotiating in good faith, assuming that the White Eyes could show reason, compassion, a willingness to bend. Instead she was imprisoned and infected.

We get a tiny echo of this feeling when we go out into the world seeking common ground and mutual benefit, only to find a regime that believes life is a zero-sum game where there is a winner and a loser and nothing in between. How do we reason with people who want to destroy us, who want us to lose? How do we compromise with a society that would rather we didn't exist? And a question that perhaps the Earth Spirits are asking themselves: How do we talk to those who won't listen?

I'm reminded of the Stokely Carmichael quote that broke my heart and blew my mind the first time I heard it, and every time since:

> *Dr. King's policy was that nonviolence would achieve the gains for black people in the United States. His major assumption was that if you are nonviolent, if you suffer, your opponent will see your suffering and will be moved to change his heart. That's very good. He only made one fallacious assumption: In order for nonviolence to work, your opponent must have a conscience. The United States has none.*[37]

I'm certainly not advocating for violence here and I don't think Stokely was either. We're just asking, under these circumstances, what do we do?

With no apparent solutions, we turn our questions over to the third voice. The ancestors, the spirits, the land, the bones, the cards, the stars, our souls for otherwise inaccessible answers. We hold our hands up to the sky and beg the heat to tell us what to do, where to turn.

Lozen tried it both ways. The warpath and the path of peaceful negotiation. And although it's tempting to feel like she failed at both, we can't. Because we don't know how many lives or maybe even generations she saved . . . what America might look like if she hadn't tried. If she hadn't felt the heat in her palms. What the future might look like if *we* don't try. We can sit back and watch, or we can fight. Educate. Donate. Celebrate. Do *something*. Anything. Anything is better than nothing at all.

Lozen had powers of divination that most of us don't, but we modern Witches, too, have powers that Lozen did not. The internet has given us the possibility of finding a global voice; feminist and civil rights leaders have secured us a modicum of self-determination, autonomy, and agency. It's better than nothing. We can organize the baby steps that will become the journey of a thousand miles. It's better than nothing at all.

And all the while, we have to keep in mind that a word like *compromise* has two meanings: 1) a deal in which both parties give a little and get a little in an effort to secure a mutual benefit or agreement; and 2) a lowering of one's standards or integrity.

So we can see Lozen in her final years, and maybe ourselves as we negotiate our paths, searching for answers in black mirrors, as one who is looking to compromise while simultaneously being very uncompromising. Such is the world of Magic—contradictions without binaries at every turn.

A few of my friends call me psychic because I always seem to text them at the exact right time; I get bad vibes from dudes they thought were cool but turned out to be duds. Before cell phones, two of my friends waited, desperately hungover, at my apartment, literally chanting and praying for me to return with pizza. I returned with pizza. I am not psychic. I use the power of divination that each and every one of us is born with, the one that cannot be purchased in a store, and so it has been demeaned as mood rather than deep knowledge: intuition.

We Witches trust our guts.

I'll grant that there are possibly spirits at work who deliver these downloads, ancestors silently guiding our choices, but for my part, my contribution to the magic? I pay attention. I can sense if something is off or wrong. I can tell the future by recognizing patterns that repeat. Context clues. Love is part of this too. As bell hooks said, love is an action. And part of that action is the divinatory process, the future-seeing of anticipating your loved ones' needs, recognizing them before, perhaps, even they do.

I often think of Sherlock Holmes, Sir Arthur Conan Doyle's fictional detective. Holmes appears to have a near-psychic power, but as elementary as it may be, his power comes from the mere act of noticing. Powers of perception lead to his mystery-solving deductions, and so it is for Witches. We can appear psychic if we are paying attention to our surroundings and the third voice. Not ours or other people's. The one that, at its core, requires no tea leaves or cowrie shells. Be quiet and listen to that part of you, informed by a hundred thousand years of data, collected in your very DNA. Your gut can be the greatest divination tool of all.

Trust your gut and be very fucking careful with divination. Not because you might release some malevolent spirit, though I'm not ruling that out, but because it can easily become addictive. I've seen friends spend hours and hours pulling and repulling cards, doing tarot spreads over and over again, then switching to other fortunetelling methods and repeating the cycle. I've read stories of mothers spending their life savings on telephone psychics.

So think of divination as a mind-expanding drug, opening the doors of perception. It must be used responsibly and only to enchant your perspective, enhance your life, not to escape it. Rootworker Beverly Smith gave us a first easy step in our pursuit of ethical divination. Ask a yes or no question. Flip a coin, use a yes/no pendulum, or throw dice (evens or odds?). Accept the answer. "If you get a yes, move forward. If you get a no, don't keep asking," she said. "Part of being an ethical magical person is that once you get your magical answer, you go with it. You don't keep nagging until you get something that you prefer."[38] A question that Beverly often poses to her deity is, "Am I justified?"

Beverly says she practices the religion of Justice saying, "I cannot separate my spirituality from my politics." She feels justified in using what she calls the left-hand path, cursing and hexing, bringing balance to unjust scales, through her use of divination. "I will do divination to ask my deities, on behalf of myself, on behalf of my clients, divine answers are requested, through divination, and only when the green light is given do I consider myself a justified worker." Divination also tells her how far to take the rebalancing. "Any type of magical work should be done by completely ethical people. When you are doing magical work to manifest results, you must be ethical. Your agenda, your heart, your head must be working toward ethical manifestation." She doesn't do divination for her close friends and family, because she knows she'd be bringing her own agenda to the reading.[39]

World changers like Minty and Lozen used their "psychic abilities" and divination tools to lead their people, to evade capture, and to win battles, but each of us has a personal power of divination. It's called intuition, and it is nurtured in the same world-changing way that Lozen and Minty nurtured their powers. By paying attention. By watching for the signs—not just in patterns of birds in flight, in stars, in cards, but in our relationships, in our thinking, in our systems, in politics, in our lives. By using our tools of divination in pursuit of freedom and justice.

Everything is alive. Everything has something to teach.

Feel the life force. Every moment has something to teach us—something to inform our wisening intuition, a whispered prediction for what lies ahead, a way of understanding what's passed. Let's stand and raise our hands, palms toward the eastern sky. Let's affirm our connection to the land. Ask to know the unknowable. Let's find the answers that are otherwise inaccessible. At the same time, we need to become more and more comfortable with not knowing, with giving dreams credence and myth credibility in our world-building.

It takes Pluto 248 Earth years to make its orbit around the sun. There are patterns of immeasurable age, patterns of planets and ancient symbols, that can potentially give us clues to a future that turns in cycles of millennia and not days. Cycles imperceptible in human lifetimes.

Turn slowly in a circle and feel the energy of the directions, the gravitational pull. Understand that places have power to shape thoughts and behaviors. Time and place will have their say. Try to sense what messages the breeze and clouds and rocks and trees and sun are sending. Knowing we may never learn their language fully, we must try to feel the wisdom, magic, and spirit of places. Witches seek the wisdom that sits in places. We yearn for it so we might serve our people.

The places will know we are listening. Witches, let's divine. Let's make listening our superpower. There are patterns that will predict the future, so let's acknowledge and cultivate our forces of perception. Compromise without compromise. Seek out the wisdom of bones and stars, inkblots and cobwebs to understand our positions in the revolution. Reach for the stars to change the world and feel the heat of a whole history of Witches burning in our palms.

Let's steal horses, singing Lozen's words all the while: This power is mine.

Incantation

This Power is mine.

I pay attention.

I see a future in patterns of seasons and suns.

Tea leaves and spiderwebs and DNA.

I get advice from the Wind and Moon.

My palms are burning with unseen wisdom.

I seek answers,

Information otherwise inaccessible.

I have a knowing

and a dreaming

within and without.

I am marked by a purposeful pursuit of my destiny.

I reach for the stars to change the world.

Ritual

The Capricorn New Moon feels overloaded with potential. The coming year can be molded in any way we choose. Capricorn's drive and determination pushes us to almost believe that a New Year is a New You.

So, instead of going shopping for divination tools, take a moment and think about your own interests, hobbies, goals, and personality and consider if there might be something in your home that you could use instead.

Maybe you're into books. Notice titles in the wild, or open a random book to a random page and search for meaning. That's bibliomancy.

Maybe you're the meditative type. Sit and watch as the sunlight throws shapes and shadows through the window and onto the wall. What might this mean? Is the light directing you somewhere? Is it fluttery or staid? Animal shaped? What message might sunlight be sending?

I began my study of tea leaves after I got hooked on looseleaf blends. Seemed a shame to let all those otherwise inaccessible answers go to waste.

Ideally, for our purposes of reframing and reimagining, you'll make up your own divination method culled from your everyday life, then sanctify it by adding "-mancy." Defined as:

combining form
  suffix: -**mancy**

divination by a specified means.[40]

Stains-on-the-wall-omancy, Hairomancy, Dustomancy, Stitchomancy ...

Set some time aside on the new moon to explore your new practice, making use of the dark sky to better see the stars (literally or metaphorically). Open yourself to the possibility of being guided by celestiality, dancing to the cellular-level choreography of our galaxy in motion. Open yourself up to the enveloping nebulae of possibility. As astrologer Loli Moon proclaims: "The only possibilities you're aware of are the ones that already exist in your mind."[41]

Enter your new practice thusly:

1. Light a candle. You can tailor this lighting to your question/ intentions. Choose a red candle for lust or courage, blue for communication and creativity, green for prosperity, yellow for clarity and confidence. Or go all in and choose purple: spirituality, intuition, ancient wisdom.

2. Sit in front of your candle and close your eyes. Take a deep breath as your eyes adjust to the darkness. Notice how the light makes its way through your eyelids in colored shapes. Think of the night sky with its shiny dots poking holes in the darkness. Think of your most ancient ancestors, two hundred thousand or so years ago, staring up at the same moon, the same stars and planets. Imagine adventures guided only by the light of a star. Feel your connection to all of human history.

3. Now open your eyes and look at your candle flame. Take a deep breath as your eyes adjust to the light. Think of Harriet Tubman following the North Star to freedom. Repeat this quote from Harriet:
   Reach for the stars to change the world.

4. Repeat steps 2–3 as necessary.

5. When you are finished, take one more big, deep breath; say: "I conjure darkness to see the stars." Blow out your candle and begin.

Bonus: Long-term project/ritual

I have a collection of tarot and oracle decks, like many Witches do, but my favorite will always be the one I made myself. Invent an oracle deck based on your interests and personality. It doesn't have to be with fancy card stock or any artistic genius. It can be words on scraps of paper. Your creation will bring new resonance to your divination.

11

New Moon in Aquarius

The Word

This circle is led by Amy
with expansions by Risa.

Like a lab technician prodding at cross-sections of a heart, the Aquarius New Moon beholds its feelings with curiosity and distrust. They feel emotions—but they want to measure that data against other facts. The Aquarius New Moon nurtures through logic, truth, and intellectual exchange. They might appreciate poetic motifs as the heart, but they'll also perceive it as a muscular organ that pumps blood through the circulatory system.

—ELIZA ROBERTSON, ASTROLOGER

WITH OUR NEW MOON IN AQUARIUS, we acknowledge that words are spells. They don't call it *spelling* for nothing.

Aquarius is a visionary. As the water carrier delivers their sacred element, so too does the writer distribute theirs: the idea. They move it from one form, one place, into another. An idea becomes a to-do list, a recipe, a love letter, or a poem, and it is concretized. The idea has moved out of the ether, out of the imaginary, and into the material world.

When we read, it is an equal yet opposite reaction: words become ideas. The material becomes ethereal.

Terry Tempest Williams wrote, "A pencil is a wand and a weapon."[1] It is a wand because it is a conduit for muses and magic. It feels like a wand in hand. A pencil is also a weapon, mightier than a sword, because this tool of communication is capable of changing hearts, minds, culture, the world.

One of my favorite things about the word *Witch*, one of the few labels I'm comfortable with, is its nebulosity. It is formless until we give it form. It's employed in equal numbers by hippies and goths, spiritualists and scientists, ancient mystics and neopagans. Cross-culturally, the word *Witch*, in and of itself, *is* a wand and a weapon. Depending on how it's used, it can uplift us or demean us. It has been used to try to destroy us. Witch hunts continue and often, an accusation, the utterance of the word *Witch* is all the evidence required to banish or condemn a person to death.

In *I, Tituba* Maryse Condé imagines the life of Tituba, the first woman to be accused in the Salem Witch trials of 1692. It's a work that Condé claims was channeled and created with the help of the Black Witch of Salem herself (Tituba). Maryse wrote:

> *The conversations went on all the time while I was writing the novel. I had the feeling that Tituba was involved in the writing. Even when I left my pages at night in my study, I believed that she would go look at them, and eventually correct what she did not like. I cannot say when we really started conversing, however. All along during my writing of the novel I felt that she was there—that I was addressing her.*[2]

Maryse writes a scene in which Tituba demands of the children in her care: "Do you know what a witch really is?" And the girls reply that a Witch is someone who has made a pact with the Devil.

In the winter of 1692, Betty and Abigail, the daughter and niece of Samuel Parris, began having "fits"—convulsing and screaming, blaming Tituba and her Witchcraft. A finger point and a single word: Witch.

Between 1692 and 1693 almost two hundred people were accused of Witchcraft in Salem village. Twenty were executed, mostly women. The girls accused Tituba and two other women from the village, Sarah Good and Sarah Osborne, both disenfranchised women who shirked the rules of Puritanism. One was poor, loud, and unkempt, the other refused to give up her property when her husband died and instead married her lover. Neither attended church. They were called Witch and condemned.

This is the power of a word.

We can harness that power too, though, for our own glorification.

Ffiona Morgan wrote, "One of the moist effective paths to breaking resistance is to name yourself a witch. In the early days of feminist witchcraft it was suggested to repeat to yourself three times, 'I am a Witch.' By naming our reality, we create it."[3]

I think we can all relate to how easy it is to believe that we are what we are called, what people call us, so we inherently understand that words have a power beyond logic. Witches, however, know that this power can be used by us and not just against us. In our first book, we suggested that the definitions of things should not be left up to only the oppressors, that we have a right and a duty to take part in the naming of things. This includes ourselves.

Genesis P-Orridge wrote, "I think changing names is a really potent form of magic. It's a technique for shedding a nostalgic connection."[4] A name is a word we use to identify ourselves. *Witch* is another. As artist Edgar Fabián Frías told us, "One thing that's really incredible for Witches is that we get to self-ordain. We get to decide that we're Witches."[5] We decide we are sacred. We choose the word that labels us. Specialties such as rootwork, herbalism, reiki, and so on all require training and education. But to declare ourselves Witches all that's required is a gut feeling. A claiming of a word.

WITCH has been made an acronym too. Woman In Total Control of Herself. And for our feminist forebearers, Women's International Terrorist Conspiracy from Hell was a network of activist groups, part of the women's liberation movement during the late 1960s.

How we use the word *Witch* has certainly changed a lot over time, but by my way of thinking, it's not the Witches that have changed so much as the values and priorities of the world around us. Witches were made into monsters with the convincing narrative of patriarchal capitalism. Do you know what a Witch really is?

Witches' houses are covered in spiderwebs. This is because Witches don't kill spiders. Spiders trap other more harmful insects. Spiders are friends. Witches are kind.

A Witch will steal your first "child." This is because the old lady in the woods could be trusted to perform a safe abortion. Witches are helpful.

A Witch can poison. This is because a Witch understands the power of plants, and the subtle tools women have needed to survive. Witches are wise.

Witches are "ugly." This is because they have no interest in performing for contemporary standards of fuckability. Witches are beautiful.

Witches are scary. This is because there is nothing more terrifying to the status quo than a confident dissident. Witches *are* scary.

Everything the stories say about us is true, but the reasons behind our actions are filled with intentions of balance, justice, freedom, kinship, and healing.

When we write, and especially when we write spells, we can play with language, manipulate letters into words, words into paragraphs, experiment with form and content in order to open our minds to new and world-changing ways of thinking.

Why do spells so often rhyme? Does cadence help to set and prime the spirits' ears to hear our cries and find in us a compromise? Are messages more apt to stick in sonnet or limerick? And how does genre change the meaning or shift which way our spells are leaning? To all these questions, I've no doubt of the answer: play and find out.

Poet Gemica Rosenberg told us, "Poetry is the only thing that makes me feel like a witch." With words as her tool, Gem becomes a medium, a channeler, a creator; she inhabits states of trance and of hyperawareness. A self-described ecofeminist, she uses her poetry to examine her relationship to craft, science, herself, humans, animals, the earth, her past, and even past lives. Her poems are memento mori, reminders of death, an acknowledgment. "Acknowledgement," she says, "is the first step in resistance."[6]

Many Witches, poets or otherwise, keep a "book of shadows," a place for magical notes, whether they are handbound leather volumes or Lisa Frank three-ring binders. I like to include secularized versions of the book of shadows in my thinking: scrapbooks, grandma's recipe collection—her spells passed down, intention-setting to-do lists, diaries, poetry, and prose—the innumerable ways we can use words to make magic. We can include journalism, scientific and political theory, too, because, at its heart, a book of shadows is a place to record what we perceive, what we've discovered, and what we've been taught in an effort to learn as much as we can from our experiences. This term *book of shadows* was popularized by the burgeoning Wicca movement in the 1940s and 50s, so you can choose to use those words to describe your handwritten magic book or not.[7] The important thing is that we write our magic down. Not just our spells, but our goals, fantasies, intentions, fears, and thoughts. They are all magic.

Judika Illes reminds us, "Not only are magical texts among the oldest surviving pieces of literature, but many scholars and anthropologists suggest that it was the need to record spells and divination results that stimulated the very birth of writing."[8]

They don't call it spelling for nothing.

We Witches build worlds with words, going letter by letter, word by word, sentence by sentence into uncharted territory, through brambles and choppy waters of thought, trying to transform our ideas into something someone else can understand. How do we articulate a vision?

It feels like a swarm of bees inside our heads that we're trying to organize in neat lines on a table top; they keep buzzing and won't sit still. But when we corral enough idea bees to make one coherent statement, sometimes we get stung, and sometimes we get honey.

As Judy Grahn told me, "Don't be scared of your ideas. Write them down."[9]

When I asked Veronica Varlow how we can beat imposter syndrome, fight the paralysis of fear, not be scared of our ideas, and conjure the bravery to write them down, she was passionate in her answer: "I need your stories and your experience and your spells to help enrich the world, so don't you dare take that away from me."[10]

Toni Morrison said, "There is no time for despair, no place for self-pity, no need for silence, no room for fear. We speak, we write, we do language. That is how civilizations heal."[11] So we can imagine reading and writing as methods not only to create culture, change culture, but also to heal. To heal ourselves and our whole civilization. Ylva Mara Radziszewski described her book-writing process to me as "healing on a deadline," adding "honesty is a radical practice of Witchcraft."[12]

The truth is that I'm scared. Scared that I don't know enough, that I'm not wise enough, Witchy enough, or poetic enough, correct or eloquent enough, that I'm not worthy of the ink. But I spill it anyway. I spill it and make grand messes of Rorschach stains. And in cleaning up the blots, sometimes I find some truth, so I write that too.

Author Christena Cleveland told us about her vision of God she writes about in her book *God Is a Black Woman*. A welcoming, unconditionally loving God. Christena said, "My mess is my sacred offering to her."[13]

A covenmate suggested once that poems are healing, confronting viruses. That we spread them from one to another and having been touched by them, we are changed. Provoked. We can spread ideas worth spreading.

But let's keep an eye on the word's will to evangelize. For better or worse. "The Word" brings to mind the most contentious, viral, power-wielding occulture collection of literature that I know: The Judeo-Christian Bible.

John 1:1: "In the beginning was the Word, and the Word was with God, and the Word was God."

The Word was God. The Word was God.

Rather than ignore it or allow it to do us harm, let's take this book and add it to our collection of tools. It can be a difficult task. After all, Exodus 22:18 says: "Thou shalt not suffer a witch to live."[14] But we can take a page from the remarkable Harriet Tubman who "took much of her biblical inspiration from the Old Testament with its focus on deliverance and was not fond of the narrative contained in the New Testament, feeling it promoted obedience among the enslaved."[15] Very shrewd.

In the New Testament, Jesus delivers his most famous speech, the Sermon on the Mount, "if anyone slaps you on the right cheek, turn to them the other cheek also. And if anyone wants to sue you and take your shirt, hand over your coat as well" (Matthew 5:39–41). We can view this as a beautiful statement of passivism, nonviolence, nonmaterialism, Zen, and the absence of greed. But we also *clearly* see how words like this could easily be manipulated by slave traders to imply that submission to oppression is the only path to salvation. This is the power of words, but also their kryptonite—they can be twisted.

I grew up in a church. I was in the choir and the youth group. I did the forty-hour famine on Christian retreats. I was lucky. We were Presbyterian, not fanatical. My mum is a Christian to the core, but she's progressive, feminist. She's also been brainwashed into a sense of Christian superiority. Hers is the way, the truth, and the light. The only way into Heaven is to formally accept Jesus Christ into your heart. As she gets older and her memory fades and her body breaks down, she clings more and more to her faith. She prays and prays and prays because, according to her rules and regulations, her bible, her Word, the Word of God, I'm not going to Heaven either. I ask how it could be Heaven if your most loved ones can't be there with you? For this, she has no answer except:

Because that is The Word of God.

Still, because of my upbringing, Jesus is my default deity. When I am in agony, his is the name I instinctually beg for relief. It took some time, but I no longer feel conflicted about my Christian heritage. I decided that Jesus was a Witch. A Conjure man who overturned the moneylenders' tables in the temple and befriended outcasts. And yet, it remained difficult for me to envision the Bible as anything more than a tool for white supremacy and religious hegemony.

In her book *Toni Morrison's Spiritual Vision*, Nadra Nittle writes that Toni Morrison's family

> *took pride in the fact that her grandfather had read the bible cover to cover five times. With reading materials limited—"there were no books, no libraries"—the Bible was the only book available to him, and his decision to read the scriptures amounted to "taking power back" since it had been illegal for enslaved African Americans to read. Following her grandfather's example, Morrison's parents had books throughout their household. "That was like resistance." she said.[16]*

We spoke to Nadra who told us that Toni's family

> *had a way of viewing the world that some would deem as magical in the sense that they believed that they had visitations from ghosts, that they had to some degree psychic abilities—so Toni grew up in this environment where these things were accepted as opposed to questioned. She grew up fully aware and fully comfortable with this idea that science didn't explain everything that went on in the world.[17]*

And neither did the Bible. Toni's family, performing activist resistance by owning books, carved a path for their daughter to win the Nobel Prize in Literature.

For those of us, and I'm especially looking at our Queer and otherwise blasphemous coven members here, who've felt personally victimized by the Bible and rightfully cry out, "Fuck that Bible noise!" I spoke to Sherry Shone, author of *The Hoodoo Guide to the Bible* and *Hoodoo For Everyone*. As a Queer, Black woman, she refuses to have the Bible taken from her, and reminds us that Zora Neale Hurston wrote: "All hold that the Bible is the great conjure book in the world."[18] Sherry has adopted and adapted this conjure book with a magic that she calls Turning a Hurtful Bible Verse into a Helpful Exercise.

Sherry admits that the Bible has been used "as a tool for the restriction, degradation, degeneration, everything that you can think of that is hatred and fear and stress." But the Bible "is also a tool that can be used to flip all of that on its head. It can be gender neutral, it can be religion non-specific, it can be a tool for us to take our power back."[19]

As I read aloud an infamous and hurtful passage, Timothy 2:12, "I do not permit a woman to teach or to assume authority over a man; she must be *silent*." Sherry takes a long deep breath and chuckles.

"Take out the pronouns. I do not permit *blank . . . blank* must be silent." Sherry explains that in her reading, the spirit of Timothy 2:12 is to invoke silence when silence is needed. To have the power, control, and autonomy to tell someone or any voice, "you need to be quiet." She also uses Timothy 2:12 for binding work. "I do not permit" Sherry lists examples, a boss, a person, a government agency, a system "to have authority over our lives, our children, our home."[20] You can fill in the blank with any force in your life that wants to demean or control you and tell it, No. What Christena Cleveland calls "The Holy No."[21]

We do not permit fear, hatred, ignorance, racist, sexist, or capitalist forces to have authority over our spirits. These forces must be silent.

We can take any words that are used against us and flip them, invert them, make verses with them, and take back their power. Even the Word of God is ours. It has been translated and retranslated countless times for thousands of years.

We can do our own translations.

As you wield your pen, keep at least this from that book: The Word became flesh. (John 1:14). Know that words become flesh. That what is said becomes truth, that what is written becomes law. Our words are tools. They are wands and weapons that we craft with play, by inverting, subverting, mixing, or simply finding new meaning in the words we've been hearing or reading.

Whatever our personal history with the Bible, Quran, Torah, the Vedas, or religious texts of any kind, when we go looking for our own tools for practical magic, these texts stand as examples of what we can do with words, for better and for worse. They can hurt and they can heal. Last thousands of years. Build civilizations and tear them down.

The Bible is such a powerful tool in the US that, by convention, incoming presidents raise their right hand and place the left on a Bible while taking the oath of office. A notable exception is John Quincy Adams, who swore on a book of law.

Laws and contracts are created by carefully arranging words to create documents by which we literally live and die.

In Lozen's story, her people, the Nde, asked, "Who could know how it stood with the White Eyes? . . . They could not make decisions themselves and were bound by the promises written down on paper—which seemed almost like Witchcraft.[22]

It seemed like Witchcraft to the Nde because it is Witchcraft, and it's useful to think of it as such. Laws and contracts are, in essence, no different than what we saw with Ursula and Ariel in *The Little Mermaid*, or scare stories of making deals with the Devil. Sign your name, the die is cast, and so mote it be.

I use this magic in my own praxis. When I want to make a serious commitment to myself, I write a contract on paper and sign it. I keep it in my book of shadows. Although my contracts with myself probably wouldn't hold up in any court, they serve as reminders that the promises we make to ourselves are as valuable as the promises we make to our employers, our loved ones. They work. Although I've broken a million promises, let myself down innumerable times, I have yet to break a written contract I have made with myself.

Judge, lawyer, and self-proclaimed Witch Melissa Bekisz told us, "before going to law school, I felt like I had no grasp of the legal system, so I do my best to explain as much as possible." The complexity of language in the law is intentionally disenfranchising. "In contracts," Melissa suggests, "it's important to try to use more plain language so that people can understand it. It's overly complicated; that is a gatekeeper."[23] She also laments another gatekeeper: the crippling cost of law school. She got by on scholarships but fears a system where only the rich can become lawyers.

Having studied Reiki, Melissa keeps symbols and stones on her bench. Her work is to open up access to justice, and she campaigns for more funding for legal aid. She uses a combination of magic and the word of the law to try to help.

Immigration lawyer and creator of the Lawyer Witch Coven group on Facebook Pamela Muñoz agrees, saying legalese is akin to a secret language; loopholes are secret knowledge. She told me, "I got a really strong sense of justice from my dad. If you're able to speak up on things that are not right, that's your duty . . . and a strong sense of feminism from my mom." Although she takes issue with the *love and light* reputation of Witchcraft, her job means facing heartbreak and injustice daily. She needs the love and light and her craft helps her to both root and detach. Pamela considers her work to be a blend of Witch and lawyer, unseparated. "An argument is spellwork," she said. "When I write a closing statement, I put in a lot of myself and my sheer will to try and influence the result of the court hearing and the decision of the judge through the use of my words. I also consider defense work to be protection magic." She's trying to "beat the system at its own game," taking the secret knowledge and secret power of words back.[24]

After our conversation, Pam published a blog post to work through her emerging identity, standing firm, loud, and proud at the intersection of lawyer and Witch. "At first glance," she wrote,

> *magick and the practice of law seem to be mutually exclusive due to the compartmentalization of every facet in our modern-day lives. Consulting the tarot deck or performing a spell on a full moon night couldn't seem further from reason and rhetoric, the main staples of legal argument and debate. But putting aside the fact that magick and science are not mutually exclusive for a moment, the work of a lawyer is akin to magick in yet another way. Ask any lawyer and they'll tell you that our work much of the time deals not with fact, but with the* perception *of facts. The same is true of magick, a system of practices and beliefs which holds that one can alter and shape her reality based on perception, intent and sheer force of will.*[25]

We need Witches on all sides. Witches writing laws. Witches enforcing them. Witches breaking them. Witches bearing witness. Whether we are lawyers or poets, words are our wands and our weapons.

Healing and wisening ourselves requires an equally essential use of our pencil as a wand, to enchant as well as resist. To create and destroy. To tear down old systems with a steady eye on how we will build new ones. Imagination preceding action, we turn to journals—blank pages that we mostly fill for no one's eyes but our own.

Language and landscape are my inspiration.[26]

So said Terry Tempest Williams in *The Hour of Land: A Personal Topography of America's National Parks*, and I think this rings true for most Witches. We do our workings and find our magic in those spaces between Creator and creation, writing tiny wish poems on bay leaves to burn, transforming our wishes to words, our words to action, action to environment. We are all a part of nature, creatures who paint landscapes with pigments and poems. We *are* language and landscape.

If you decide to dive into the rocks and sand, the beautiful and terrifying landscape of Terry's work, I don't suggest you go alone. Terry Tempest Williams is honest about desolation, silence, rage, cancer, confusion, fear, and loss. She asks: "How do we find the strength not to look away from all that is breaking our hearts?"[27] And we sense in her question a million tiny heartbreaks: personal, political, spiritual—finding beauty in a broken world. So, if you're anything like me, trying your best not to look away, you'll need a therapist, a priest, or a mystic, your coven, a trusted and sympathetic friend, *or* at the very least, an empty journal, a blank page . . . something or someone willing to be a sounding board to the discomfort that Terry, unearthing her own truths, inevitably digs up in you.

But this is what all word Witches have in common. Reporters, lyricists, or diarists: they find the strength to not look away from all that is breaking their hearts. They face it. They write it.

I got to page two of Terry's book *When Women Were Birds* and had to put it down for a couple days . . .

I don't want to start you off thinking that Terry is some nihilistic, hopeless Debbie Downer; she's not. She wrote: "we need not lose hope, only locate where it dwells."[28] For Terry, hope, like most things, is tangible, actionable. She doesn't wait for hope to come to her, she goes out and finds it—taking us with her along the rugged, stumbling path of its discovery.

As a child, Terry was raised under that thinly veiled racism and sexism sometimes found in the Mormon church. As a child, Terry saw a mushroom cloud explode. Nine women in her family have had mastectomies. Seven have died of cancer, her mother included. Doctors say it is a matter of when—not if—she will be stricken with cancer.[29]

Terry and her family are called "downwinders," people the US government knowingly exposed to radiation during nuclear testing in Nevada in the 1950s and 60s. For Terry, the connection between environment and self, the joy and pain that that entails, is very fucking real.

But equally important in her work and life is the commonly mislabeled "unreal"—the intangible, the unseen, and unseeable. The spirit beneath and behind the science. Like Migene Gonzáles-Wippler, WhiteFeather Hunter, and other glorious science witches of the earth, for Terry, the universe *is* magic.

Terry is the kind of Witch whose message resonates most deeply with me. She doesn't seek out the supernatural, but sees mysticism every day in the *air quotes* real world. She graduated from the University of Utah in 1978 with a degree in English and a minor in Biology, and this is so witchy to me, balancing one's education between poetry and petri dishes, music and molecules, seeking a holistic understanding of life itself and humanity's place in that life. The non-Witch sees a line of delineation between the real and the unreal, the real and the surreal, the seen and unseen. For the Witch, no such lines exist.

In one of my favorite passages from *When Women Were Birds* she wrote about a childhood moment when her education met up with her enlightenment: "Four gasses create air: Nitrogen—78.084%, Oxygen—20.9476%, Argon—0.934%, Carbon dioxide—0.0314%. This gave me confidence. The unseen world was real."[30]

Learning the invisible dance of molecules did not diminish but rather gave credence to the Magic that Terry felt vibrating in the very air she breathed.

Terry wrote:

Emily Dickinson wrote poems in her bedroom and kept them largely secret. . . . The poet Susan Howe writes, "She may have chosen to enter the space of silence, a space where power is no longer an issue, gender is no longer an issue, voice is no longer an issue, where the idea of a printed book appears as a trap." "To write," Marguerite Duras remarked, "is also not to speak. It is to keep silent. It is to howl noiselessly."

These essays are my howl.[31]

In Nature, a howl is simply a wolf's way of saying "I am here," and that is perhaps the most profound statement of all. I am here.

I am here.

This is the power of our wand and weapon: to make a mark with paper, with pens, or posts with pixels is to make a mark on the world. To declare, "I am here." This is what I've seen. This is what I've heard. This is what I know.

In her book *Refuge*, Terry continued her examination of the isolated, eccentric poet: "When Emily Dickinson writes, 'Hope is the thing with feathers that perches in the soul,' she reminds us, as the birds do, of the liberation and pragmatism of belief."[32] Pragmatism of belief. Pragmatism, with its focus on practical application, is not a word most people would use to describe a bird-fostered belief system, but, for Terry, bird magic has real-world benefits. She wrote, "Once upon a time, when women were birds, there was the simple understanding that to sing at dawn and to sing at dusk was to heal the world through joy. The birds still remember what we have forgotten, that the world is meant to be celebrated."[33]

Beautiful right? The idea that joy is world-healing. Because if we think of joy as healing, we can see play as important work and gleeful bird-watching as a productive earner, an investment in the future.

When joy is acknowledged to be healing, all acts of love and pleasure (to borrow a phrase from Doreen Valiente) can be viewed as a damn good use of time. Sorry, grinding, striving, patriarchal capitalist meat wheel; compared to that, your system just doesn't measure up.

Our undoing is also our becoming. Like The Tower card of the tarot symbolizes, sometimes our destruction is our revelation. Sometimes a good cry makes you feel *better*—(side rant: crying is your body's way of releasing stress hormones. When you stop yourself from crying you are literally and scientifically keeping that stress inside your body— patriarchal brainwashing is fucking bizarre). *So*, let's bathe in our bummers a little while longer until we can transform them into hope or the impetus for change. Build sandcastles on the shores of our rivers of tears.

Before Terry Tempest Williams's mother died, she told Terry, "I am leaving you all my journals . . . but you must promise me that you will not look at them until after I am gone."

Terry wrote:

On the next full moon, I found myself alone in the family home. I kept expecting Mother to appear. Her absence became her presence. It was the right time to read her journals. They were exactly where she said they would be: three shelves of beautiful clothbound books; some floral, some paisley, others in solid colors. The spines of each were perfectly aligned against the lip of the shelf. I opened the first journal. It was empty. I opened the third. It, too, was empty, as was the fourth, the fifth, the sixth—shelf after shelf after shelf, all my mother's journals were blank.[34]

In the book, these words are followed by *twelve* blank pages that the reader is forced to flip through, the silence resonating and multiplying inside the emptiness. It is one of the loudest silences I have ever experienced.

All my mother's journals were blank.

I've also been left with blank pages. I once found, in a box in the basement, a baby memory book that had been gifted to my mother when I was born. There were no entries. It was blank. My father had

Alzheimer's and my mother has multiple sclerosis–related neurological impairment. She doesn't remember. When I have questions, there's no one out there with the answers.

The good thing about a blank journal though, is that you can fill it up yourself.

I want you to know that Terry Tempest Williams wrote *When Women Were Birds* on the pages of her mother's blank journals.

But oh, the blank page; equal parts confronting silence and limitless potential . . . fill it with what? Terry has some ideas:

I write to make peace with the things I cannot control. I write to create red in a world that often appears black and white. I write to discover. I write to uncover. I write to meet my ghosts. I write to begin a dialogue. I write to imagine things differently and in imagining things differently perhaps the world will change. I write to honor beauty. I write to correspond with my friends. I write as a daily act of improvisation. I write because it creates my composure. I write against power and for democracy. I write myself out of my nightmares and into my dreams. I write in a solitude born out of community. I write to the questions that shatter my sleep. I write to the answers that keep me complacent. I write to remember. I write to forget. . . .

I write because I believe in words. I write because I do not believe in words. I write because it is a dance with paradox. I write because you can play on the page like a child left alone in sand. I write because it belongs to the force of the moon: high tide, low tide. I write because it is the way I take long walks. I write as a bow to wilderness. I write because I believe it can create a path in darkness. . . .

I write as ritual. I write because I am not employable. I write out of my inconsistencies. I write because then I do not have to speak. I write with the colors of memory. I write as a witness to what I have seen. I write as a witness to what I imagine. . . .

I write because it is dangerous, a bloody risk, like love, to form the words, to say the words, to touch the source, to be touched, to reveal how vulnerable we are, how transient we are. I write as though I am whispering in the ear of the one I love.[35]

We write for so many reasons, and once again, as we examine our tools of magic, we find that the spiritual benefits are echoed in the practical. Studies have shown that the act of journaling reduces stress, improves immune function, and sharpens memory.

Journaling habits evolve over time, and so writers become more in tune with their health as they connect with inner worlds and wants and desires. Journaling helps us stay present, and it offers perspective. It allows for catharsis and helps our brains regulate emotions. It gives us more self-confidence and self-identity. Expressive writing has even been shown to help people construct more structured, adaptive, and integrated schemes about themselves, others, and the environment. Writing activates and stimulates right-brained creativity, allowing you to use all of your brainpower. Journaling does, in fact, promote growth.

Journaling is good for you—physically, mentally, and emotionally.[36]

When hefty thoughts or the heaviness of emptiness weighs us down, we can unburden ourselves onto paper and lighten our loads.

We can use words to journal, to keep records just for ourselves, or as resources for our descendants. And we know that this individual Witchcraft ripples out into the world in its own way, but there is also that viral, public usage of this tool of magic. Publishing.

Risa: Diane di Prima grew up in an Italian family in New York. Her grandfather introduced her to poetry, opera, and to Italian philosophers on the margins writing about light as a unifying principle.

Her father abused her sexually, some of which she remembered very clearly up until that very bad year that she didn't remember at all. He introduced her to Machiavelli, and a sense of nothingness, and the true smell and feeling of fascism.

She went away to school and—miracle and wonder—found a coven, just an incredibly powerful gang of teenage girls including Audre Lorde, and they called themselves The Branded. A group of eight women who met to practice telepathy, trance, and communications with the dead, especially Keats and Shelly.[37]

265

Di Prima later published Lorde's work in her Poets Press.

She was determined to listen to the voices she was longing to hear—either in trance or by publishing them herself. Publishing is a powerful act of extending our listening to the voices we think matter out into the world. With Amiri Baraka, crucial Black poet of the Beat Generation, di Prima coedited the literary magazine The Floating Bear. *They ran it together and then Diane kept it all afloat herself, from 1961 to 1971—sending out electrifying new writing directly to a community of writers every few weeks. They paid out of pocket or with small donations to publish Beat writers, poets of the New York School, Black Mountain, and other revolutionary writers of the time.*

Di Prima also cofounded the Poets Press and the New York Poets Theatre and founded Eidolon Editions and the Poets Institute. She cofounded the San Francisco Institute of Magical and Healing Arts. In 2009 she was named the poet laureate of San Francisco.

Di Prima was a poet and a publisher because, as she wrote, "the war is the war of the imagination."

Dominique di Prima (daughter of Diane and Amiri) said, after her mother passed:

> *The war is the war of the imagination, right? . . .*
>
> *When you talk about the protests and everything here and around the world, you know, that's what we were raised to do as children of Di Primas, as children of Barakas, to be part of that change. And it is about re-imagining. I mean, if you listen to Black Lives Matter and if you listen to poets, it's about re-imagining what we think we live like, what we think people interact like . . . and what we think policing is going to be.*[38]

The war is the war against the imagination. We resist with the Word.

Trading words is a societal foundation. It's the reason that several rankings have named Johannes Gutenberg's printing press the greatest invention of the past thousand years. A mighty weapon.

In the twenty-first century, it has never been easier to make our words public. Your tweet has a greater reach in two seconds than Plato or Shakespeare had in their whole lifetimes. Everything we write on the internet has a potential, immediate global audience. And although it's tempting to dismiss the slacktivism of keyboard warriors, they too have consciousness-raising, world-changing power. Just ask Cintoya Brown.[39]

Audre Lorde said, "Words had an energy and a power and I came to respect that power early."[40] She used her words to channel frustration, to open doors and dialogues that a lot of us are too scared to even approach. One night she was driving and heard on the news that a ten-year-old boy had been shot by police. She pulled over and wrote her poem "Power," a poem about magic and imagery as tools to transform hatred into power. She pulled over and wrote a poem; she wrought power from despair using a pen as a wand, like conducting energy with a baton at symphony. We are not lost. We have magic and imagery. We can write hatred and destruction into power.

Despite the patriarchy's best attempts to keep women uneducated and silent, new ways of writing have often been developed by women, determined to have their voices heard. Enheduanna is humanity's first known poet. Humanity's first-known novel was written in 1010 CE by Japanese poet and "lady-in-waiting" Murasaki Shikibu. Our earliest example of science fiction is *The Blazing World*, written by Margaret Cavendish in 1666. History is brimming with marginalized voices who wrote regardless of what anyone told them about their worth, and in doing so, they changed the course of humanity, of literature, of how we perceive and understand written language. They played with the unknown and changed the known.

But before our love poems to words push us into the ever-lurking capitalist trap of discrimination, let's screech our heels and remember that there is life outside the linear realm of syntax and semiotics.

Now don't get me wrong, I'm a language junkie, and when I was a kid, I was a little shit and a real stickler for "proper" grammar, a condescending nine-year-old brat who wanted to prove that I was not only smart, but smarter than you. Thanks be to the Great Unknown, I grew out of that pretentious way of thinking. Sadly, some people never do.

Being smug and arrogant, they think one can determine a person's worth by their level of fancy book learnin'. Or determine their intelligence by their proper or improper use of grammar. It goes beyond feelings of intellectual superiority and into classism, racism, and sexism. Poor people, people of color, women, and people of marginalized sexualities and genders have historically been kept out of polite society and formal education. But, as we saw, this did not stop them from having vast knowledge of their own, and maybe, more importantly, ideas.

We can safely add slang and emoji into our spells because, for me, and I think for the listening Universe, if your ideas are good, who gives a fuck if your participle is dangling? We'd be crazy to care.

Harriet Tubman, for example, could not read, and yet there is no doubt in my mind that she was smarter, braver, more knowledgeable, and more magical than I can ever hope to be, no matter how many letters I acquire after my name. Listen now, Witches, if you ever think, or dear Lord forbid, if someone ever tells you that you're not educated enough to make a difference, that your vocabulary's not grand enough for your voice to have value, if anyone tries to make you feel small (you know the type: they can be found dismissively saying shit like, "Ohhhh, you've never read Dostoyevsky???"), remind them and yourself that Harriet Tubman could not read. And yet . . . Ideas . . . Maybe you haven't read a ton of books. Maybe you're the next Harriet Tubman.

As part of my introduction to Ayurveda, my guide gave me a mantra: Ham Ram Shrim Sham. She told me, "A Mantra is a seed of intention that is either heard, spoken, sung, thought, written, reflected upon, seen, touched, felt, expressed, or received in one form or another. It is most often chanted repeatedly or thought repeatedly with the belief that the vibration created by this seed thought will effectively change and transform matter."

Words become flesh.

The message we repeat becomes our reality.

Let us choose our words carefully.

Because the Word is God and what we say becomes our flesh. What we write becomes our Word.

As Word Witches, we make text our offering. It is exhilarating and terrifying. Humbly yet confidently presenting our visions, our versions.

Setting ourselves up for scrutiny, mockery, critique, continued obscurity, but with extra steps. Or maybe . . . just maybe . . . (y)our words might inspire a future Witch to re-enchant the world. With the odds stacked against us Witches, to write, to be read, is a gamble. We throw the dice and they tumble into infinity. In our lifetimes we won't see how they land.

Risa and I joke that we tricked ourselves into writing our first book. We had already been looking for Witches, and when we found them, we wrote emails that became podcast scripts that became a book. I had spent most of my life assuming that no one cared what I thought, but with the Missing Witches project, I wrote it anyway. Much to my surprise, people listened. People cared about what I wrote and I learned that while the world already had infinite books, articles, and five-hundred million tweets a day to read, what the world didn't already have, what had been as yet unwritten, was my perspective. And that perspective mattered.

The same is true for every Witch. What is left to be written? Your side of the story.

Our words are world-builders, so let us build worlds, banishing fear by conjuring the voice of Audre Lorde, whispering with warm breath we can feel in our ear: "Your silence will not protect you." And in the other ear, Judy Grahn's voice echoing: "Don't be afraid of your ideas. Write them down."

As Witches, to write is to break our own silence. To read is to resist the powers that would keep us ignorant and uninspired.

Let us do the unsilenced howl of writing, choose our words carefully, mold them into intentions and rhyming couplets, song lyrics and love letters, new dictionaries, new bibles, new laws, new identities, and new perspectives. Imagine your pen is carving your intentions into the cosmos—write them down for the Universe, and maybe for some future Witch, looking for a voice that resonates, a message that makes sense, to read.

Take a blank page and make a mark. They don't call it spelling for nothing.

Ritual

On this Aquarian New Moon, as the prospect of spring seems real, but distant, make a commitment to and for yourself. Keep a journal from this new moon to the next based on a schedule that is realistic. Journal every day, twice a week, or only on Sundays, but start on this new moon and stick to the visionary vow of beginning you make in the dark.

Make this a ritual with a blanket, a candle, or a cup of tea. Pick a favorite pen and use it just for this purpose.

If you need a jumping-off point or already keep a journal and want something fresh for your new moon, try the following exercise: define, for yourself, one more word: *success*. Because the financial version, collecting points to save our lives like in video games, is hollow and false. Because some of history's greatest minds (Zora Neale Hurston, William Blake, Oscar Wilde, to name a few) died penniless, buried in paupers' graves. Their life, their legacy, could not be measured in dollars and cents. They were, in my estimation, successful. They changed the world with a currency of resilience and imagination that cannot be reduced to dollars and cents. Let us Witches focus our lens on this word *success* and ask ourselves what it means. Friendship? Family? Education? Philanthropy? Creativity? Define *success* and make that a spell of intention. Write it down. Create a new dictionary. A mantra.

The malleability and wholly interpretive nature of language is proven by the existence of sarcasm. We can say what we mean by saying the exact opposite of what we mean. This manner of playing with language, according to *Scientific American*, spurs creative thinking because it requires us to think abstractly.[41]

Try it.

Or try the gift that Risa and I gave each other for Yule one year: picture your most powerful council of spirits, ancestors, animals, and like-minded soulmates, and then write a love letter of recommendation for the person you most want your council to know in the ways that you know them. Describe their best characteristics as if you are nominating them for an award. Then share this letter with that person. This is a powerful spell, and its effects are immediate for the caster and the cast upon.

Incantation

Words are spells
Words are made flesh
My pencils and pens
Are Wands
And Weapons
I wield them with tenderness
And might
Ink and graphite
and dried tree pulp
Combine with my will to make magic.
My keystrokes
Are a stroke of luck
Strokes of genius
The stroke of midnight ringing from a Witch's clock.
There is no time for despair,
no place for self-pity,
no need for silence,
(my silence will not save me)
no room for fear.
I do my own translations.
I speak, I write, I do language.
That is how civilizations heal.
I am a Witch.
I am a Witch.
I am a Witch.

12

New Moon in Pisces

Art

This circle is led by Risa
with expansions by Amy.

*The new moon in Pisces has been and will always be two-headed—
a collaboration between mystical and physical bodies. Luna refreshes
before the muses and dives into the domains of all we can and cannot see.*

—THEA ANDERSON, ASTROLOGER

ALL NEW MOONS MAKE A SPACE. Without the brightness of the sun reflecting on the moon and casting big shadows, we can more clearly see the depths. Pisces New Moon swims deep in those waters following the luminescence that is down there—not a reflection, but a living glow all its own.

One new moon, I sat at the bottom of the ocean in the middle of the night. We turned off our headlamps and breathed through our regulators in the cold pressing depth, in what should have been ultimate dark, and saw what hadn't been visible before. Our every breath, our every gesture stirred up a gentle bioluminescence that was all around us. There was light there, living light. The coral bloomed in the night and drew their long pink skeletal fins through the water gathering microorganisms. Everything was lit, everything brilliantly alive, everything more beautiful than I ever could have imagined from the surface.

On this new moon, I invite you to slip down to the depths of your psychic Piscean mind and make art from what you find there. With that art, help to make visible totally new possibilities for your life, and for the world.

All Witches are artists. We have crafting in common at our very core. We dance with all the layers of personal and collective shadow involved in carving out the space to turn ourselves outward and to draw forth new forms.

Every altar is an artform, every ritual a performance piece. Whether you are performing for your community, or your ancestors, or your shadow, or your past or future selves, your crafting makes a container for the place where your soul meets the universe. Art calls this uncanny known/unknown realm into sensory space. Marion Peck told us, "Painting is like trying to remember your dreams."[1]

Witchcraft uses art as a tool, especially when the new moon is in Pisces.

Where we live, Pisces season is a time of waters melting, cracks opening in the ice or between worlds. It's a time to make an opening in the dark for the utterly new. Using art for Witchcraft is the practice of dedicating time to all your senses, including your intuition. Crafting in this art-way liberates you. "Art is magic delivered from the lie of being truth," as Adorno has it, and it allows you to resist the oppression of a present that wants you to forget the possibility of magic.[2]

Art as Witchcraft can awaken us to astonishing magic that is always with us in the world. Art as a magical practice works on the mind in this way: tricking us out of our expectations and awakening us to our senses. Art-making magic brings us back to the astonishing realities that are already here—back into the glittering, weird now. When our expectations are defied, we see the world again.

This is the first piece of using art for your Witch practice: soak in it. Let your body experience art. Wait for the feeling of being lit up on the inside. When Leonora Carrington first encountered Max Ernst's art, it struck her heart, and decades later, she would remember how it felt: "a burning, inside; you know how when something really touches you, it feels like burning."[3] That burning was a flicker of her future life, a life of the surrealist art-making and storytelling that lay ahead for her. And I think following that feeling helped her survive great loss and darkness. I think for all of us, finding art that makes us burn can fuel our resistance, our resilience, and our delight.

Marion Peck is a covenmate and goddess artist of movements described both as "Lowbrow" and "Pop Surrealist." In an interview with us, she told of a moment when art school had nearly broken her. It required this tough critical stance that was destroying her love and personal language of art. So she took the last of her student loan money and went to Italy. She was walking around looking at the Colosseum and thinking: this is all patriarchy. What can I do with this? She felt the oppression of centuries that was somehow related to the choking feeling she had felt in school and she felt totally lost. Until suddenly, she stumbled on a work of a minor master, an artist she's not even sure the name of. And it was just, beautiful. Something about the greenery lit her up and eased her mind.

"I came home and painted a young girl in a similar greenery, peeing on it. That was me peeing on everything I'd learned." And the spell was broken, and she was free.[4]

Sometimes art is an argument, sometimes it's a manifesto, sometimes it's a hammer; and sometimes it rescues beauty and play from a utilitarian, war-like world. What Marion says was electric about Lowbrow in the early 2000s was that it felt like "we were saying fuck you, this stuff you think is garbage? This is where Soul has been living."[5] The work of resistance and re-enchantment is to look for where soul has been living. To sing out the truth of the spirit that comes to Marion when she paints: that beauty *is*.

Chaos magic is a practice that makes deliberate use of the summoning power in art. One of its core tenets is that the doctrines and cultural specificities of spiritual and occult practices don't matter. What works is always the same. What works is raising energy and directing it toward a focused desire in a symbolic language that speaks to the subconscious. In this practice, Witches create sigils, iconic symbols that you draw or carve with your own hands and fill with energy. Do this and then let it drift in your unconscious mind, slipping past the locks of ego and doubt and normalcy to draw up new possibilities from the impossible depths of the universe-mind, body-mind, lunar-mind.

The method for sigil crafting developed by queer magic artist Austin Osman Spare (who is problematic and ranty and deeply hard to read, but deliciously effective nonetheless—and who Genesis P-Orridge considered to be the greatest of all the occultists they had studied) is to write the phrase that encapsulates what you want, remove all duplicate letters, and then arrange the remaining letters; to play with them until they converge in an image that resonates.[6] Grant Morrison takes this practice further. They describe their graphic novel *The Invisibles* as a hypersigil: "a dynamic miniature model of the magician's universe, a hologram, microcosm or 'voodoo doll' which can be manipulated in real time to produce changes in the macrocosmic environment of 'real' life."[7]

Sigil crafting in the tradition of chaos magic is fun and powerful, and the idea of stripping all cultural specifics seems liberating in one way, but also totally barren. An idea for the children of colonizers who long to forget. It's missing the deep roots, the living Earth magic of real places and specific bodies. Leonora Carrington said "All religions are real . . . But you have to go through your own channels."[8] What would a feminist, antiracist, rooted version of art and symbol magic look like?

Afro-futurist artists give us a pretty good idea. Costume designer Ruth E. Carter drew on the Adinkra symbol-language of the Bono people of Gyaman to create the visual world of *Black Panther*, and in doing so, she suggests a joyful other way to approach the crafting of hypersigils in our lives and in culture.[9] Digging into the symbol language of our ancestors to craft and wear icon messages that speak beyond words, in a visual, emotional language of the worlds we want to live in draws those possibilities into the living, moving, breathing sweaty present.

In Wakanda, the Adinkra symbol for cooperation is emblazoned on capes that move like fabric blankets until a gesture unlocks their secret technology and they become shields. She used Adinkra symbols that date from at least the 1600s and were developed to make points of connection between tribes with different dialects and also to communicate truths too complex for words. Like runes, the symbols themselves have power. They are not similes for the spirits they stand for; they are, in some fundamental way, the spirits themselves. The costume capes with their ancient symbols borrowed from the real world are a humming, rippling piece of the utopian magic of that film.

Mequitta Ahuja is a contemporary painter included in the wide scope of Afro-Futurism. She builds her imagery in layers from performance to photography to paint. She draws in her ancestors in Africa, India, and her childhood in Connecticut, and she centers her own vision, her own unique body. She always carefully, lovingly depicts her amblyopia—one eye seeing differently—a condition still used to justify violence against women in the name of Witch hunting today.[10] She lovingly depicts her strange body and other-sight, and in doing so, she calls out to the truth of strangeness in all bodies. This is not chaos magic, but Mequitta's images are a kind of hypersigil for a future that is alive with its past, and bodies that are alive with their own perspective and power.

Often nude, the artist's self-portrayals have been described as femi-nist because they depict emboldened women who battle tigers, climb trees, fell their enemies, build monuments, carry heavy loads, sprout wings and manes of roots or snakes, suckle children, run, leap, play, toil and rejoice with dramatic gestures in landscape settings.[11]

Mequitta paints Black women as heroes and Black hair in a way that celebrates possibility, spiral connection.

Where hair grows voluminously from the protagonist's head and takes the form of tree branches or snakes, the reference is to "the psychic proportions hair has in the lives of black people," explains Ahuja ... If turned upside down, as is a head with tree-branch hair in the top left of Ahuja's 2012 collage drawing Macoonama, *the inversion indicates the realm of fantasy; and the tree branch hair symbolizes endless possibilities of self-transformation.[12]*

She uses photography, and then a layered practice moving through different media to draw her self out beyond its known edges into the infinite. She paints herself in a universe of stars or bioluminescence in *Rhyme Sequence: Jingle Jangle*, or reveling in tiny, fungal flowering detail in *Generator*. She suggests that we can make new contexts for ourselves that exceed the canvas of what seems possible now. Mequitta shows Black women and children overlapping and becoming-with, bones and flesh curling tenderly, embracing and birthing each other in an oil-on-drafting-film work called *Merge*; and women with their arms entangled in a circle, leaning back, in a piece called *Gather*. Bodies in this kind of art-magic are resonating through each other, supporting each other, creating. This is the coven we all want, and making pictures of it calls it forth.

Mequitta wrote, "My work has brought me the things I most desire."[13]

Art as antiracist Witch practice can build on sigil magic and go cracking past its limitations by taking up the cloaks and utopias of our own ancestors, bringing them into communion with each other, to conjure the world we desire.

The mother of Afro-Surrealism, Suzanne Césaire, wrote:

Finally those sordid contemporary antinomies of black/white, European/African, civilised/savage will be transcended. The magical power of the mahoulis will be recovered, drawn forth from living sources. Colonial stupidity will be purified in the blue welding flame. Our value as metal, our cutting edge of steel, our amazing communions will be recovered.[14]

Find your roots, reach for your grandmothers and kids, remember your value, and together, make art that recovers amazing communions.

Indigenous artist of Utopia, Urapuntja (Australia), Emily Kame Kngwarreye leads viewers deep underground, to intertwined, infinite root bundles. In her hundreds of paintings, curators see resonance with other art movements around the world, but for Emily the story of her paintings was always in the lives of the species of plants, animals, insects, and stones where she lived.[15] Where do we go when we follow those roots and routes? Similarly, Janet Forrester Ngala encodes sacred knowledge from an art practice that is thirty thousand years old; knowledge about our original star homes and the meeting place of life origin and ancestor spirits.[16] In *Milky Way Dreamin* that knowledge is abstracted, both to preserve its secrets and to transmit them without words into our own dreamings.

Austin Osman Spare describes the power in a sigil as bypassing our ego and consciousness to connect directly to the undercurrent of power in the universe that makes magic.[17] This is the realm we connect to through the dreaming. What Janet and Emily show us are the more-than-human kin that have been dreaming here, long before we came.

Marion Peck told us artists might not admit it but they all should: art is channeling. Marjorie Cameron—artist, elemental—knew the many beautiful and painful sides of this: being used as a tool in someone else's channeling of the new world, crafting her own life of sigils, being burnt up, and being the one to do the burning.

Cameron's story is about wild creation in liminal spaces, magical thinking, and a remarkable artist Witch who had to figure out who she was outside of a man's powerful idea about her destiny. Her husband, rocket scientist Jack Parsons, performed an act of Crowlian/Enochian ceremonial magic called the Babalon Working out in the desert and believed that in doing so, he summoned Cameron, and that she was a Fire Elemental. And maybe in a way she was. But she was also and entirely her own self.

> *In a letter to his wife . . . Parsons attempted to impress upon her that "the invocation of lesser forces [including angels, demons, and elementals] is far more dangerous than the invocation of Gods." The lower work, he continued, is "an act of science," while "in the higher work you are actually wooing the god—it is an act of art.". . . [M]aybe we can conclude that Cameron, the elemental herself, was invoking only God, the higher force, in her work—leaving us with her art."[18]*

If sciences are an invocation of the elements, and art is making love with God, then Witchcraft weaves a way through both.

Parsons believed Cameron's art magic was a crux in the rebirth of the world. He wrote:

> *You, Cinderella of the Wastelands have chosen the way of the hero— and the gods alone may guess the end of your path.[19]*

Her path was a struggle and it didn't go in straight lines. And there isn't that much of her art left, since she sent much of it up in flames.

> *Decades later, Anger explained, "She [was] releasing the spirit that she put in the drawing into the fire," meaning Cameron sacrificed her art as an act of conscious, occult-inspired transmutation. Once the art moved beyond her imagination, it had also served its purpose and became unnecessary, providing Cameron the opportunity to emancipate herself from it physically. "It was release," Anger continued. "In other words, if she'd kept them as drawings or paintings she would have been enchained to them."[20]*

She burned the art that chained her, but still, some beautiful work remains. She let them live. She must have believed that they were different—art that wooed God in a way that nourished them both and didn't leave them diminished or imprisoned.

The most comprehensive retrospective of her work was at the LA Museum of Contemporary Art in October 2014. The final pieces in her collection are a humming, resonant series of line drawings that look like maps of sound waves, or like singing messages from the universe. They are called *Pluto Transiting the Twelfth House*. These are so different from the rest of her work, but they are my favorite, and here in the twelfth chapter in the house ruled by Pisces, they feel like a homecoming. A reminder of the current of watery light moving through our particles at all times.

In Cameron's last public performance, she reads her poetry. She is steady, gray hair wild and candle-haloed.

She says these things and much more:

I am that dream of wings . . .
I pried all truth and lies to shreds to appease the doubt until at last not
    through a single act but through all acts I find myself in the landscape
    of your star . . .
Mother all life has fed at your golden breast. All dreams are spun from
    your silken lyre. Oh mother you have come at last out of the earth
    born from the corn . . .
Oh the many steps of the way.[21]

Cameron has spent a lot of time as a side note in other men's stories—Jack Parsons, L. Ron Hubbard, Kenneth Anger—or as a lurid caricature of pre-Beat sex Witch. So I want to begin her story with *Pluto Transiting the Twelfth House* and Cameron the poet because I want you to hold this image of her in your mind. See the steady crone poet in the candlelight, a landscape of burnt art behind her, spirits released, chains burned, waves of Pluto singing from her, lifelines that dreamed of wings, the landscape of a star, life as a cup, a message, as elemental, as channeler, expanding around all of us, rising ever brighter now. Both frail and infinitely powerful. Both flawed and wildly brave. Make it a picture that makes love to the gods.

Cameron was born April 23, 1922, in Belle Plaine, Iowa. She was an artist Witch who broke the hearts of girls and boys in Iowa and beyond, briefly ran a sex cult in the desert, and saw ghosts all her life. And she was a gifted artist from childhood. Belle Plaine residents remembered when, still a kid, she was commissioned by the town to make art in patterns along the banks of a roadway for a town celebration. At fifteen she became pregnant and her mother performed an abortion at home.[22] And she started to visit the local cemetery, late at night.

Ironically, Cameron's ticket out of small-town America and toward the counterculture came through the United States Navy, which she joined in 1943 as part of a women's initiative spearheaded by Eleanor Roosevelt. She became a mapmaker for the Joint Chiefs of Staff in Washington, DC.[23]

In the military, she became Cameron. She was among the first women to ever join the US armed forces. We know she drew maps and designed sets and costumes for propaganda efforts, that she had to recycle bloodied uniforms with pockets full of heartbreaking mementos to do her work, and that she was haunted by her involvement, even at a distance, in the machinery of war. Her brother got hurt in the fighting and she went AWOL to see him and was confined to the base upon her return, but then she was granted an honorable discharge that raises questions about the classified parts of her military history.[24]

She made her way to California. One day she stepped into the house in Pasadena folks called the Parsonage—Jack Parsons's mansion, which he'd turned "into a boarding house for artists, bohemians, drop outs, and occultists," where rocket scientists and sci-fi writers hung with Aleister Crowley's students and Freemasons lodge members, and the greatest magicians of all were the musicians improvising all night long.[25] Black and white men and women lived together illegally and it was a great, messy, electric pleasure dome.

Jack Parsons is an occult conspiracy theorist's goldmine. He used rituals dedicated to Pan to get some of the first rockets to fly and helped found the Jet Propulsion Lab that would contribute to that insane piece of unfathomable magic that sent Earth animals off their mother planet to the moon.

Parsons was a member of Crowley's Thelema order at this time, and an honored one at that, until an encounter with a powerful con artist derailed his life. Parsons was married to a woman named Betty, and though they had a happy, open marriage, when she began an affair with L. Ron Hubbard, it tore Jack up. The loss worked on Parsons's mind and became entangled with his ceremonial magic in a way that was fed and manipulated by the conman Hubbard. At this time Hubbard was immersing himself in Crowley's work, and living his life in a way that would show the violence in Crowley's doctrine: "do what thou wilt is the whole of the law."[26]

"Driven to distraction by the loss of Betty . . . Parsons threw himself into the only other part of his life he could control: his magic. And so began the fevered weeks of the Babalon Working. He began by tracing five-pointed stars in the air . . . Strewn around him on the floor were paper "tablets" covered with arcane symbols and languages . . . The ritual called for focused masturbation—what the Golden Bough would have recognized as sympathetic magic—as Parsons tried to "fertilize" the magical tablets around him and bring his elemental to life."[27]

The whole process took hours, but he was in a frenzy of loss and longing, so he repeated the whole process twice a day, for a week. "He began to use his own blood instead of semen."[28] All this time, his wife was sleeping with L. Ron Hubbard across the hall.

Once I had a lover cheat on me after biting and bruising me over and over, sometimes to my pleasure and sometimes not. I thought I could forgive him. I wanted to be that kind of person, I guess, and also I wanted back the life I had imagined. So we agreed that he should move into the apartment downstairs from me, and we would be friends and lovers and treat each other well from then on. Only once he moved in did I realize how paper-thin the floor was, how impossible it actually was for me to build a new life for myself with no space for my senses to spread out away from him. I could hear the voices of my girlfriends downstairs as my ex tried to seduce them, I could hear his pounding music all night and into the early morning, and I could hear my own anger and shame blowing around the creaking walls of that crumbling old building. And then the explosions started, as a new condo development began dynamiting the backyard to put in an underground parking lot. I was shaking thin and seeing ghosts everywhere. I had chosen so much of this and brought it swirling and crashing around me and I felt paralyzed. Not for the first or last time.

But I wasn't trapped. The strange magic of my own leaping choices, of my life as art practice, was circling around for me. I had said yes to a wild invite months before and got a cheap ticket before I even knew I'd need one, and I got the fuck out of town. I flew to Shanghai and worked in Shanghai and Beijing for a couple weeks at an underground indie art festival that doesn't exist anymore. I played music in tiny bars in the Beijing hutongs, roofs open to the stars and ancient trees growing in the middle. I managed the acts on the two stages at the art fair where people sold the crafts they'd made, and I whirled in circles with the Beijing roller derby team while an Appalachian folk band called out square dancing changes. I wasn't there very long and wasn't able to contribute much to this brilliant community of people who kept music and art going for as long as they could, until they collapsed under the pressure of the constant demands for bribes, having their gear confiscated, armed soldiers in the art market. I escaped my day-to-day reality only for a little while. I met artists working and resisting and making beauty, and it was enough to bring me back to life.

Amy hosted two friends at my place while I was gone. When I came home, we all sat up together into the night. One had a box of blank wooden matryoshka dolls—Russian nesting dolls—and she would take them out one by one to draw on, and while she turned them over in her hands she let the stories come out of the abusive relationship that waited for her back home. We sat on my back porch overlooking a pit dynamited into the earth, the hops plant I had given my ex creeping its tendrils up along the wrought iron.

I told her what lurked for me in the apartment below. She handed me a doll. The wood warmed in my hands and I loved her generous curve, that mother doll with secrets inside her, and slowly I started to trace the images I saw in the wood grain. The messes of my life entangled in line drawings. Images from my travels, images from my life before. I integrated my changes and scrawled them on those wood-mother bodies. We talked and drew all night and never saw each other again, though I tried to reach her.

I can't keep that night still in my mind; it slides around through my memory. But I know I kept drawing on those wooden dolls as I moved out, drew in new loves, got betrayed again, shed another skin, and looped around.

I kept drawing the cycle I was emerging from, spiral by spiral, until I drew this moment to me, where you read these stories that are like matryoshka dolls. Witches leading to other Witches, and dozens of matryoshka dolls sit happy and well fed on my altar, next to my first book, and alongside the wooden spoons Marc had carved while he was on his way to me. He was sitting at a spot in the Rocky mountains called the "Wait a Bit Creek" as I drew those first dolls, carving those wooden spoons one by one. I think we called forth our life together on those pieces of wood. Perhaps we are each other's elemental.

Drawing on the wooden dolls drew me to my future, and also connected me back to my teenage self. Black ink drawings used to come off the margins of all school books onto my skin, my clothes, walls, and bookshelves. I used to illustrate everything in my world in winding black ink. This was a practice I lost when I lost myself. Coming back to it was a kind of madness for a while and then a kind of meditation, and it helped me conjure a new life.

Amy: Years later Risa drew on a wand carved from a tree branch in this same black ink style and gave it to me for my birthday. It is rough in some spots and smooth in others, adorned with a bird and vines of leaves that creep toward its pointed tip. I use it to conjure strength. To grow toward sharpness with the courage of a bird and the patience of leaves.

All this to say, I see some of myself in the Babalon Working. As he continued to perform the increasingly frantic ritual, Parsons heard strange taps and voices in the night. He traveled with Hubbard into the Mojave desert to the intersection of two power lines, and did the working one more time.

> *At sunset the two men stood beneath them and suddenly Parsons felt the tension snap. "I turned to him and said 'It is done'... I returned home, and found a young woman answering the requirements waiting for me."... In a letter to Crowley, Parsons declared, "I have my elemental!" describing her as fiery and subtle, determined and obstinate, sincere and perverse, with extraordinary personality and intelligence." He immediately began performing sex magick rituals with her.[29]*

When Cameron appeared, it felt like magic, and the two didn't leave the bedroom for a week. Parsons was trying to summon Babalon, a goddess or female messiah, a new possible world, and when Cameron arrived, he moved on to the next stages of ritual with her, but he didn't include her. "They worked with me without telling me what was going on. Everybody assumes that I was in on it—that I really knew. But I didn't know."[30]

Consider this a lesson from the patriarchy about how *not* to do sex magic. The power that you draw to yourself in such a working is likely to slip through your fingers. Parsons believed Cameron was Babalon, a female goddess whose arrival marked the beginning of a new era of free love and anti-authoritarianism. He believed she was nothing short of epoch changing and "even after Parsons death, the Babalon Working would stay with Cameron, infusing her life with a narrative of epic proportions."[31] But Cameron was utterly her own person, not a conjured elemental, bound to him and his work. She was an artist and Witch in her own right, and after two weeks in bed, she left the Parsonage to make her own magic.

In 1948, she left for Europe, and then travelled to Mexico where she would live and make art for two years after she and Parsons agreed to an open marriage. "I associated with homosexuals, I had lovers among bullfighters, I went nude bathing with mariachis, I danced in a whorehouse."[32] In Mexico, where the socialist government had offered citizenship to refugees from fascism,[33] Cameron met other surrealist art Witches who had escaped the war—Remedios Varo, Renate Druks. They found each other, and there was a sense of homecoming and of transformation for these women who had—all in their own ways—been terrorized by World War II and used by the patriarchs of the art world.

Not much has been published about Cameron's time in San Miguel de Allende, but I want to imagine it anyway. When Cameron was there, meeting these powerful women, these incredible artists, she didn't know yet she had been used in sex magic workings or that her husband saw her as an elemental he had summoned. And she hadn't lost him yet, and she hadn't begun to make the body of surrealist, romantic, mythological, alchemical art that would become her testimony. I think these Witches shared pieces of their world views, maps they had drawn on their journeys through the underworld. Cameron made friends in Mexico who would become golden threads in her life, and those threads would unspool into artwork. Through Renate Druks she would later meet Kenneth Anger when he was casting *Inauguration of the Pleasure Dome*. Anaïs Nin "was lined up to star, but when Anger found his Scarlet Woman the film immediately changed course . . . [Anaïs] wrote in her diary about 'the dark spirit of the group' whose 'paintings were ghostly creatures of nightmares.'"[34] Cameron was the dark spirit, and for her art would become a praxis for conjuring dreams, and transmuting nightmares.

While Cameron was making love and art in Mexico, Parsons fell down the last of the rabbit hole set up for him by L. Ron Hubbard. He put his entire savings into a scheme for Hubbard and Betty to buy yachts in Miami and sail them to California, which ended up being a setup for them to travel the world on Parsons's dime. Parsons realized he'd been manipulated and crafted a ritual that raised a windstorm, turned the tide, and brought them back to shore. But the money was long gone.

Shortly after, Hubbard published a Dianetics essay in *Astounding Science Fiction*, and it was a hit. In this essay he does away with the complexities of psychiatry to offer an alien mythology instead, and for only $600 you can start to "go clear." Dig into your shadow experiences, let your new leader put it all on tape, turn over the exhausting work of navigating life, and you'll soon be free. Within months he published a book based on this essay that became a national bestseller. Hubbard was beginning to put up the tentpoles of the great pyramid scheme of Scientology, playing on dreams and fears in ways he'd already shown himself well versed in back at the Parsonage.

I feel empathy for Parsons, a Pan-lover who dreamed of the moon and peace on Earth, who got scammed by one of the world's great scam artists. And I feel love for Cameron, this Witch of the wild and the wastelands. She made it out of Belle Plaine and out of the war machine and found the joyful uninhibited jazz magic of the Parsonage. She found a love who used her and also who thought she was pure fire goddess magic, thought her art was holy. And together they believed in helping bring about a better day. Love under patriarchy is always broken in some way. "Chances are if you are reading this then you too are living in a dead and dying world. The colonized or so-called first world is the underworld."[35] Witches and artists journey through it, and the journey itself is art.

After Mexico, Cameron returned to California and to Jack, and they had a few brilliant years together. Then they were preparing to leave California to return to San Miguel de Allende together when Jack was caught in the mysterious explosion that would end his life.

After, Cameron made her way to the desert. She made a home out there, no electricity or running water, but it was beautiful nevertheless, the home of an artist freed to wander late at night and mourn. Cameron would talk to the moon and welcome travelers and beautiful friends of all genders and races. They would get deeply high together, and sometimes they would practice sex magic or just fun kinky play. Cameron used other bodies in her workings, playing out the patterns enacted on her by Jack. Trauma echoes. Cameron learned about Jack's workings by reading through the papers that remained after his death. After he was gone, out there in the desert, she attempted her own ritual work to magically create their child. "This she called her 'Wormwood Star,' a name taken from Parsons's writings about a dark star that crashes to earth. The ritual didn't succeed, but as she explained in a letter to Wolfe, the pregnancy was never meant to be 'the actual growth of a human child but the spiritual child of a psychic union.'"[36]

People like to talk about this part of her life as if she was trying to start a sex cult, teetering on the brink of madness, but what it sounds most like to me is a Witch in mourning. It makes me think of that other California goddess, Joan Didion, and her book *The Year of Magical Thinking*, about how impossible it is to adjust to the coming absence of those we love.

Lately, my daughter has been crying for her ancestors, we think this is her way of coping with the fact that her grandmother is dying. She likes to tell me of the times when she was an adult before she was born, and about what she'll be after she dies. I told her that we become the earth, trees, and stars and from this she makes her own mythologies. Maybe that's what Cameron meant by the Wormwood Star; symbol systems that give hope are our psychic children.

Years after Jack's death, and after she came out of the desert, Cameron exchanged letters with Joseph Campbell about *The Hero's Journey*. I wonder if she told him about making love in the desert, about going deathward to the womb, birthing possible worlds in spirals of loss, clouds of starfire, black hole collapse, and inversion into multiverses on the other side. Cameron's journey was that of an uncontainable woman in postwar, post moon-landing America. Modern and mythic. A journey of losing safety and going to the underworld, the other world, the desert or the moon, and then the long, slow, painful process of crafting a new skin and building that dream of wings.

We mostly have to peer through keyholes to see her art and the worlds she conjured. A camera lovingly moves through the landscape of her paintings in *Wormwood Star*. "The film *Wormwood Star* is really about Cameron's work as a painter, and the thrust of the film is to present the artist as an alchemist who, through her creative work, becomes herself transmuted into gold."[37] Biographies of Cameron focus mostly on *Wormwood Star* and *Inauguration of the Pleasure Dome*, alongside a couple other times when she flickers into light in the popular history of the emerging counterculture, like the time in 1957 when her drawing "Peyote Vision" got Wallace Berman's Ferus gallery shut down.

But in the late 1950s, Cameron was not just the erotic image of the Scarlet Woman in *Pleasure Dome*, or the scandalous creator of pornographic, hallucinatory, persecuted "Peyote Vision." She was also a woman in an ailing body, sick with allergies, rotten teeth, and an untreated ulcer. Married for the second time, though it wouldn't work out. She was a human with no health insurance in a country that—decades later—still ties a person's right to care to the whims of employers and the market. She was sick and making art on her journey through it. She performed poetry and spent much of her time at The Unicorn Coffee House on the Sunset Strip, the first real beat hangout in the city, where Allen Ginsberg, Maya Angelou, and Lenny Bruce all came to perform new material.

The owner of The Unicorn said:

Beat had changed already by 1959. It was exploited. Shops were selling black leotards and berets. Kerouac to me was like Bob Dylan later, they both wrote about people who were doing it. They articulated it. They were the messengers. Times they are a-changing, but they didn't change the time—Cameron and people around her were the ones who were doing it."[38]

She was changing the world with the fierceness of her vision: "her creative drive governed her life, there was no compromising whatsoever. Cameron's work was not viewer friendly, it was viewer disturbing."[39] She found love many times, she was admired and adored, and she was often alone. She painted rocks out in the desert where she felt everything was alive and sacred, and out there, she received communications from the sky. Visions of time travel and of other dimensions.

Cameron had dreamed of getting pregnant with Parsons, and after he died, of getting magically pregnant with a child that would be the outcome of their workings. When she did get pregnant with her daughter many years later, she named her for that perfect complex magical structure: the crystal. She was in the midst of traveling and making art, and living with men and women who inspired her; she was part of a movement that was trying to birth a freer, loving, peaceful world, and she brought Crystal with her everywhere. I understand why she wanted to upend the rules of the Man's world to invent a new reality for Crystal. And I can also understand how that made a life that didn't always feel safe.

> *She let me stay out of school . . . I started being bullied because I couldn't read or write back in first grade, because I had dyslexia, and they didn't know that it was dyslexia. They thought I was retarded . . . So instead of pushing me to stay, she just kind of let me, you know, do what I wanted.*[40]

Cameron gave her a creative life, a life outside the system that taunted her and misunderstood her, but maybe she went too far.

> *She let me experience things with her that maybe other mothers would say, 'Why did Cameron do this?' You know, she let her daughter experience LSD with her when I was about 9 years old.*[41]

Crystal ended up stuck for a while in the orbit of addiction and abuse. But she made it out alive. So, let her story ring for us at the edges of too far: when we creatively destroy systems that are making us sick, keep stability and foundations enough so the next generation can build without being victimized yet again.

Because so many of us are descendants of these kinds of days, children of a generation that longed to bring about a new world, one where art and music, fungi and magic would help open the doorways of perception. One where many got hurt by accident, tripped up, or were victimized by those who sit waiting to prey on the vulnerable.

But the parents grew up, and so did their art and their magic. "By the end of 1973, Cameron was a grandmother, and she settled into the role by forgoing her nomadic lifestyle in favor of fostering bonds with her grandkids," her first-born grandchild, Iris Hinzo, said. "My grandmother was the backbone of the family." While her parents lived their own shadow journeys "freebasing, brawling and calling the police,"

Cameron made her home in West Hollywood, behind the bamboo shield, a refuge.

In her later years, Cameron gardened, cooked organic food, drank tea, smoked pot and earned a teaching certificate in Tai Chi. She also became interested in the Hopi culture and homeopathy. She'd still perform rituals at every solstice, burning candles, lighting incense, and ringing bells, 'like priests do' Hinzo says with a smile.[42]

I take so much comfort in this image of Cameron as grandmother, backbone, priestess. I love getting older so much. I turned 39 when I started writing on Cameron, I'll be 43 by the time it comes out, maybe in my 50s by the time these words make their way to you. Maybe I'll be in the trees and stars by then, who knows. Every year I feel one more layer of something shed. I am ready to own the crone. The art-making of my life is bringing me around in spirals in ways that help me smile at the disasters that came before.

Our voices get clearer, and somehow it becomes easier to just know the things you know. To apologize when you've fucked up. To love and share the odd and godly thing that you are. To make art and make ritual and make gatherings and make a life. This crafting transmutes me.

If you are in pain, or feel far from your voice, the art Witch tradition blesses you right now on your path to finding your practice. Feel this surge come down the wire. Follow your art practice through the death of everything that dies, of everything you thought you knew. Make with the world as it changes.

All that you touch
You Change.
All that you Change
Changes you.
The only lasting truth
Is Change.
God
Is Change.[43]

Capitalist patriarchy has used you like a sex magician, working on you without your consent, but your true power always slips through their grasp. Make with the world to change the world.

Amy: If you have a blockage when it comes to the art-making process, try automatic painting. Gather whatever materials you can find, no need for fine pigments and horsehair brushes here. I've used leftover house paint and sidewalk chalk . . . Close your eyes, and just paint or draw, or sculpt with playdough made from flour, water, and cooking oil, with no notion of a final product. In this way, you cannot fail. If you try to draw an apple and it doesn't look much like an apple, you can feel defeated, but if you set out to draw an amorphous message from the universe, there is no wrong answer. If you sit down to fingerpaint, get lost in the flow of joy and freedom and creativity for an hour, and then hold up the finished piece and don't like it, don't find it aesthetically pleasing, and declare that it sucks, then you've lost the point. The magic was in that hour of creation, not in that split second of judgment. There is no wrong answer in art. Only a million questions, unfolding through the viscous squish of colors and imagination. I love painting. I am not a good painter, but I have a good time. I've often said that both in art and life, I'm more of a Jackson Pollock than a Seurat. More likely to throw a bucket of paint than to spend years meticulously pointilizing a beach scene from tiny dots. I've designed album covers and drawn the illustrations for this book, but my favorite art project ever was when I felt compelled to make these big, wearable, alien heads out of papier-mâché. For no reason other than that my imagination pushed me there. I got into papier-mâché in the first place because I had no art supplies, but I had flour and water and a newspaper. What artist Jer Ber Jones has dubbed Availablism. Using what's around, mundane junk, to make magic, art, and costumes. Experience this mode of art-making. No cost. No stakes. Just the Witchcraft of transmogrifying from imagination to material. Open this gate laughing, not with fear or judgment. Laughing. Throwing paint. You may find a Witch in there, in the laughter, in the squish. The magic in the making. Imagination by necessity, preceding invention. See the value of your work without the lens of capital or profitability, reassured that the Art World (that's Art Business) is a lot of money laundering for the elite. We Witches don't need that kind of validation.

For Cameron her practice was her throughline. It brought her through:

> *What clearly was her saving grace through it all was her work. It is difficult in the context of today's art world—its climate of production and acquisition and impenetrable levels of social status—to comprehend a practice as personal as Cameron's was, but just as the Witch Woman drawings were part of her mourning process, so was all her art a means of reckoning with reality.*[44]

This reality can be hard to reckon with. But your making, even on the smallest scale, spreads a dream of wings throughout the universe. Changes in culture happen like in the body: in the dark corners, in those overlooked places that hold everything together; the myofascia and the gut. It happens in the Unicorn Coffee Houses, in the tiny box of the voting booth, in the petri dish, in solstice rituals, and in the soft click of the keyboard in the night.

Wormwood Star ends with a refrain from Cameron's poem "Cinderella of the Wastelands," familiar to any heart-tired member of the faithful: "how long beloved god, how long."[45]

We sing this refrain, still, as we craft the art that is the weaving of the world, that is the visionary work of resistance and re-enchantment. We call out, alongside the Cinderella of the Wastelands, alongside all those whom patriarchy has used and war machines have traumatized, this loving, lonely call. We lift our hearts to the sky and feel our roots reach down into Earth as we join with her in song, in reverence, with the passion and bravery of a fire elemental, and the gentle steely backbone of an artist, grandmother, priestess.

> I have heard your voice singing lonely songs of desire in the wild wind, i
>   remember the artistry of fingers that held the rose in wonder…
> how long my beloved god, how long, how long, how long[46]

Ritual

Artist Emmie Tsumura told us:

> *I did a residency on the West Coast . . . and elders there did some work on how settlers can place themselves on this land in a good way, and part of that is understanding your own ancestries, speaking to your own ancestral spirits . . . if you know your ancestral medicine, it's going to be here as well, so you just need to . . . find it again here.*[47]

And so this is the invitation for the end:

Come to the land you are on with knowledge of your own ancestors. Nikki Sanchez, in her work "Decolonization is for Everyone," asks us to research the history of the land where our grandmothers were born.[48] What is the colonization story in that place?

Go looking into your history so that you have something to offer. What were the colors, the plants, the patterns, the archetypes, the choices and heartbreaks and disasters that shaped your grandmother? What was her colonization story?

Use this investigation to inspire a new self-portrait, let it become a hypersigil that entangles you into the brilliant world that is and can be.

Incantation

My work has brought me the things I most desire.
I am elemental, I am fire.
All that I touch
I Change.
My art and the universe sing:
I am that dream of wings.

13

Thirteenth Moon

Technology, Anarchy, and the Web

This circle is led in collaboration.

THIS IS THE END THAT KEEPS THE STORY OPEN. This is the Black Moon, the extra new moon, the moon for those years when the calendar can't keep up with the sky. For the Thirteenth New Moon, let's embrace the edge of what seems possible. The anarchy of sometimes but not always. Let's embrace the virtual and speculative and explore one of Witchcraft's greatest tools: technology. Remember that the word *technology* at its root means "science of craft."

As coauthoring, podcasting Witches collaborating during these plague years, we find each other, our people, and our protests online. We are Woods Witches and Tech Witches. We are lovers of forests, lakes, and cityscapes, musty books and PDFs, hand drums and midi tracks. We are digital and analog, and while we love to dig in soil, we also love these tiny supercomputers we get to carry around with us all the time. Our magic bridges the gap and questions if the gap exists at all.

Maria Mies and Vandana Shiva opened the introduction of their book *Ecofeminism* with a section entitled "Why We Wrote This Book Together," writing:

> *Some women . . . find it difficult to perceive commonality both between their own liberation and the liberation of nature, and between themselves and "different" women in the world. This is because capitalist patriarchy or "modern" civilization is based on a cosmology and anthropology that structurally dichotomizes reality, and hierarchically opposes the two parts to the other: the one always considered superior, always thriving and progressing at the expense of the other. Thus, nature is subordinate to man; woman to man; consumption to production; and the local to the global and so on."[1]*

We collaborate for liberation. We collaborate as an act of defiance and resistance. We collaborate because while society trains us to compete, Nature gives us a model of cooperation and mutual aid. We collaborate to transgress against hierarchy. We collaborate because the tech means we can work together, even from inside homes, inside forests.

For us, and like our practice of Witchcraft, the answer to Why We Write Books Together is because we can. As we send and receive each other's feedback in real time, we imagine those Witch collaborators who came before us. Monica Sjöö and Barbara Mor crafting *The Great Cosmic Mother* across an ocean, waiting for weeks for the manuscripts in the mail, Diedre English and Barbara Eirenrich laboring over *Witches, Midwives, and Nurses*, without the ease of Google docs and Zoom check-ins.

As we reach out across the internet, laying webs upon webs, we find new worlds, new modes of complexity, and understanding. We find them, and when we don't, we make them.

Witchcraft is a practice of attunement with the more-than-human world, with the spectrum of possibilities in the past as well as the future, within ourselves and our communities, in order to call forth our dreaming.

Many have been branded with the word *Witch specifically* to break us from that radical polyphony we sense is possible. And so we gather up— in our seed bags, cauldrons, web communities, and grimoires—practices to resist that breakage, tools with which we incant the re-enchantment.

We sense in the vice grip of capitalism, patriarchy, and colonialism a fear of decentralized communion. Kyriarchy fears the lack of control implicit in becoming-with the animacy in everything, including the digital; the lack of control that is inevitable when we are being sporulated by the sacredness that is everywhere. But Veronica Varlow's Bohemian Witch grandmother taught us fear is forgetting everything is all right. We are not afraid of what the collective needs, of where the most marginalized will lead us, or of what truths Earth will tell. We are ready to walk through the sorrow caves of the present singing, knives bright and at the ready, offering our bodies to Earth, together crafting rituals and ceremonies for what comes next. We ready ourselves with every new moon to tend our gardens, feed our circles, tell our stories, sing our songs, and in these ways, together, conjure the pre-utopia. Together we call it forth by refusing to forget that our magic is real, that flourishing is still possible.

This praxis calls for a shift in our understanding of resources. And so for us, there are practical, political implications to being a Witch.

Political Witchcraft is a land back movement. Earth's remaining wildernesses and "crown" lands and fundamental resources must shift to being coordinated by communities of Indigenous scientists and knowledge keepers who can lead us in reestablishing kinship with the more-than-human world.

Political Witchcraft is a reparations movement. The hoarded wealth of billionaires resting on centuries of slave trade must be distributed with guiding principles of reparations for communities and individuals brutalized by colonialism.

Political Witchcraft is a basic income movement. The right to the pursuit of happiness and the right to social security require that each person, regardless of immigration status or incarceration history, be guaranteed a livable income and healthy living environment. We need to stop using Earth's resources to perpetuate planet murder and systemic injustice and start using them to end poverty for all.

Political Witchcraft goes to work. We find our roles in the revolution and support the decentralized activism that makes change in real-world networks like tenants' rights groups, food banks and community kitchens, lake associations, knitting circles, and covens.

Political Witchcraft is anarchic tech. We are an open-source movement; we are in all the code. The re-enchanted world will be planned and improvised using collaboratively built and maintained ethical open-source systems, sharing open data, guided by open governance.

Political Witchcraft is platform agnostic. We will use technology when it suits us, but we have no loyalty to brands or systems, only to each other, only to the living principle itself.

In *The Energy of Slaves*, Leonard Cohen wrote:

All that we disclose of ourselves forever
is this warning
Nothing that you built has stood
Any system you contrive without us
will be brought down.[2]

Blessed Fucking Be.

Ariel Gore, in *Bluebird: Women and the New Psychology of Happiness*, tells this story about Diane di Prima:

Diane had promised her babysitter that she'd be back at 11:30 that night, and 11:30 starts rolling around, so Diane bids her farewells. "Whereupon, Kerouac raised himself up on one elbow on the linoleum and announced in a stentorian voice: "DI PRIMA, UNLESS YOU FORGET ABOUT YOUR BABYSITTER, YOU'RE NEVER GOING TO BE A WRITER."[3]

The voices who build this starving world call out: "Forget your promises, abandon your children, burn your care for others in the flames of your own ambition and you will prosper." But there are other voices. Tune your tools in the dark of the new moon, imagine you can hear them and you will. The war is the war for the human imagination.

I considered this carefully, then and later allowed that at least part of me thought he was right. But nevertheless I got up and went home . . . I'd given my word to my friend, and I would keep it. Maybe I was never going to be a writer, but I had to risk it. That was the risk that was hidden (like a Chinese puzzle) inside the other risk of: can I be a single mom and be a poet?[4]

Looking back, she knows that if she'd followed Kerouac's advice "there would be no poems. That is, the person who would have left a friend hanging who had done her a favor, also wouldn't have stuck through thick and thin to the business of making poems. It is the same discipline throughout."[5]

On this Thirteenth Moon, in every liminal time, remember: we are the poets who keep our word. We craft re-enchantment with our relationships. We are Witches who cast that most astonishing spell of telling the truth. We build bodies we can be proud of, bodies extended across the living systems we are symbionts with, including the digital web that, in places, aids the interface.

In *Revolutionary Letters*, di Prima writes, "Be strong. We have the right to make the universe we dream. No need to fear 'science' groveling apology for things as they are, ALL POWER TO JOY, which will remake the world."[6]

All power to joy, joy will remake the world. All power to the fertile margins, to the places where the mysteries have been hiding. The isolation of rugged individualism leaves us missing the context, skipping not just the women and the kids and the Queer family and the sores and the chores and the woods, but also just skipping the joy, the beauty, and the magic.

> *We're in the same position that we've always been in with our great minds, of wanting to take part of the package and leave the rest, like let's take Newton's laws of mechanics and forget his alchemy. Let's decide that poor John Dee was a great mathematician but he must have gone crazy when he started conjuring . . . I think we're at the point where the magic or the spiritual, whatever you want to call it, the part of ourselves that we have been keeping out of the spotlight because of being caught in a few hundred years of Rationalism Civilization, has got to come back into the work.*[7]

Let's infuse the technocrats with magic, let's commune together on every plane, and make rituals and spells in moonlit groves and Zoom rooms. Let's open up our sources, tell the painful and magical histories, and weave our lives back together to include what we've been missing. di Prima thought the history we were missing was "essentially aimed at human liberation" and crucially, she believed that "anarchism, gender equality, communal property and sexual freedom were interlinked concepts."[8] Political Witchcraft knows that the relationship between *gender equality*—the freedom to love and celebrate all consensual acts of joy and pleasure—and *communal property* holds a key to human liberation.

Common land, public space, basic income, open source technologies, public research: these are interrelated spaces where our liberation breathes and weaves like so much ancient mycelia. These places and practices are among the techne of re-enchantment.

This is what our tools are for: the liberation of Earth and all who live here. And though this burden is heavy, and fascists are fucking exhausting, our tools can also help us remember the purpose and spirit of all our workings.

Emma Goldman, feminist hero and foundational anarchist activist, wrote:

> *I did not believe that a Cause which stood for a beautiful ideal, for anarchism, for release and freedom from conventions and prejudice, should demand the denial of life and joy. I insisted that our Cause could not expect me to become a nun and that the movement should not be turned into a cloister. If it meant that, I did not want it. "I want freedom, the right to self-expression, everybody's right to beautiful, radiant things." Anarchism meant that to me, and I would live it in spite of the whole world—prisons, persecution, everything. Yes, even in spite of the condemnation of my own comrades I would live my beautiful ideal."[9]*

Live your beautiful ideal, live it radiantly. Do what you need to in order to call back your power, and incant that vision into this world.

Not all forms of anarchy harmonize with our own evolving, personal philosophies, but we love the idea that "anarchists offer a positive theory of human flourishing, based upon an ideal of non-coercive consensus building."[10] A communal flourishing based on independent choices, woven together through consensus building rather than coercion. Or, as Julie Nowak of The Seasonal Body put it in one of our monthly New Moon Gatherings, "we can't rely on the government to always take care of us but we can make resilient communities to take care of each other no matter what the government does."[11] We can't rely on our right to abortion to be guaranteed, but we can support those organizations that have, for decades, woven networks for safe abortion access. We will craft routes and roots past those who would deny our autonomy and liberation. We can't rely on every political party to tax the rich appropriately and fairly distribute those funds, but we can continue to work out ways into positions of power, seen and unseen, build openness into every level of government and technocracy, expose the truth, become the rising tide. And in the meantime, we will distribute our resources ourselves and reincarnate our care. In our diverse, intergenerational, Queer families we will re-weave the bonds of support that help us flourish, and cultivate epochs of refuge.[12]

This is why we return to the moon. To the Thirteenth New Moon where hidden possibilities are born. Here marginalized voices are streaming from beyond the violent, coursing mainstream.

This is why we return to the web of which the internet is just a piece. The web of all that lives and all the tools we use to reach and uplift each other. We return to connection, education, and experimentation.

In a *Wired* article on Technopagans from 1995, Brenda Laurel is quoted as saying:

> *Pagan spirituality on the Net combines the decentralizing force that characterizes the current stage in human development, the revitalizing power of spiritual practice, and the evolutionary potential of technology. Revitalizing our use of technology through spiritual practice is an excellent way to create more of those evolutionary contexts and to unleash the alchemical power of it all.[13]*

Brenda Laurel's game company, Purple Moon, told stories about girls—girls in a forest world, using their magic—before other game companies paid any attention to that audience. Her writing about Gaia and theatre used Renaissance Faires as examples of fractal interactivity that could be applied to distributed computing games. Her groundbreaking research turned VR into a tool for flight. Her book *Computers as Theatre* became a classic of computing theory and begins: "computers flourished as the engineers lost control of the activists, the homebrew clubs, the artists and the visionaries."[14] Beyond the illusion of control, there is the fertile wilderness of art and activism. The homebrew clubs upended ideas of property so they could work together on wildly complex problems. Busting out of digital enclosures, the homebrew clubs invented open-source software by remembering the commons.

Brenda Laurel compared the possibilities and medium of computers not to a transaction machine, but to an activist philosophy of theatre. This is the world of Augusto Boal and the Theatre of the Oppressed, where the play exists beyond the illusion of control. "The play is adapted in conversation with the audience, it is about 'acting' rather than just talking. In Theatre of the Oppressed, the audience is not made of spectators but 'spect-actors.' Through the evocative language of theatre, everyone is invited to share their opinion on the issues at hand."[15] What's possible is cocreated. Laurel calls for—calls out to—an activist, anarchist, becoming-with spirit in how we use and design technology. She conjures the Goddetc right into the heart of the machine. Her work is a Trojan Horse full of theatre nerds and solstice rituals aimed right at the heart of contemporary capitalism: video games, war games, the vast copy-pasting of war.

In a commencement address at California State University at Monterey Bay, in May of 2000, Brenda Laurel said:

> *Don't marginalize yourself. This is activist error number one. You are not an outsider. You are not prowling around the edges of society. You are at the center. You are America's heart and its conscience and its hands. You have a moral duty and a legitimate voice . . . It's time to bring your judgment of yourself inside your own heart. Speak from your own experience. Honor your own voice. Be your own moral compass. Know your power.*[16]

You are the center. Know your power. This new moon praxis of resistance and re-enchantment that we call Witchcraft (but you might know it by other names) isn't a cult and there is no single answer. Honor your voice. Beware anyone who offers you the opportunity to turn your questioning off. Ask every question. Cast the radical spell that tells the truth.

Witchcraft is not the Word, it is the Work. It's not a product, it's a process.[17] It's not an easy answer or a guru. It is not a religion; it's a technology. Witchcraft is a methodology for improvisation, education, evolution; the expression of our questions; and the connection with the vast and minute realm of answers. It is a praxis—a lens through which we see and become-with the world—a way to make pathways toward flourishing, both for ourselves and our ecosystems.

In "Designed Animism," Brenda writes in favor of using technology and design to "act as if" every tree and rock and field and river were alive.[18] She skips over the debate about what is animate to ask: What can we create if we *imagine* everything is?

> *Designed animism may help us make crucial changes in how we frame the world and how we behave in the face of enormous environmental challenges . . . Sensors that gather information about wind, or solar flares, or neutrino showers, or bird migrations, or tides, or processes inside a living being . . . We have, for the first time, the capacity to create entities that can sense and act autonomously, or with one another, or with living beings. They can learn and evolve. They can reveal new patterns, extend our senses, enhance our agency and change our minds."[19]

This is technology meeting wildcraft, and Witchcraft. And this is where we want to live. We don't want to destroy the built world; we want to lichenize it. Live in the places where technology meets ancient nature knowledge. Extend our senses all the way into communion with the webs of the world.

> *If I had more sensors, my body could be the earth. With matching effectors, I become a 'Gaian Gardener,' responsible for and enacting the health of the living planet.*[20]

We treat our web worlds like gardens, gently tend them, watch what grows, follow the spark of life, learn from what doesn't work, let it feed us. We reach out and extend our sensors.

All of us here, now, are world-builders, blending and coloring past the outlines of our reality. We are in circle together, spiraling outside the rules of linear time with this ancient magical technology of writing and reading, painting and perceiving. We will meet you in digital spaces, we will send our love out along the wires.

We want to own this as another mode of Witch. Women, men, the genderqueer, and neuroqueer, the technopagans, all those who have found themselves fractured and furious in a world of monumental inequality, all those alone and staring at screens, we invite you into this circle that is a spiral always opening, all lines meeting somewhere. Unmask with us in the dark of the Thirteenth Moon so we can reach for one another.

So we can extend ourselves—via technologies and emergent properties—over Earth. So we can be in the rhythm of change, the fractal pink noise of music, like water striders taking up the right amount of space in balance with other entities. In gentleness.

So we can be Gaian Gardeners and cyberpunks too. So we can dance through data to cast the ultimate spell of telling the truth.

So we can create our Selves and create our worlds.

So we can make our own rules and build consensus.

So we can see every interaction as collaboration.

So we can know our power.

So we can "unleash the alchemical power of it all."

Ritual

For this Thirteenth New Moon of the year, which may or may not exist, we invite you to embrace both anarchy and technology. Don't follow any rules. Extend kindness in a new direction. Research something random; put it in your spells. Create your own ritual, and write your own incantation. Do whatever you want. Use technology to disrupt or connect or create.

We leave these sections blank, inviting you to collaborate with us in the creation of this book. Like our new moons, the empty space is open for you, awaiting what seems possible.

My Incantation

My Ritual.

NOTES

Introduction

1 Cunningham, *Earth Power*, 71.
2 Federici, *Caliban and the Witch*, 143.
3 Federici, *Re-Enchanting the World*, 1.
4 Feldmann, "Like Witchcraft."
5 Grahn, "Our Bonding."
6 Donna Haraway, *Staying with Trouble*, Location 547.
7 adrienne maree brown, "for George Floyd: fire."
8 Lorde, *Sister Outsider*, 110.
9 Redmond, *When Drummers Were Women*, 13.
10 González-Wippler, *The Santeria Experience*.
11 West, "Yes, This Is a Witch Hunt."
12 Thea Anderson, "Harriet Tubman" and "The Past Is Right Here."
13 We choose they/them pronouns for the moon because they are alive to us, and beyond binaries.
14 Silverstein, "Invitation," 9.

Chapter 1

1 Callie Little, conversation with author.
2 Callie Little, conversation with author.
3 Callie Little, conversation with author.
4 Goodall, conversation with the authors.
5 Goodall, conversation with the authors.
6 Cleveland, "God Is a Black Woman."
7 Wikipedia, "Gebel el-Arak Knife." Again, we choose they/them pronouns for Venus.
8 Wikipedia, "Gebel el-Arak Knife."
9 Cady Stanton, Anthony, Gage, and Harper, "The Suffragists."
10 Kahina, "Free People."
11 Kahina, "Free People."

12 Andy Morgan, "What Do the Tuareg Want?"
13 Mark, "Kahina."
14 "Kahina, Queen of Berbers."
15 Naaim, "How to Treat Women."
16 Mattingly et al., "Burials, Migration and Identity," 17–18.
17 Editorial Team, "Queen Tin Hinan."
18 Garcia, *Initiated*, 282.
19 Kwekudee, "Tuareg People."
20 Hirschberg, "The Problem of the Judaized Berbers," 339.
21 Brett, Michael, and Elizabeth Fentress, *The Berbers*, 35.
22 Herodotus, *Histories Book 4*.
23 Rasmussen, "Tuareg," 366–69.
24 Becker, "Female Face of Berber History."
25 Becker, "Female Face of Berber History."
26 Kahina, "Free People."
27 Yeats, "The Second Coming."

Chapter 2

1 Nimbin Apothecary, "Heart Is Not Just a Pump."
2 *Missing Witches*, "Samhain Circle—Look for the Door."
3 Looi, "The Human Microbiome."
4 Silvia Federici, as quoted in Gago, "Spirituality as Force of Rebellion."
5 Cosmogyny, "Your Body Is an Ancestor."
6 This classic trope of horror stories gets picked up by RuPaul (@RuPaul, Twitter post, April 12, 2011) and others to become a metaphor for self-sabotage. Amy says this to me when I am spinning up a self-doubt specter.
7 Earthbound Futures, "QUEER the Heroes Journey."
8 Earthbound Futures, "QUEER the Heroes Journey."
9 "2SLGBTQ+" stands for Two-Spirit, Lesbian, Gay, Bisexual, Transgender, Queer (or questioning), the plus sign represents other sexual identities including asexual.
10 Strand, "I Will Not Be Purified."
11 Grahn, "Our Bonding."
12 Favale, "Bingen's Vital Contribution."
13 Hildegard, quoted in Newman, "Hildegard of Bingen," 164.
14 Strand, "We Are the Product of Anarchic Queer Love Making."
15 Sacks, *Migraine*, 757.
16 Fox, Introduction to Hildegard von Bingen's Mystical Visions.
17 Fox, Introduction to Hildegard von Bingen's Mystical Visions.

18 Magloire, "Oh My Body."

19 Norton, "4 Gay Heretics and Witches."

20 "United States' Child Marriage Problem."

21 Wikipedia, "Child Marriage in the United States."

22 Wikipedia, "Nevertheless, She Persisted."

23 Chitnis, "The Original Tree Huggers."

24 Arya, "Mother of Chipko Movement."

25 *Missing Witches*, "Samhain Circle—Look for the Door."

26 Clifton, two-headed woman.

27 Magloire, "Spirit Writing."

28 Magloire, "Spirit Writing."

29 Lucille Clifton, *Good Woman*, iBooks locator 175.

30 Poetry Foundation, "Lucille Clifton."

31 Magloire, "Spirit Writing."

32 Magloire, "Spirit Writing."

33 BioArt Coven, "The BioArt Coven Manifesto."

Chapter 3

1 McLeod, "Why Do We Garden?"

2 Belcourt, *Medicines to Help Us*, xiii.

3 Cunningham, *Encyclopedia of Magical Herbs*.

4 Beyer, "Know 10 Plants Deeply."

5 Bennett, "Garden," 81.

6 Strand, "Your Body Is an Ancestor."

7 Grahn, *Blood, Bread, and Roses*, 231.

8 Many witches will tell you that a large, yet ever-growing collection of random empty jars is a key component of their practice.

9 Tolle, "Flowering of Human Consciousness."

10 Gray, "The Wisdom of the Natural World."

11 Oda, *I Opened the Gate, Laughing*, 66.

12 DNA Tests, "How Much DNA Do Humans Share?"

13 Buggs, "What If Agriculture Could Heal?"

14 Buggs, "What If Agriculture Could Heal?"

15 Faun, "On Interspecies Humility."

16 Akst, "Influence of Soil."

17 Paddock, "Soil Bacteria Similar to Antidepressants."

18 Oda, "Wheel of Dharma."

19 Oda, *I Opened the Gate, Laughing*, 61.

20 Oda, *I Opened the Gate, Laughing*, xv.

21 Kowalczyk, "What Is Dharma in Hinduism?"

22 williams, *Radical Dharma*, iii.

23 Oda, *Sarasvati's Gift*, 4.

24 Oda, *I Opened the Gate, Laughing*, 63.

25 Oda, *I Opened the Gate, Laughing*, xiv.

26 Oda, *I Opened the Gate, Laughing*, x, 17.

27 Oda, *I Opened the Gate, Laughing*, 6.

28 Oda, *I Opened the Gate, Laughing*, 15.

29 Oda, *I Opened the Gate, Laughing*, 21.

30 Oda, *I Opened the Gate, Laughing*, 71.

31 Pedersen, interview with author.

32 Pedersen, interview with author.

33 Pedersen, interview with author.

34 Sreechinth, *Thich Nhat Hanh Quotes*, 125.

35 Stewart, *Feminist Weed Farmer*, 13.

36 Stewart, *Feminist Weed Farmer*, 11.

37 Ally, "Tree Lady of Brooklyn."

38 Kimmerer, *Braiding Sweetgrass*, 126.

39 Kimmerer, *Braiding Sweetgrass*, 122.

40 Ledesma, "Grief Is a Dancer."

41 Okpala, "26 Peculiar Benefits."

Chapter 4

1 Barnstaple and DeSouza, "Dance Is Healing Medicine."

2 Samuels, "Dance as a Healing Force," 161.

3 Planetary Dance, "The Story."

4 Planetary Dance, "The Story."

5 Planetary Dance, "The Story."

6 Schechner and Halprin, "Anna Halprin: A Life in Ritual," 67.

7 Halprin and Stinson. *Circle the Earth Manual*. Excerpted here: https://dimutara.com/planetary-dance.

8 Stine, "Modern Shaman in Seoul."

9 Stine, "Modern Shaman in Seoul."

10 Lola, "Spirit for EVERYBODY!"

11 Winton-Henry, *Dance—The Sacred Art*, 4.

12 Winton-Henry, *Dance—The Sacred Art*, 4.

13 Halprin, *Returning to Health*, 30.

14 Halprin, *Returning to Health*, 30.

15 Halprin, *Returning to Health*, 34.

16 Halprin, *Returning to Health*, 34.

17 Barnstaple and DeSouza, "Dance Is Healing Medicine."

18 Asante and Mazama, *Encyclopedia of African Religion*, 131.

19 "In philosophy, systems theory, science, and art, emergence occurs when an entity is observed to have properties its parts do not have on their own, properties or behaviors that emerge only when the parts interact in a wider whole." Wikipedia, "Emergence."

20 di Prima, "War for Human Imagination."

21 Ferre, "Marinette."

22 Michel and Bellegarde-Smith, "Vodou," 1366.

23 Michel and Bellegarde-Smith, "Vodou," 1367.

24 Danticat, *Krik? Krak!*, 194.

25 Magloire, "Quest for Abolition."

26 Gay, *Ayiti*, 381.

27 Sparks, "Magical Thinking for Girls."

28 Beete, "Make Good Trouble."

29 Fick, *The Making of Haiti*, 42.

30 Dunham, *Island Possessed*, 67.

31 Cognitive Behavioral Therapy Los Angeles, "Act as If."

32 Boisvert, "Colonial Hell and Female Slave Resistance," 69. Quoting Jean Fouchard.

33 Michel et al., "From the Horses' Mouths," 70.

34 Magloire, "Quest for Abolition."

35 Magloire, "Quest for Abolition."

36 Lawler, "Bee Dances and 'Sacred Bees,'" 103–06.

37 Lawler, "Bee Dances and 'Sacred Bees.'"

38 Despret, *What Would Animals Say If We Asked the Right Questions?* 80.

39 Samuels, "Dance as a Healing Force," 164.

Chapter 5

1 Huebner, *Seduction Through Witchcraft*.

2 "And those who were seen dancing were thought to be insane by those who could not hear the music" is a quote often attributed to Friedrich Nietzsche but there's no substantive evidence that Nietzsche wrote or said it. It's a wonderful, Witchy notion nonetheless.

3 Mithen, *Singing Neanderthals*, Location 4479.

4 Kauai's Hindu Monastery. "The World of Siva's Sacred Song."

5 Yes, I was a contestant on a "reality" singing competition. Having had my brushes with the exploitive, masturbatory ego orgies of the Music Business,

I had no interest in being a pop star. As a curious person, Witch, and journalism student, knowing I was a good enough singer to make the cut, I discovered that I needed a peek behind the curtain. The experience only confirmed my lack of any desire for pop stardom, so with the curtain open, secrets exposed, and my questions answered, I left the competition when the numbers were being whittled down to a precise forty finalists. It wasn't my dream, but far be it from me to take the place of someone whose dream this truly was. I had perhaps already taken the joke too far. Many times, through multiple audition rounds, I would get nervous, and then have to stifle my laughter. It was silly and I treat the memory as such. That said, there was one part, one moment of the audition process, that I carry in my heart. Two friends graciously agreed to accompany me to the first audition—a shopping-mall-filling cattle call. The wait was hours. My friends stepped out of line to use the bathroom and get something to drink, so I was alone in the crowd. An old woman, straight out of a David Lynch movie with her disquieting demeanor, came deliberately toward me and asked: What are all these people doing here? I responded, "Oh it's a singing competition and this is the line ..." She cut me off: "No no. I mean, what are all these people doing here when there's real work to be done?" I was astounded. She was absolutely right. When my friends returned I told them we should leave. They convinced me to stay by appealing to my unsatisfied curiosities, but the old lady was right. There was real work to be done, and that experience solidified my stance.

6 Harrison, "We Are One."

7 Harrison, "We Are One."

8 Translated by Rita Steblin in *A History of Key Characteristics in the 18th and Early 19th Centuries*.

9 *Missing Witches*, "Music Witches, Music as Witchcraft."

10 *Missing Witches*, "Music Witches, Music as Witchcraft."

11 *Playboy*, "Wendy/Walter Carlos."

12 *Playboy*, "Wendy/Walter Carlos."

13 Wikipedia, "Wendy Carlos."

14 Lamoureux, "Witches Found Spirit."

15 Redmond, *When the Drummers Were Women*, 3.

16 Fancourt et al., "Effects of Group Drumming."

17 Tsumura, "You Have to Believe in Magic."

18 Witch Camp (Ghana), *I've Forgotten Now Who I Used to Be*.

19 Witch Camp (Ghana). *I've Forgotten Now Who I Used to Be*.

20 Wel, "Healing Power of Sound."

21 Wel, "Healing Power of Sound."

22 J. R. Miller, Residential Schools and Reconciliation, 4.

23 Warner, *Buffy Sainte-Marie*, 17.

24 Warner, *Buffy Sainte-Marie*, 36.

25 CBC Radio, "What Does Buffy Believe?"

26 *Time*, "Folk Singers: Solitary Indian," 53.

27 Warner, *Buffy Sainte-Marie*, 58.

28 Gamblin, "LAND BACK!"

29 Buffy tells these stories throughout Andrea Warner's *Buffy Sainte-Marie*.

30 Warner, *Buffy Sainte-Marie*, 70.

31 Warner, *Buffy Sainte-Marie*, 95.

32 Alchetron, "Buffy Sainte Marie."

33 CBC Radio, "What Does Buffy Sainte-Marie Believe?"

34 Warner, *Buffy Sainte-Marie*, 266.

Chapter 6

1 Varlow, *Bohemian Magick*, 9.

2 Beth, *The Hedge Witch's Way*, 36.

3 Chapman, *Advanced Magick for Beginners*, 37.

4 Mui, "Queering the Church."

5 Wikipedia, "Cremation of Care."

6 Frías, "Hopeful for the Magical We Are Weaving."

7 It bears repeating: "If I didn't define myself, I would be crunched into other people's fantasies for me and eaten alive." Audre Lorde said this during a speech entitled "Learning from the 60s" at Harvard University in February of 1982.

8 Gino and Norton, "Why Rituals Work."

9 Most Canadian Witches will recognize this as a reference to Lucy Maud Montgomery's *Anne of Green Gables* in which the feisty iconoclast title character uses poetry and her imagination to change the lives of everyone she meets.

10 Harvard Health, "Power of Placebo Effect."

11 Migene Gonzalez-Wippler, *The Complete Book of Spells*, xxi.

12 Granddaughter Crow, "What a Person Believes."

13 Oursler, *Synesthesia*.

14 Simpson, "Genesis P-Orridge."

15 Sandberg, "Genesis P-Orridge: Alter Everything."

16 P-Orridge, *Nonbinary*, 274.

17 Granddaughter Crow, "What a Person Believes."

18 Harvard, "Power of Placebo Effect."

19 *Goddetc* is a term coined by artist Maria Molteni to describe an expansive, unending, and inclusive notion of God.

20 Strand, "We Are the Product."

21 Hunter, "Making Manifestos."

22 Gonzáles-Wippler, from her blog https://migenegonzalezwippler.typepad .com/about.html.

23 P-Orridge, *Non Binary*.

24 P-Orridge, *Thee Psychick Bible*, 37.

25 P-Orridge, *Three Psychick Bible*, 276.

26 P-Orridge, *Three Psychick Bible*, 271.

27 Britannica, "Sacrifices."

28 P-Orridge, *Non Binary*, 397 (Kindle).

29 Vogt, "World's Oldest Ritual Discovered."

30 Smith, "Anything That We Do."

31 Smith, "Anything That We Do."

32 Maya Angelou via Twitter.

33 Oxford dictionary. Oxford Languages online.

34 Oxford dictionary. Oxford Languages online.

35 Varlow, "The World Will Trick You."

36 González-Wippler, *What Happens After Death*, 10.

37 Frías, "Hopeful for the Magical We Are Weaving."

38 Tsumura, "You Have to Believe in Magic."

39 Gonzalez-Wippler, *The Santeria Experience*, 209.

40 Sandberg, "Genesis P-Orridge: Alter Everything."

41 P-Orridge, *Non Binary*, 13, 399 (Kindle).

Chapter 7

1 Via private message to the authors, October 4, 2021.

2 Jarod K. Anderson, Twitter feed.

3 Carrington, "Down Below," 236.

4 Wertheim, " Wonderful, Mysterious, Beautiful."

5 Diggins, *String, Straightedge and Shadow*, 81.

6 Debakcsy, "Theano of Croton."

7 Morelle, "Ancient Babylonians."

8 Waxman, "Where Do Zodiac Signs Come From?"

9 "Mesopotamian Priests and Priestesses," History on the Net.

10 Massey, "Power-Geometry," 61.

11 Social Science Space, "Geographer of Space and Power."

12 Massey, "Space of Politics," 291.

13   DuQuette, *Aleister Crowley's Thoth Tarot*, 8.
14   Dickens and Torok, *Missing Witches*.
15   Kaczynski, "Frieda Lady Harris." O.T.O.
16   Caduceus Books, "Lady Frieda Harris."
17   Kaczynski, "Frieda Lady Harris." O.T.O.
18   Caduceus Books, "Lady Frieda Harris."
19   Kaczynski, "Frieda Lady Harris," Hermetic Library.
20   Hermetic Library, "Correspondence between Crowley and Harris."
21   Hermetic Library, "Correspondence between Crowley and Harris."
22   Crowley to Stubbins, April 22, 1942.
23   Hermetic Library, "Correspondence between Crowley and Harris."
24   Lupec.org, "Queens of Tarot Frontier."
25   Sklar and Sklar, *Mathematics in Popular Culture*, 328.
26   Sklar and Sklar, *Mathematics in Popular Culture*, 328.
27   Farmelo, "Dirac Hidden Geometry."
28   Farmelo, *Strangest Man*, 16.
29   Adams, *Physical and Ethereal Spaces*.
30   Hoffman, "Projective Synthetic Geometry."
31   Melt, "Lady Frieda Harris."
32   af Klint, *Notes and Methods*, 150.
33   Brooklynn, "Sonic Witchcraft, Neurodiversity."
34   Vanessa Oliver-Lloyd in a voicemail to the authors, October 4, 2021.
35   Varlow, "The World Will Trick You."
36   Letzter, "Mathematician Wins $3 Million."

Chapter 8

1   Rutledge, "Psychological Power of Storytelling."
2   Grahn, "Our Bonding."
3   Federici, *Witches, Witch-Hunting, and Women*, 88.
4   Dimmick, "Inspired by Ruth Bader Ginsburg."
5   Libera, "Creating Circles," 3.
6   Starhawk, *The Spiral Dance*, 36.
7   Wigington, "Perfect Love, Perfect Trust."
8   Page, "Powerful Women Work Together."
9   Harris, "Healing Through (Re)Membering," 258, 262.
10   Harris, "Brave Together."
11   Goode, "We Are Waking Up."
12   Goode, "We Are Waking Up."
13   Armour-Lynx and Beausejour. "Storytelling and Healing."

14 Armour-Lynx and Beausejour. "Storytelling and Healing."

15 Absolon, "Indigenous Wholistic Theory."

16 Lorde, "A Woman Speaks."

17 Lorde, "A Woman Speaks."

18 Lorde, "Open Letter to Mary Daly," 70.

19 Lorde, *Sister Outsider*, back cover.

20 AfroMarxist. "Contemporary Woman Poets."

21 Angela Davis, "Angela Davis on Audre Lorde."

22 Lorde, "Age, Race, Class and Sex," 116.

23 Berano, "Introduction," 8–9.

24 Smith, "Anything That We Do."

25 Audre Lorde, "Learning from the 60s," speech at Harvard University, February 1982.

26 Lorde, "Age, Race, Class and Sex," 116.

27 Evans, "Crushing on Brené Brown."

28 Lorde, "Coal."

29 Lorde, "Transformation of Silence into Language and Action," 41–44.

30 Lorde, *Zami*, 4.

31 Lorde, *Zami*, 81.

32 Lorde. *Zami*, 98.

33 Lorde, "Age, Race, Class and Sex," 114.

34 De Veaux, *Warrior Poet*, 14.

35 De Veaux, *Warrior Poet*, 17.

36 Lorde, "A Woman Speaks."

37 Lorde, "A Woman Speaks."

38 Lorde, "Open Letter to Mary Daly," 66–71.

39 Wikipedia, "Mary Daly."

40 Lorde, "Open Letter to Mary Daly," 66–71.

41 Lorde, "Open Letter to Mary Daly," 66–71.

42 Lorde, "Open Letter to Mary Daly,"66–71.

43 Lorde, "Open Letter to Mary Daly," 66–71.

44 Lorde, "From the House of Yemanja" and "The Winds of Orisha."

45 Lorde, "Reading at Amerika Haus Berlin, 1984."

46 Lorde, "Equinox."

47 Lorde, *Cancer Journals*, 61.

48 From poems "House of Yemanjá" and "A Woman Speaks."

49 Lorde, "Age, Race, Class, and Sex," 123.

Chapter 9

1 Madeline Miller, *Circe*, 343.

2 Shaw, "Cerridwen, Dark Goddess."

3 Haraway, *Staying with Trouble*, 396.

4 Beyer, "Know 10 Plants Deeply" (lightly edited for clarity).

5 Skinner, "The Hidden Cosmos."

6 Beyer, "Know 10 Plants Deeply."

7 Beyer, "Know 10 Plants Deeply."

8 Strand, "We Are the Product."

9 Schulke, *Veneficium*, 25.

10 Matyssek and Lüttge, "Gaia."

11 Madeline Miller, *Circe*, 428.

12 Haraway, *Staying with Trouble*, Location 704.

13 Strand, "What Is Poison?"

14 Thompson, "How Witches' Brews Helped."

15 Thompson, "How Witches' Brews Helped."

16 Chidgey, "Abortion Democracy."

17 Rippey, "I Started to See."

18 Boisvert, "Colonial Hell and Female Slave Resistance," 70.

19 Campbell, "Abortion Remedies."

20 O'Brien, "Eat Like a Medieval Saint."

21 Mangelsdorf, "Beerstory 101."

22 Skinner, "Collaborate with These Beings." (Edited for clarity.)

23 Beyer, "Folk Magic of von Bingen."

24 Uehleke et al., "Correct Herbal Claims?"

25 Medievalists.net, "Herbal Cures of von Bingen."

26 Maddocks, *Woman of Her Age*, 136.

27 Strand, "We Are the Product."

28 Hey, "Attunement and Multispecies Communication."

29 Hey, "Attunement and Multispecies Communication."

30 Hey, "Attunement and Multispecies Communication."

31 Sender et al., "Revised Estimates for Bacteria Cells."

32 Hey, "Attunement and Multispecies Communication."

33 Strand, "We Are the Product."

34 Frost, *You Are the Medicine*, xviii, and "You Are The Medicine."

35 Beyer, "Know 10 Plants Deeply."

36 Chin, "How to Feed a Protest."

Chapter 10

1 Woolfolk, *Only Astrology Book*, 54.

2 Huxley, *Doors of Perception*.

3 Peek, *African Divination Systems*, 2.

4 Esselmont, "Hi, I'm Brigit."

5 Mui, "Queering the Church."

6 *Missing Witches*, "Stellar and Star Studded Astrology."

7 *Missing Witches*, "Stellar and Star Studded Astrology."

8 *Missing Witches*, "Stellar and Star Studded Astrology."

9 *Missing Witches*, "Stellar and Star Studded Astrology."

10 Sparkly Kat, *Post-Colonial Astrology*, 302.

11 *Missing Witches*, "Stellar and Star Studded Astrology."

12 Alberto, Interview with authors.

13 González-Wippler, *Santeria*, 121.

14 Wikipedia, "Patience Worth."

15 I hope you don't need me to tell you this, but ... please, for the love of all that is sacred, *do not* attempt to give yourself a head injury to obtain psychic powers. It won't work and you'll just hurt yourself.

16 Rucker, "Conjure, Magic, and Power," 85.

17 Utu, *Conjuring Harriet*, 16–18.

18 *Missing Witches*, "Stellar and Star Studded Astrology."

19 Thea Anderson, "Harriet Tubman as Magical."

20 *Missing Witches*, "Stellar and Star Studded Astrology."

21 *Missing Witches*, "Stellar and Star Studded Astrology."

22 Marie, "Book Is Written by White Eyes."

23 Sanchez, "Decolonization Is for Everyone."

24 Cleveland, "God Is a Black Woman."

25 Wikipedia, "Ojo Caliente Hot Springs."

26 American Experience, "Native Americans and Mount Rushmore."

27 Wise, "This Is the Frightening Way."

28 National Park Service, "Apache Before 1861."

29 Wikipedia, "Victorio."

30 Mingren, "Lozen: Warrior Woman."

31 Aleshire, *Warrior Woman*, 55–57.

32 Trent, "Southern Writers."

33 Wikipedia, "Lozen."

34 Wikipedia, "Victorio's War."

35 Aleshire, *Warrior Woman*, 1.

36 Wise, "What Everyone Can Learn."
37 Olsson, *The Black Power Mixtape 1967–1975.*
38 Smith, "Anything That We Do."
39 Smith, "Anything That We Do."
40 Oxford Languages online.
41 *Missing Witches*, "Stellar and Star Studded Astrology."

Chapter 11

1 Terry Tempest Williams, *When Women Were Birds*, 39.
2 Condé, *I, Tituba*, 200.
3 Ffiona Morgan, *Wild Witches Don't Get the Blues*, 162.
4 P-Orridge, *Nonbinary*, 86.
5 Frías, "Hopeful for the Magical We Are Weaving."
6 Rosenberg, "Poetry Is the Only Thing."
7 Valiente, "All Acts of Love."
8 Illes, *Element Encyclopedia of 1000 Spells*, vi.
9 Grahn, "Our Bonding."
10 Varlow, "The World Will Trick You."
11 Toni Morrison, "No Place for Self-Pity."
12 Radziszewski, "World Needs You Witch."
13 Cleveland, "God Is a Black Woman."
14 In the Quran too, Witchcraft and sorcery are condemned by God (2:102).
15 Utu, *Conjuring Harriet*, 16.
16 Nittle, *Toni Morrison's Spiritual Vision*, 3.
17 Nittle, "Nadra Nittle on Toni Morrison's Spiritual Vision."
18 Hurston, *Mules and Men*, 280; Shone, "Reclaiming the Bible."
19 Shone, "Reclaiming the Bible."
20 Shone, "Reclaiming the Bible."
21 Cleveland, "God Is a Black Woman."
22 Aleshire, *Warrior Woman*, 57.
23 Bekisz and Muñoz, "Witches Found Justice!"
24 Bekisz and Muñoz, "Witches Found Justice!"
25 Lawyer Witch, "Lawyers Work Magick."
26 Terry Tempest Williams, *The Hour of Land*, 1.
27 Terry Tempest Williams. *Erosion*, Location 66 (Kindle).
28 Terry Tempest Williams. *Erosion*, Location 333 (Kindle).
29 Spoiler alert: as of this writing, Terry is alive and well. You can follow her on Twitter and I suggest you do.
30 Terry Tempest Williams, *When Women Were Birds*, 40.

31 Terry Tempest Williams, *Erosion*, 14.

32 Terry Tempest Williams. *Refuge*, 90.

33 Terry Tempest Williams, *When Women Were Birds*, 225.

34 Terry Tempest Williams, *When Women Were Birds*, 1–2.

35 Terry Tempest Williams, *Red*, 112.

36 Bailey, "5 Powerful Health Benefits."

37 Calonne, *Diane Di Prima*, 64–89.

38 Goodyear, "Beat Poet Diane di Prima."

39 Cintoya Brown was convicted of murder at age sixteen when she shot a man to whom she had been trafficked for sex. Cintoya was released from prison after her case went viral, attracting the attention of celebrities and other supporters who campaigned for her clemency.

40 De Veaux, *Warrior Poet*, 22.

41 *Scientific American*, "Sarcasm Spurs Creative Thinking."

Chapter 12

1 Peck, "Remember Your Dreams."

2 Adorno, *Minima Moralia*.

3 Carrington, *Down Below*, 19.

4 Peck, "Remember Your Dreams."

5 Peck, "Remember Your Dreams."

6 Riikka Ala-Hakula, "Asemic Occultism," 45.

7 Grant Morrison, "Pop Magic!" 21.

8 Carrington, *Down Below*, 133.

9 Ryzik, "Afrofuturistic Designs of 'Black Panther.'"

10 Specter, "In Modern Russia."

11 Iona Rozeal Brown, "Additional Artist Biographies."

12 Iona Rozeal Brown, "Additional Artist Biographies."

13 Baker Artist, "Mequitta Ahuja's Portfolio.

14 Richardson, *The Refusal of the Shadow*, 7.

15 Gagosian Gallery, "Emily Kame Kngwarreye."

16 Gayoso, "Janet Forrester Ngala."

17 Grant, "Austin Osman Spare."

18 Nelson, "Witch of Art World."

19 Nelson, "Witch of Art World."

20 Laden, "Witch Woman Sings."

21 Parsons, "Cinderella of the Wastelands."

22 Kansa, *Wormwood Star*, 21.

23 Nelson, "Cameron, Witch of the Art World."

24 Kansa, *Wormwood Star*, 35.

25 Atlas Obscura, "The Parsonage."

26 Wikipedia, *Thelema*.

27 Pendle, *Strange Angel*, 260.

28 Pendle, *Strange Angel*, 261.

29 Pendle, *Strange Angel*, 263–64.

30 Laden, "Cameron's Connections to Scientology."

31 Laden, "Cameron's Connections to Scientology."

32 Laden, "Witch Woman Sings."

33 With a bias against unwealthy Jews. See Argote, "Jewish Migration to Mexico," 1.

34 Nelson, "Witch of Art World."

35 Feliz, "Cure Is in Venom."

36 Nelson, "Witch of Art World."

37 Nelson, "Witch of Art World."

38 Kansa, *Wormwood Star*, 189.

39 Kansa, *Wormwood Star*, 189.

40 Laden, "Witch Woman Sings."

41 Laden, "Witch Woman Sings."

42 Laden, "Witch Woman Sings."

43 Octavia Butler, *Earthseed*, 16.

44 Nelson, "Witch of Art World."

45 "Cinderella of the Wastelands."

46 "Cinderella of the Wastelands."

47 Tsumura, "You Have to Believe in Magic."

48 Sanchez, "Decolonization Is for Everyone."

Chapter 13

1 Mies and Shiva, *Ecofeminism*, 5.

2 Leonard Cohen, *The Energy of Slaves*.

3 Gore, *Bluebird*.

4 Gore, "Can You be a Writer AND a Mother?"

5 Gore, "Can You be a Writer AND a Mother?"

6 Harriet Staff, "Diane di Prima."

7 Calonne, *Diane di Prima*, 693.

8 Calonne, *Diane di Prima*, 639.

9 Goldman, *Living My Life*, 56.

10 Fiala, "Anarchism."

11 *Missing Witches*, "Afterparty!!"

12   Haraway, *Staying with Trouble*, Location 547.
13   Erik Davis, "Technopagans."
14   Laurel, *Computers as Theatre*, 359.
15   Boal, "Theatre of the Oppressed."
16   Laurel, "Activism for a New World."
17   Hunter, " Magic Is Anti-Capitalist."
18   Cognitive Behavioral Therapy Los Angeles, "Act as If"; Laurel, "Design Animism."
19   Laurel, "Design Animism."
20   Laurel, "Design Animism."

BIBLIOGRAPHY
FOR NEW MOON MAGIC

Absolon, Kathy. "Indigenous Wholistic Theory: A Knowledge Set for Practice." *First Peoples Child and Family Review* 5, no. 2 (2010): 4–123. https://doi.org /10.7202/1068933ar.

Adams, George. *Physical and Ethereal Spaces*. London: Rudolf Steiner Press, 1965. https://archive.org/stream/AdamsGeorgePhysicalAndEtherealSpaces /Adams%20George%20-%20Physical%20and%20ethereal%20spaces_djvu.txt.

Adorno, Theodor. *Minima Moralia: Reflections from Damaged Life*. Translated by E. F. N. Jephcott. New York: Verso Books, 2020.

af Klint, Hilma. *Notes and Methods*. Christine Burgin, ed. Chicago: University of Chicago Press, 2018.

AfroMarxist. "Contemporary Woman Poets with Audre Lorde and Marge Piercy." YouTube. https://www.youtube.com/watch?v=8Jfp5Vc758s&list=PLjj3W4i3 WnZ6lfdXu2Zziz6vFZJmHXh3l&index=2.

Ahuja, Mequitta. *Tress IV*. Minneapolis Institute of Art. Accessed September 10, 2022. https://collections.artsmia.org/art/108869/tress-iv-mequitta-ahuja.

Akst, Jef. "The Influence of Soil on Immune Health." *The Scientist*. January 8, 2020. www.the-scientist.com/news-opinion/the-influence-of-soil-on-human -health-66885.

Ala-Hakula, Riikka. *"Asemic Occultism: The Magical System of Austin Spare's Sigils."* In *Understanding the Unknown* edited by Laura Thursby, 45–52. Interdisciplinary Press, 2016.

Alberto, Angela. Interview with authors. February 2022.

Alchetron. "Buffy Sainte Marie." alchetron.com. Last updated April 11, 2022. https://alchetron.com/Buffy-Sainte-Marie.

Aleshire, Peter. *Warrior Woman: The Story of Lozen, Apache Warrior and Shaman*. New York: St. Martin's Press, 2015. Kindle.

Ally. "Hattie 'The Tree Lady of Brooklyn' Carthan." Brooklyn Library blog. February 8, 2017. www.bklynlibrary.org/blog/2017/02/08/hattie-tree-lady-brooklyn.

American Experience. "Native Americans and Mount Rushmore." Accessed September 8, 2022. www.pbs.org/wgbh/americanexperience/features/rushmore -sioux/.

Anderson, Jarod K. (@JarodAnderson). "Dear Science, Humans Conceptualize Complex Ideas through Metaphor Not Jargon." Twitter feed. December 15, 2021. https://twitter.com/jarodanderson/status/1471056936137285636.

Anderson, Thea. "Harriet Tubman as a Magical, Mercurial Figure: An Astrological Analysis of the Combahee River Raid." *Mountain Astrologer*. June 7, 2021. www.astro.com/astrology/tma_article210706_e.htm.

———. "The Past Is Right Here, It's Pressing on Us." *Missing Witches* (podcast), Episode 135 Witches Found. April 21, 2022. www.missingwitches.com /2022/04/21/ep-135-wf-thea-anderson-the-past-is-right-here-its-pressing -on-us/.

Angelou, Maya (@DrMayaAngelou). "Try to Live Your Life in a Way That You Will Not Regret Years of Useless Virtue and Inertia and Timidity." Twitter post. May 2, 2021. https://twitter.com/drmayaangelou/status /138891213125415936?lang=en.

Argote, Gisela. "The Jewish Migration to Mexico during Nazi Germany." *Pathways: A Journal of Humanistic and Social Inquiry* 1, no. 3 (February 2021): 1–14. https://repository.upenn.edu/cgi/viewcontent.cgi?article=1035&context =pathways_journal.

Armour-Lynx, Amanda, and Michelle Beausejour." Storytelling and Healing." *Missing Witches* (podcast), Episode 53 Witches Found Pink Moon part 2. April 14, 2020. www.missingwitches.com/2020/04/14/pink-moon-part -2-with-amanda-amour-lynx-and-michelle-beausejour-storytelling-and -healing/.

Arya, Shaurya. "Gaura Devi: Mother of Chipko Movement." *Himalayan Buzz*. Accessed August 1, 2022. www.himalayanbuzz.com/gaura-devi-1925-91 -mother-of-chipko-movement/.

Asante, Molefi Kete, and Ama Mazama. *Encyclopedia of African Religion*. Thousand Oaks, CA: Sage Publications, 2009.

Atlas Obscura. "The Parsonage." Accessed September 10, 2022. https://www .atlasobscura.com/places/the-parsonage-jack-parson-s-burned-down-house -pasadena-california.

Bailey, Kasee. "5 Powerful Health Benefits of Journaling." Intermountain Healthcare. July 31, 2018. https://intermountainhealthcare.org/blogs/topics/live -well/2018/07/5-powerful-health-benefits-of-journaling/.

Baker Artist. "Mequitta Ahuja's Portfolio." Baker Artist Portfolios. Accessed September 10, 2022. https://bakerartist.org/portfolios/mequitta-ahuja.

Barnstaple, Rebecca, and Joseph FX DeSouza. "Dance Is a Healing Medicine." *Hidden Witches* (podcast), Episode 96 WF. July 23, 2021. www.missingwitches .com/2021/07/23/ep-96-wf-rebecca-barnstaple-and-joseph-fx-desouza-dance -is-a-healing-medicine/.

Becker, Cynthia. "The Kahina: The Female Face of Berber History." *Mizan.* October 26, 2015. https://mizanproject.org/the-kahina-the-female-face-of -berber-history/.

Beete, Paulette. "Artists Reflect on What It Means to Make Good Trouble." *National Endowment for the Arts* (blog). February 24, 2021. www.arts.gov /stories/blog/2021/artists-reflect-what-it-means-make-good-trouble.

Bekisz, Melissa, and Pamela Muñoz, "Witches Found Justice! Litha 2020 with Melissa Bekisz and Pamela Muñoz." *Missing Witches* (podcast), Episode 58. June 20, 2020. www.missingwitches.com/2020/06/20/justice-litha-2020 -with-melissa-bekisz-and-pamela-munoz/.

Belcourt, Christi. *Medicines to Help Us: Traditional Métis Plant Use.* Saskatoon, Canada: Gabriel Dumont Institute, 2007.

Bennett, Marguerite. "Garden." In *Becoming Dangerous: Witchy Femmes, Queer Conjurers, and Magical Rebels.* Katie West and Jasmine Elliott, eds. 81. Newburyport, MA: Red Wheel/Wiser, 2019.

Berano, Nancy K. "Introduction." In *Sister Outsider* by Audre Lorde, 8–12. Berkeley, CA: Crossing Press, 2007.

Beth, Rae. *The Hedge Witch's Way: Magical Spirituality for the Lone Spellcaster.* Marlborough, Wiltshire: Robert Hale, 2001.

Beyer, Rebecca. "The Folk Magic of Hildegard von Bingen's Herbs." Blood and Spicebush. Accessed September 7, 2022. www.bloodandspicebush.com/store /p116/The_Folk_Magic_of_Hildegard_von_Bingen%27s_Herbs.html.

———. "You Can Know 10 Plants Deeply and Be a Wonderful Healer." *Missing Witches* (podcast), Episode 120 WF. January 27, 2022. www.missingwitches .com/2022/01/27/ep-120-wf-rebecca-beyer-you-can-know-10-plants-deeply -and-be-a-wonderful-healer/.

BioArt Coven. "The BioArt Coven Manifesto." *Occult Studies Vol 2: Revolution.* Snake Hair Press, Fall 2021.

Boal, Augusto. "Theatre of the Oppressed." ImaginAction. Accessed September 11, 2022. https://imaginaction.org/media/our-methods/theatre-of-the -oppressed-2.

Boisvert, Jayne. "Colonial Hell and Female Slave Resistance in Saint-Domingue." *Journal of Haitian Studies* 7, no. 1 (2001): 61–76.

Brake, Justin. "How Canada Can Give Land Back." *Breach Media.* January 29, 2022. https://breachmedia.ca/how-canada-can-give-land-back/.

Brett, Michael, and Elizabeth Fentress. *The Berbers: The Peoples of Africa*. Oxford, UK: Blackwell, 1996.

Britannica. s.v. "Sacrifices." Accessed August 25, 2022. www.britannica.com/topic/prehistoric-religion/Sacrifices.

Brooklynn. "Sonic Witchcraft, Neurodiversity and Being in Stillness." *Missing Witches* (podcast), Episode 116 WF, December 30, 2021. www.missingwitches.com/2021/12/30/ep-116-wf-brooklynn-sonic-witchcraft-neurodiversity-and-being-in-stillness/.

brown, adrienne maree. "for George Floyd: fire." May 29, 2020. http://adriennemareebrown.net/2020/05/29/for-george-floyd-fire/.

Brown, Iona Rozeal. "Additional Artist Biographies." In *African-American Art: A Visual and Cultural History*, by Lisa Farrington. Oxford University Press, 2016. Accessed August 28, 2022. https://global.oup.com/us/companion.websites/9780199995394/ch14/bio/.

Buggs, Sophia. "What If Urban Agriculture Could Heal Not Just Our Bodies, But Our Souls"? *TEDx Mansfield*. YouTube. April 24, 2019. www.ted.com/talks/sophia_buggs_what_if_urban_agriculture_could_heal_not_just_our_bodies_but_our_souls.

Butler, Octavia. *Earthseed: Parable of the Sower and Parable of the Talents*. New York: Open Road, 1999.

Caduceus Books. "Lady Frieda Harris, Masonic Tracing Boards." Accessed August 27, 2022. www.caduceusbooks.com/nextlist-7-17/index.htm.

Calonne, David Stephen. *Diane di Prima: Visionary Poetics and the Hidden Religions*. New York: Bloomsbury Academic, 2020. iBooks.

Calkin, Sydney, and Monika Ewa Kaminska. "Persistence and Change in Morality Policy: The Role of the Catholic Church in the Politics of Abortion in Ireland and Poland." *Feminist Review* 124, no. 1 (March 2020): 86–102. https://doi.org/10.1177/0141778919894451.

Campbell, Olivia. "Abortion Remedies from a Medieval Catholic Nun(!)." *JSTOR Daily*. October 13, 2021. https://daily.jstor.org/abortion-remedies-medieval-catholic-nun/.

Carrington, Leonora. *Down Below*. New York: New York Review Books, 2017. iBooks.

CBC Radio. "What Does Buffy Sainte-Marie Believe? Tapestry. Last updated December 30, 2016. www.cbc.ca/radio/tapestry/what-does-buffy-sainte-marie-believe-1.3524933.

Chakraverti, Ipisita Roy. *Beloved Witch: An Autobiography*. N.p.: Harper Collins Publishers India, 2010. EPUB 2. Adobe DRM.

Chapman, Alan. *Advanced Magick for Beginners*. London: Aeon Books, 2008.

Chidgey, Red. "Abortion Democracy: An Interview with Sarah Diehl." *Feminist Review* 99, no. 1 (November 1, 2011): 106–112. https://doi.org/10.1057 /fr.2011.37.

Chin, Monica. "How to Feed a Protest." *The Verge*. August 31, 2020. https:// www.theverge.com/21377132/mutual-aid-solidarity-protests-food-assistance -police-brutality.

Chitnis, Rucha. "The Original Tree Huggers: Let Us Not Forget Their Sacrifice." *Women's Earth Alliance*. April 22, 2013. https://womensearthalliance.org /wea-voices/the-original-tree-huggers-let-us-not-forget-their-sacrifice-on -earth-day/.

"Cinderella of the Wastelands, A Poem by Marjorie Cameron." Tsunami Books, November 23, 2016. https://tsunamibooks.jimdofree.com/2016/11/23 /cinderella-of-the-wastelands-a-poem-by-marjorie-cameron/.

Cleveland, Christena. "God Is a Black Woman." *Missing Witches* (podcast), Episode 123WF. March 3, 2022. www.missingwitches.com/2022/03/03/ep-123 -wf-christena-cleveland-god-is-a-black-woman/.

Clifton, Lucile. *Good Woman: Poems and a Memoir 1969–1980*. Rochester, NY: BOA Editions, 2018. iBooks.

Cognitive Behavioral Therapy Los Angeles, "Act as If." (blog). Accessed August 23, 2022. https://cogbtherapy.com/cbt-blog/2013/8/26/act-as-if.

Cohen, Leonard. *The Energy of Slaves*. London: Jonathan Cape Ltd., 1972.

Condé, Maryse. *I, Tituba: Black Witch of Salem*. Charlottesville, VA: University of Virginia Press, 1992.

Cosmogyny. "Your Body Is an Ancestor." Instagram post. October 30, 2021. www.instagram.com/p/CVqBtklFXh9/.

Crowley, Aleister, to Ben Stubbins. April 22, 1942. Yorke Collection, Warburg Institute Archives, University of London, NS 117.l.c.

Cunningham, Scott. *Earth Power: Techniques of Natural Magic*. St. Paul, MN: Llewellyn Publications, 2003.

———. *Cunningham's Encyclopedia of Magical Herbs*. St. Paul, MN: Llewellyn Publications, 1985.

Daly, Mary. Letter to Audre Lorde, reprinted www.historyisaweapon.com/defcon1 /lordeopenlettertomarydaly.html.

Danticat, Edwidge. *Krik? Krak!* New York: Soho Press, 1993.

Davis, Angela. "Angela Davis on Audre Lorde." March 23, 2014. www.youtube.com /watch?v=EpYdfcvYPEQ.

Davis, Erik. "Technopagans: May the Astral Plane Be Reborn in Cyberspace." *Wired*. July 1, 1995. www.wired.com/1995/07/technopagans/.

Debakcsy, Dale. "Theano of Croton and the Pythagorean Women of Ancient Greece." *Women You Should Know.* February 27, 2019. https://womenyoushouldknow.net/theano-of-croton-pythagorean/.

Despret, Vinciane. *What Would Animals Say If We Asked the Right Questions?* Translated by Brett Buchanan. Minneapolis: University of Minnesota Press, 2016. iBooks.

De Veaux, Alexis. *Warrior Poet: A Biography of Audre Lorde.* New York: W. W. Norton, 2004.

Dickens, Risa, and Amy Torok. *Missing Witches: Recovering Histories of Feminist Magic,* Chapter 8. Berkeley, CA: North Atlantic Books, 2021.

Diggins, Julia E. *String, Straightedge, and Shadow: The Story of Geometry.* Boulder, CO: Jamie York Press, 2021.

Dimmick, Robert B. "Inspired by Ruth Bader Ginsburg." *Etiquetteer* 19, no. 53 (September 20, 2020). www.etiquetteer.com/columns/2020/9/20/inspired -by-ruth-bader-ginsburg-vol-19-issue-53.

———. "The War Is the War for the Human Imagination." *Missing Witches* (podcast), episode 82 MW. March 28, 2021. www.missingwitches.com/2021/03 /28/ep-82-mw-diane-di-prima-the-war-is-the-war-for-the-human -imagination/.

DNA Tests. "How Much DNA Do Humans Share with Other Animals and Plants?" Accessed August 12, 2022. https://thednatests.com/how-much -dna-do-humans-share-with-other-animals/.

Dunham, Katherine. *Island Possessed.* Garden City, NY: Doubleday, 1969.

DuQuette, Lon Milo. *Understanding Aleister Crowley's Thoth Tarot.* Newburyport, MA: Red Wheel/Weiser Books, 2017.

Earthbound Futures. "QUEER the Heroes Journey and Find Your Inner Ally." *Missing Witches* (podcast), Episode WF LITHA 2021. June 20, 2021. www .missingwitches.com/2021/06/20/wf-litha-2021-earth-bound-futures-queer -the-heroes-journey-and-find-your-inner-ally/.

Editorial Team. "Queen Tin Hinan: Founder of the Tuaregs." *Think Africa.* January 10, 2019. https://thinkafrica.net/tin-hinan/.

English, Diedre, and Barbara Eirenrich. *Witches, Midwives, and Nurses: A History of Women Healers.* 2nd ed. New York: The Feminist Press, 2010.

Esselmont, Brigit. "Hi, I'm Brigit." Biddy Tarot. Accessed September 7, 2022. www.biddytarot.com/about/.

Ethical Source. "Ethical Source: Open Source, Evolved." December 2022. https://ethicalsource.dev/.

Evans, Marci. "Crushing on Brené Brown." Marci RD Nutrition. October 2, 2013. https://marcird.com/brene-brown/.

Fancourt, Daisy, Rosie Perkins, Sara Ascenso, Livia A. Carvalho, Andrew Step-
toe, and Aaron Williamon. "Effects of Group Drumming Interventions on
Anxiety, Depression, Social Resilience and Inflammatory Immune Response
among Mental Health Service Users." *PLOS One.* March 14, 2016. https://
journals.plos.org/plosone/article?id=10.1371/journal.pone.0151136.

Farmelo, Graham. "Dirac's Hidden Geometry." *Nature* 437, no. 323 (2005).
www.nature.com/articles/437323a.

———. *The Strangest Man: The Hidden Life of Paul Dirac, Mystic of the Atom.* New
York: Basic Books, 2009. www.softouch.on.ca/kb/data/Strangest%20Man
%20(The).pdf.

Faun. "On Interspecies Humility." *Queer Nature: Critical Naturalist* (blog). April
2019. www.queernature.org/criticalnaturalistblog.

Favale, Abagail. "Hildegard of Bingen's Vital Contribution to the Concept of
Woman." *Church of Life Journal.* December 11, 2018. https://churchlifejournal
.nd.edu/articles/hildegard-of-bingens-vital-contribution-to-the-concept-of
-woman/.

Federici, Silvia. *Caliban and the Witch: Women, the Body and Primitive Accumula-
tion.* Brooklyn, NY: Autonomedia, 2004.

———. *Re-Enchanting the World.* Oakland, CA: PM Press, 2018.

———. *Witches, Witch-Hunting, and Women.* Oakland, CA: PM Press, 2018.

Feldmann, Erica. "Like Witchcraft, Anti-capitalism Is a Practice." *Missing Witches*
(podcast), Episode 145 WF. June 2, 2022. www.missingwitches.com/2022
/06/02/ep-145-wf-erica-feldmann-like-witchcraft-anti-capitalism-is-a
-practice/.

Feliz, Star Catherine. "The Cure Is in the Venom," *BLUE.* Accessed August 28,
2022. https://b-l-u-e.online/star-catherine-feliz/.

Ferre, Lux. "Marinette." *Occult World.* August 3, 2017. https://occult-world.com
/marinette/.

Fiala, Andrew. "Anarchism." *Stanford Encyclopedia of Philosophy.* October 3, 2017.
https://plato.stanford.edu/entries/anarchism/.

Fick, Carolyn E. *The Making of Haiti: Saint Domingue Revolution from Below.*
Knoxville: University of Tennessee Press, 1990.

Fox, Matthew. Introduction to *Hildegard von Bingen's Mystical Visions: Translated
from Scivias.* Trans. Bruce Hozeski. Oakland, CA: O.P. Holy Names College,
1985.

Frías, Edgar Fabián. "I'm Hopeful for the Magical We Are All Weaving . . . We Are
Transforming Hierarchies." *Missing Witches* (podcast), Episode 137 WF. April 28,
2022. www.missingwitches.com/2022/04/28/ep-137-wf-edgar-fabian-frias-we
-are-transforming-hierarchies-we-are-transforming-age-old-societal-structures/.

Frawsen, Ulbani Ait, and L'Hocine Ukerdis. "The Origins of Amazigh Women's Power in North Africa: An Historical Overview." *Al-Raida Journal* 1 (2003), 17–23. https://doi.org/10.32380/alrj.v0i0.418.

Frost, Asha. *You Are the Medicine: 13 Moons of Indigenous Wisdom, Ancestral Connection, and Animal Spirit Guidance.* Carlsbad, CA: Hay House UK Limited, 2022.

———. "You Are the Medicine." *Missing Witches* (podcast), Episode 139 WF. May 5, 2022. www.missingwitches.com/2022/05/05/ep-139-wf-asha -frost-you-are-the-medicine/.

Gago, Veronica. "Spirituality as a Force of Rebellion: The Movement for Legal Abortion in Argentina." *Verso* (blog). June 18, 2018. www.versobooks.com /blogs/3886-spirituality-as-a-force-of-rebellion-the-movement-for-legal -abortion-in-argentina.

Gagosian Gallery, "Emily Kame Kngwarreye. Accessed September 21, 2022. https://gagosian.com/artists/emily-kame-kngwarreye/.

Gamblin, Ronald. "LAND BACK! What Do We Mean?" *4Rs Youth Movement.* Accessed August 24, 2022. http://4rsyouth.ca/land-back-what-do-we-mean/.

Garcia, Amanda Yates. *Initiated: Memoir of a Witch.* New York: Grand Central Publishing, 2019.

Gary, Gemma. *Traditional Witchcraft, A Cornish Book of Ways.* Cornwall, UK: Troy Books, 2008.

Gay, Roxanne. *Ayiti.* New York: First Grove Atlantic Press, 2018. iBooks.

Gayoso, Adrienne L. "5 Fast Facts: Janet Forrester Ngala." *Broad Strokes* (blog). National Museum of Women in the Arts. Accessed August 28, 2022. https:// nmwa.org/blog/from-the-collection/5-fast-facts-janet-forrester-ngala/.

Gino, Francesca, and Michael I. Norton. "Why Rituals Work: There Are Real Benefits to Rituals, Religious and Otherwise." *Scientific American.* May 14, 2013. www.scientificamerican.com/article/why-rituals-work/.

Godley, A. D. (ed/trans.) *Herodotus: The Histories.* Cambridge, NJ: Harvard University Press, 1920.

Goldman, Emma. *Living My Life.* New York: Knopf, 1934.

González-Wippler, Migene. *The Complete Book of Spells, Ceremonies and Magic.* Woodbury, MN: Llewellyn Publications, 1978.

———. "How Infinite My Possibilities." *Missing Witches* (podcast), Episode 40. October 13, 2019. www.missingwitches.com/2019/10/13/missing-witches -migene-gonzalez-wippler-how-infinite-my-possibilities/.

———. *The Santeria Experience.* Hoboken, NJ: Prentice Hall, 1982.

———. *Santeria: The Religion: Faith, Rites, Magic.* St Paul, MN: Llewellyn Publications, 2018.

———. *What Happens after Death: Scientific & Personal Evidence for Survival*. St. Paul, MN: Llewellyn Publications, 1997.

Goodall, Emily. Unpublished conversation with the author. May 2022.

Goode, Starr. "We Are Waking Up . . . Popping the Bubble of Patriarchy's Spell." *Missing Witches* (podcast), Episode 85 WF. April 7, 2021. www.missingwitches .com/2021/04/07/ep-85-wf-starr-goode-we-are-waking-up-popping-the -bubble-of-patriarchys-spell/.

Goodyear, Sheena. "Beat Poet Diane di Prima Taught Her Kids to Question Authority and Believe in Their Own Creativity." *CBC Radio: As It Happens*. Last updated October 27, 2020. www.cbc.ca/radio/asithappens/as-it-happens -tuesday-edition-1.5778707/beat-poet-diane-di-prima-taught-her-kids-to -question-authority-and-believe-in-their-own-creativity-1.5778900.

Gore, Ariel. *Bluebird: Women and the New Psychology of Happiness*. New York: Farrar, Straus and Giroux, 2010.

———. "Can You Be a Writer AND a Mother?" *Psychology Today*. April 14, 2010. www.psychologytoday.com/ca/blog/women-and-happiness/201004/can -you-be-writer-and-mother.

Grahn, Judy. *Blood, Bread, and Roses: How Menstruation Created the World*. Boston: Beacon Press, 1994.

———. "Our Bonding Is What Makes a Revolution Happen." *Missing Witches* (podcast), Episode 129 WF. March 31, 2022. www.missingwitches.com /2022/03/31/ep-129-wf-judy-grahn-our-bonding-is-what-makes-a -revolution-happen/.

Granddaughter Crow. "What a Person Believes Constitutes How They Behave in the World." *Missing Witches* (podcast), Episode 148 WF. June 16, 2022. www.missingwitches.com/2022/06/16/ep-148-wf-granddaughter-crow-what -a-person-believes-constitutes-how-they-behave-in-the-world/.

Grandjean, Philippe. "Paracelsus Revisited: The Dose Concept in a Complex World." *Basic and Clinical Pharmacology and Toxicology* 119, no. 2 (August 2016): 126–32. https://doi.org/10.1111/bcpt.12622.

Grant, Kenneth. "Austin Osman Spare: An Introduction to His Psycho-Magical Philosophy." *Pastelegram* 8 (Fall 2014). http://pastelegram.org/e/126.

Gray, Joy "Granddaughter Crow." "The Wisdom of the Natural World." *Missing Witches* (podcast), Episode 100. September 29, 2021. www.missingwitches .com/2021/09/29/e100-wf-granddaughter-crow-the-wisdom-of-the-natural -world/.

Halprin, Anna. *Dance as a Healing Art: Returning to Health with Movement and Imagery*. Mendocino, CA: LifeRhythm Books, 2000.

Halprin, Anna, and Allan Stinson. *Circle the Earth Manual: A Guide for Dancing Peace with the Planet.* Kentfield, CA: Anna Halprin, 1987.

Haraway, Donna. *Staying with the Trouble: Making Kin in the Chthulucene.* Durham, NC: Duke University Press, 2016. iBooks.

Harriet Staff. "Diane Di Prima, Denise Levertov, Nikki Giovanni, & More Protest Poets to Read Now." *Harriet* (blog), Poetry Foundation. February 9, 2017. https://www.poetryfoundation.org/harriet-books/2017/02/diane-di-prima-denise-levertov-nikki-giovanni-more-protest-poets-to-read-now.

Harris, Lakeesha. "Brave Together." *Missing Witches* (podcast), Episode 94 Juneteenth. June 19, 2021. www.missingwitches.com/2021/06/19/ep94-juneteenth-w-lakeesha-harris-brave-together/.

———. "Healing Through (Re)Membering and (Re)Claiming Ancestral Knowledge about Black Witch Magic. In *Black Women's Liberatory Pedagogies: Resistance, Transformation, and Healing Within and Beyond the Academy*, edited by Olivia N. Perlow, Durene I. Wheeler, Sharon L. Bethea, and BarBara M. Scott. New York: Palgrave Macmillan, 2018.

Harrison, Michaela A. "We Are One." *Missing Witches* (podcast), Episode 143. May 19, 2022. www.missingwitches.com/2022/05/19/ep-143-wf-michaela-a-harrison-we-are-one/.

Harvard Health Publishing, "The Power of the Placebo Effect: Treating Yourself with Your Mind Is Possible, But There Is More to the Placebo Effect Than Positive Thinking." Harvard Medical School. December 13. 2021. www.health.harvard.edu/mental-health/the-power-of-the-placebo-effect.

"The Herbal Cures of Hildegard von Bingen—Was She Right?" Medievalists.net. Accessed December 16, 2022. www.medievalists.net/2016/07/the-herbal-cures-of-hildegard-von-bingen-was-she-right/.

Hermetic Library. "Correspondence between Aleister Crowley and Frieda Harris." Harris to Crowley, May 10, 1939. https://hermetic.com/crowley/crowley-harris.

"Herodotus Book 4: Melpomene [170]." Sacred-texts.com. Accessed November 22, 2022. www.sacred-texts.com/cla/hh/hh4170.htm.

Hey, Maya. "Attunement and Multispecies Communication in Fermentation." *Feminist Philosophy Quarterly* 7, no. 3 (2021): 1–25. https://ojs.lib.uwo.ca/index.php/fpq/article/view/10846/11376.

Hirschberg, H. Z. (J. W.). "The Problem of the Judaized Berbers." *Journal of African History* 4, no. 3 (1963): 313–39.

Hoffman, Claas. "Projective Synthetic Geometry in Lady Frieda Harris' Tarot Paintings and in Aleister Crowley's *Book of the Law.*" Parareligion. Accessed August 28, 2022. www.parareligion.ch/dplanet/stephen/claas/olive_e.html.

Huebner, Louise. *Seduction Through Witchcraft.* Warner Brothers, 1969.

Hunter, WhiteFeather. "Magic Is Inherently Anti-Capitalist." *Missing Witches* (podcast), Episode 43 WF, October 23, 2019. www.missingwitches.com/2019 /10/23/witches-found-whitefeather-hunter/.

———. "Making Manifestos w WhiteFeather Hunter of BioArt Coven." *Missing Witches* (podcast), Episode 98 Mabon 2021. September 21, 2021. https:// whitefeatherhunter.net/2021/09/21/e98-mabon-2021-making-manifestos -w-whitefeather-hunter-of-bioart-coven/.

Hurston, Zora Neale. *Mules and Men.* New York: Harper Collins, 2008.

Huxley, Aldous. *The Doors of Perception.* New York: Harper & Row, 1954.

Illes, Judika. *The Element Encyclopedia of 1000 Spells: The Ultimate Reference Book for the Magical Arts.* New York: Harper Element, 2004.

Kaczynski, Richard. "Frieda Lady Harris." Hermetic Library. Accessed November 22, 2022. https://hermetic.com/sabazius/frieda-lady-harris.

———. "Frieda Lady Harris." United States Grand Lodge Ordo Templi Orientis. Accessed August 27, 2022. https://oto-usa.org/usgl/lion-eagle/frieda-lady -harris/.

Kahina, Nuuja. "Free People: The Imazighen of North Africa." *Independent Uncompromising Indigenous.* March 12, 2013. https://intercontinentalcry.org/ free-people-the-imazighen-of-north-africa/.

"The Kahina, Queen of the Berbers." *Black History Buff* (blog). March 6, 2019. www.blackhistorybuff.com/blogs/the-black-history-buff-blog/the-kahina -queen-of-the-berbers-ruled-688-705-ad.

Kansa, Spencer. *Wormwood Star: The Magickal Life of Marjorie Cameron.* Oxford: Mandrake of Oxford, 2020. Kindle.

Kauai's Hindu Monastery. "The World of Siva's Sacred Song." himalayanacademy .com. Accessed August 24, 2022. www.himalayanacademy.com/looklisten/music.

Kimmerer, Robin Wall. *Braiding Sweetgrass: Indigenous Wisdom, Scientific Knowledge and the Teachings of Plants.* Minneapolis, MN: Milkweed Editions, 2013.

Kowalczyk, Devin. "What Is Dharma in Hinduism?" Study.com. Last modified December 29, 2021. https://study.com/academy/lesson/what-is-dharma-in -hinduism-definition-lesson-quiz.html.

Kwekudee. "Tuareg People: Africa's Blue People of the Desert." *Trip Down Memory Lane* (blog). February 20, 2014. https://kwekudee-tripdownmemory- lane.blogspot.com/2014/02/tuareg-people-africas-blue-people-of.html?m=1.

Laden, Tanja M. "Cameron's Connections to Scientology and Powerful Men Once Drew Headlines, But Now Her Art Is Getting Its Due." *LA Weekly.* October 8, 2014. www.laweekly.com/camerons-connections-to-scientology -and-powerful-men-once-drew-headlines-but-now-her-art-is-getting-its-due/.

———. "The Witch Woman Sings." *LA Weekly*, October 9, 2014. http://
digitalissue.laweekly.com/publication/?m=3660&i=228808&view=
articleBrowser&article_id=1834523&ver=html5.

Lamoureux, Annie. "Witches Found Spirit." *Missing Witches* (podcast), episode 8.
October 10, 2018. www.missingwitches.com/2018/10/10/episode-3a-witches
-found-spirit/.

Laurel, Brenda. "Activism for a New World." Commencement Address at California State University at Monterey Bay, May 19, 2000. www.tauzero.com
/Brenda_Laurel/Recent_Talks/CSUMBCommencmentSpeech.html.

———. *Computers as Theatre*, 2nd ed. Toronto: Addison-Wesley, 2013.

———. "Designed Animism." In *(Re)Searching the Digital Bauhaus*, edited by
Thomas Binder, Jonas Löwgren, and Lone Malmborg, 251–74. London:
Springer-Verlag, 2009.

Lawler, Lillian B. "Bee Dances and 'Sacred Bees.'" *The Classical Weekly* 47, no. 7
(Feb 15, 1954): 103–106. www.jstor.org/stable/4343554.

The Lawyer Witch (blog), "Lawyers Work Magick (aka Witchcraft!) Here, I'll
Show You." October 11, 2020. https://ladylawyerwitch.org/2020/10/11
/lawyers-work-magick-aka-witchcraft-here-ill-show-you/.

Ledesma, Loretta. "Grief Is a Dancer, a Teacher. Grief Is Spiralling, It Is the
Depth of Me." *Missing* Witches (podcast), Episode 171 Samhain 2022. October 31, 2022. www.missingwitches.com/2022/10/31/ep-171-samhain-2022
-grief-is-a-dancer-a-teacher-grief-is-spiralling-it-is-the-depth-of-me/.

Ledesma, Loretta (@). "I am not of the cosmos. I am primordial mud." Instagram.

Ledesma, Loretta, and Angela Alberto. "A Good Death." *Missing Witches* (podcast), Episode 73, Samhain 2020. October 31, 2020. www.missingwitches
.com/2020/10/31/samhain-2020-w-loretta-ledesma-and-angela-alberto-a
-good-death/.

Letzter, Rafi. "Mathematician Wins $3 Million Breakthrough Prize for 'Magic
Wand Theorem.'" *Live Science*. September 5, 2019. www.livescience.com
/breakthrough-prize-mathematics-2019-winners.html.

Libera, Caitlin. *Creating Circles of Power and Magic: A Woman's Guide to Sacred
Community*. Crossing Press, 1994.

Little, Callie. Unpublished conversation with author. June 22, 2022.

Little, Nadra. "On Toni Morrison's Spiritual Vision." *Missing Witches* (podcast),
Episode 107. October 24, 2021. www.missingwitches.com/2021/10/24/ep
-107-nadra-nittle-on-toni-morrisons-spiritual-vision/.

———. *Toni Morrison's Spiritual Vision: Faith, Folktales, and Feminism in Her Life
and Literature*. Augsburg Fortress Publishers. 2021.

Lola, Mama. "Spirit for EVERYBODY!" *Missing Witches,* Episode 11. October 21, 2018. www.missingwitches.com/2018/10/21/episode-5-mama-lola -spirit-for-everybody/.

Looi, Mun-Keat. "The Human Microbiome: Everything You Need to Know about the 39 Trillion Microbes That Call Our Bodies Home." *Science Focus.* July 14, 2020. www.sciencefocus.com/the-human-body/human-microbiome/.

Lorde, Audre. "Age, Race, Class, and Sex: Women Redefining Difference." In *Sister Outsider: Essays and Speeches.* Berkeley, CA: Crossing Press, 2007.

———. *The Cancer Journals.* New York: Penguin Classics, 2020.

———. "Coal." In *The Collected Poems of Audre Lorde.* New York: W. W. Norton and Company, 1997. Accessed at www.poetryfoundation.org/poems/42577 /coal.

———. "Equinox" www.tumblr.com/ineedtoreadmorepoetry/180940180024 /equinox-by-audre-lorde.

———. "From The House of Yemanja" www.poetryfoundation.org/poems/42578 /from-the-house-of-yemanja.

———. "Open Letter to Mary Daly," 66–71. In *Sister Outsider: Essays and Speeches.* Berkeley, CA: Crossing Press, 2007.

———. "Reading at Amerika Haus Berlin 1984." Audre Lorde in Berlin. Youtube. www.youtube.com/watch?v=7ZdlJcwgMuk.

———. *Sister Outsider: Essays and Speeches.* Berkeley, CA: Crossing Press, 2007.

———. "The Transformation of Silence into Language and Action," in *Sister Outsider: Essays and Speeches.* Berkeley, CA: Crossing Press, 2007.

———. "'A Woman Speaks'—Reading at Amerika Haus Berlin 1984." YouTube. October 24, 2016. www.youtube.com/watch?v=h059j-vBKEw.

———. *Zami: A New Spelling of My Name.* Berkeley, CA: Crossing Press, 1982.

Lundy, Garvey F. "Fatiman, Cécile." In *Encyclopedia of African Religion.* Edited by Molefi Kete Asante and Ama Mazama, 262–63. Thousand Oaks, Sage Publications Inc., 2009.

Lupec.org. "Queens of the Tarot Frontier: Lupec Salutes Artists Pamela Colman Smith and Lady Frieda Harris." Accessed August 28, 2022. www.lupec.org /events/2003/tarot/fharris.html.

Lynskey, Dorian. "Witch Camp (Ghana): I've Forgotten Now Who I Used to Be Review—Magical Sound of the Marginalised." *Guardian.* March 13, 2021. https://www.theguardian.com/music/2021/mar/13/witch-camp-ghana-ive -forgotten-now-who-i-used-to-be-review-magical-sound-of-the-marginalised.

Maddocks, Fiona. *Hildegard of Bingen: The Woman of Her Age.* New York: Crown Publishing Group, 2003.

Magloire, Marina. "Oh My Body, Make of Me Always a Woman Who
  Listens." *Missing Witches* (podcast), Episode 87 WF. April 14, 2021. www
  .missingwitches.com/2021/04/14/ep-87-wf-dr-marina-magloire-oh-my
  -body-make-of-me-always-a-woman-who-listens/.

———. "In the Quest for Abolition, America Must Learn from Haiti." *Scalawag*.
  July 6, 2020. https://scalawagmagazine.org/2020/07/haitian-protest-miami/.

———. "The Spirit Writing of Lucille Clifton." *The Paris Review*. October 19,
  2020. www.theparisreview.org/blog/2020/10/19/the-spirit-writing-of-lucille
  -clifton/.

Mangelsdorf, Rob. "Beerstory 101: St. Hildegard of Bingen." *The Growler*. March
  6, 2017. https://bc.thegrowler.ca/features/beerstory-101-st-hildegard-of
  -bingen/.

Marie. "The Book Is Written by White Eyes, But It's Better Than Nothing at All."
  Community review, Goodreads. January 17, 2012. www.goodreads.com/book
  /show/301777.Warrior_Woman.

Mark, Joshua J. "Kahina." *World History Encyclopedia*. March 16, 2018. www
  .worldhistory.org/Kahina/.

Massey, Doreen. "Power-Geometry and a Progressive Sense of Place." In *Mapping
  the Futures: Local Cultures, Global Change*, edited by Jon Bird, Barry Curtis,
  Tim Putnam, George Robertson, and Lisa Tickner, 59–69. New York: Rout-
  ledge, 1993.

———. "Spaces of Politics." In *Human Geography Today*, edited by Doreen
  Massey, John Allen, and Philip Sarre, 279–94. Cambridge: Polity Press, 1999.

Mattingly, David J., Maria Carmela Gatto, Martin Sterry, and Nick Ray. "Burials,
  Migration and Identity: The View from the Sahara." In *Burials, Migration and
  Identity in the Ancient Sahara and Beyond*, edited by M.C. Gatto, D. J. Mattingly,
  N. Ray, and M. Sterry. Cambridge, UK: Cambridge University Press, 2019.

Matyssek, Rainer, and Ulrich Lüttge, "Gaia: The Planet Holobiont." *Nova Acta
  Leopoldina* 114, No. 391 (2013): 325–344. www.leopoldina.org/fileadmin
  /redaktion/Probekapitel_NAL391.pdf.

McLeod, Jamie. "Why Do We Garden by the Moon?" *Farmers' Almanac*. May 2,
  2022. www.farmersalmanac.com/why-garden-by-the-moon-20824.

Medievalists.net. "The Herbal Cures of Hildegard von Bingen—Was She Right?"
  Accessed September 7, 2022. www.medievalists.net/2016/07/the-herbal
  -cures-of-hildegard-von-bingen-was-she-right/.

Melt. "Lady Frieda Harris." Visualmelt.com. Accessed August 28, 2022. https://
  visualmelt.com/Lady-Frieda-Harris.

"Mesopotamian Priests and Priestesses." History on the Net. Accessed November
  22, 2022. www.historyonthenet.com/mesopotamian-priests-and-priestesses.

Metzger, Richard. *Book of Lies: The Disinformation Guide to Magick and the Occult.* Los Angeles: Disinformation, 2003.

Michel, Claudine, and Patrick Bellegarde-Smith. "Vodou." In *Encyclopedia of Global Religion,* edited by Mark Juergensmeyer and Wade C. Roof, 1365–68. Thousand Oaks, CA: SAGE Publications, Inc., 2012. http://dx.doi.org /10.4135/9781412997898.n775.

Michel, Claudine, Patrick Bellegarde-Smith, and Marlene Racine-Toussaint. "From the Horses' Mouths: Women's Words/ Women's Worlds." Chapter 7 in *Haitian Vodou: Spirit, Myth, and Reality,* edited by Patrick Bellegarde-Smith and Claudine Michel. Bloomington: Indiana University Press, 2006.

Mies, Maria, and Vandana Shiva. *Ecofeminism.* Black Point, Nova Scotia: Fernwood Publications, 1993.

Miller, Madeline. *Circe.* New York: Little, Brown and Company, 2018. iBooks.

Mingren, Wu. "Lozen: An Intelligent and Brave Apache Warrior Woman." *Ancient Origins.* May 14, 2016. www.ancient-origins.net/history-famous-people/lozen -intelligent-and-brave-apache-warrior-women-005889.

Missing Witches. "Afterparty!! Coven Meet Audio—The Elements." May 28, 2022. www.patreon.com/posts/afterparty-coven-67002437.

———. "Music Witches, Music as Witchcraft." *Missing Witches* (podcast), Episode Missing Witches Beltane Special. May 1, 2019. www.missingwitches.com/2019/05/01/ missing-witches-beltane-special-music-witches-music-as-witchcraft/.

———. "Samhain Circle—Look for the Door into the Unknown Country." *Missing Witches* (podcast), Episode 109. October 31, 2021. https://www .missingwitches.com/2021/10/31/missing-witches-samhain-circle-look-for -the-door-into-the-unknown-country/.

———. "A Stellar and Star Studded Astrology Panel—We Are Still Here." *Missing Witches* (podcast), Episode 121 Imbolc 2022. February 2, 2022. www .missingwitches.com/2022/01/24/missing-witches-imbolc-circle-we-are -still-here/.

———. "Monica Sjöö: The Earth Is a Witch and the Men Still Burn Her." *Missing Witches* (podcast). October 14, 2018. www.missingwitches.com/2018/10/14 /episode-4-monica-sjoo-the-earth-is-a-witch-and-the-men-still-burn-her/.

Mithen, Steven. *The Singing Neanderthals: The Origins of Music, Language, Mind, and Body.* Cambridge, MA: Harvard University Press, 2007. Kindle.

Morelle, Rebecca. "Ancient Babylonians 'First to Use Geometry.'" *BBC News.* January 29, 2016. www.science.org/doi/full/10.1126/science.aad8085.

Morgan, Andy. "What Do the Tuareg Want?" *Aljazeera: Opinions.* January 9, 2014. www.aljazeera.com/opinions/2014/1/9/what-do-the-tuareg-want.

Morgan, Ffiona. *Wild Witches Don't Get the Blues.* Daughters Of The Moon, 1991.

Morrison, Grant. "Pop Magic." In *Book of Lies: The Disinformation Guide to Magick and the Occult*, edited by Richard Metzger. San Francisco: Red Wheel Wiser, 2003.

Morrison, Toni. "No Place for Self-Pity, No Room for Fear." *The Nation.* March 23, 2015. www.thenation.com/article/archive/no-place-self-pity-no-room-fear/.

Morton, Oliver P. In *The History of Women's Suffrage*, Volume 2, Chapter 24. Ed. Elizabeth Cady Stanton, Susan B. Anthony, Matilda Joslyn. 1887. Accessed July 29, 2022, https://en.wikisource.org/w/index.php?title=History_of _Woman_Suffrage/Volume_2/Chapter_24&oldid=10709145.

Mui, Bex. "Queering the Church with Spiritual Playspace." *Missing Witches* (podcast), Episode 112 WF. December 2, 2021. www.missingwitches.com/2021/12/02 /ep-112-wf-bex-mui-queering-the-church-with-spiritual-playspace-2/.

Naaim, El Houssaine. "Amazigh Civilization: A Lesson in How to Treat Women." *Morocco World News.*" February 2, 2015. www.moroccoworldnews.com/2015 /02/149995/amazigh-civilization-lesson-treat-women/.

National Park Service (NPS.gov). "Apache Before 1861." Accessed September 14, 2022. www.nps.gov/chir/learn/historyculture/pre-apache-wars.htm.

Nelson, Steffie. "Cameron, Witch of the Art World." *Los Angeles Review of Books.* October 8, 2014. https://lareviewofbooks.org/article/cameron-witch-art-world/.

Newman, Barbara. "Hildegard of Bingen: Visions and Validation." *Church History* 54, no. 2 (June 1985): 163–75.

Nimbin Apothecary. "The Heart Is Not Just a Pump." Facebook post. June 16, 2021. https://www.facebook.com/NimbinApothecary/posts/pfbid026Q7x FUy4SHH3vjhfHJcFCoG6ZYsT9w9bHVRQRHoon7RsJE2icEY Z6Az66mNJX98fl.

Nittle, Nadra. "Nadra Nittle on Toni Morrison's Spiritual Vision." *Missing Witches*, Episode 107 WF, October 24, 2021. www.missingwitches.com/2021/10/24 /ep-107-nadra-nittle-on-toni-morrisons-spiritual-vision/.

———. *Toni Morrison's Spiritual Vision: Faith, Folktales, and Feminism in Her Life and Literature.* Minneapolis, MN: Fortress Press, 2021.

Norton, Rictor. "4 Gay Heretics and Witches." *A History of Homiphobia.* Updated February 18, 2011. http://rictornorton.co.uk/homopho4.htm.

O'Brien, Sam. "Eat Like a Medieval Saint." *Atlas Obscura.* September 20, 2021. www.atlasobscura.com/articles/medieval-cookie-recipe.

Oda, Mayumi. *I Opened the Gate, Laughing: An Inner Journey.* San Francisco: Chronicle Books, 2002.

———. *Saravati's Gift: The Autobiography of Mayumi Oda—Artist, Activist, and Modern Buddhist Revolutionary.* Boulder, CO: Shambala Publications, 2020.

————. "Wheel of Dharma." Accessed August 12, 2022. https://mayumioda.net
/collections/wheel-of-dharma-1.

Okpala, Blessing. "26 Peculiar Benefits of Scallion." *Recipes for Life* (blog). *Global
Foodbook.* July 15, 2016. https://globalfoodbook.com/26-peculiar-benefits
-of-scallion-spring-onion.

Olsson, Goran Hugo. *The Black Power Mixtape 1967–1975.* Story AB, Louverture
Films, and Sveriges Television AB, 2011. Premiered February 9, 2012. www
.pbs.org/independentlens/documentaries/black-power-mixtape-1967-1975/.

Oursler, Tony. *Synesthesia: Genesis P. Orridge.* YouTube. July 14, 2018. https://www
.youtube.com/watch?v=ebd2p0g8BTM.

Paddock, Catharine." Soil Bacteria Work in Similar Way to Antidepressants."
MedicalNewsToday. April 2, 2007. www.medicalnewstoday.com/articles
/66840#1.

Page, Christine. "Powerful Women Work Together." YouTube. June 25, 2017.
www.youtube.com/watch?v=fhqlTjgEkMs.

Parr, John. "Man in Motion." *St. Elmo's Fire* (Man in Motion) Soundtrack. Atlantic, 1984.

Parsons, Cameron. "Cinderella of the Wastelands." YouTube. February 22, 2013.
www.youtube.com/watch?v=NxMJONFDw_E.

Peck, Marion. "Making Art Is Like Trying to Remember Your Dreams." *Missing
Witches* (podcast), Episode 110 WF. November 18, 2021. www.missingwitches
.com/2021/11/18/ep-110-wf-marion-peck-making-art-is-like-trying-to
-remember-your-dreams/.

Pedersen, Lisa. Interview with authors, September 2, 2021.

Peek, Phillip M. *African Divination Systems: Ways of Knowing.* Bloomington, IN:
Indiana University Press, 1991.

Pendle, George. *Strange Angel: The Otherworldly Life of Rocket Scientist John White-
side Parsons.* New York: Harper Collins, 2006.

Planetary Dance. "The Story." Accessed August 23, 2022. https://planetarydance
.org/the-story/.

Playboy. "Wendy/Walter Carlos: A Candid Conversation with the 'Switched-On
Bach' Composer Who, for the First Time, Reveals Her Sex-Change Operation and Her Secret Life as a Woman." May 1979.

Poetry Foundation, "Lucille Clifton, 1936–2010." Accessed November 18, 2022.
https://www.poetryfoundation.org/poets/lucille-clifton.

P-Orridge, Genesis. *Nonbinary: A Memoir.* New York: Abrams Press, 2021.

————. *Thee Psychick Bible: The Apocryphal Scriptures ov Genesis Breyer P-Orridge
and Thee Third Mind ov Thee Temple ov Psychick Youth.* Port Townsend, WA:
Feral House, 2006.

Radziszewski, Ylva Mara. "The World Needs You, Witch." Missing Witches (podcast), Episode 104 WF. October 13, 2021. www.missingwitches.com/e104 -wf-ylva-mara-radziszewski-the-world-needs-you-witch/.

Rasmussen, Susan J. "Tuareg." In *Encyclopedia of World Culture, Volume 9: Africa and the Middle East*. Edited by David Levinson. New York: G. K. Hall, 1996.

Redmond, Layne. *When the Drummers Were Women: A Spiritual History of Rhythm*. New York: Three Rivers Press, 2018.

Richardson, Michael. *The Refusal of Shadow: Surrealism and the Caribbean*. New York: Verso, 1996.

Rippey, Phyllis. "I Started to See Breastfeeding as Central to the Construction of Gender . . ." *Missing Witches* (podcast). Episode 113 WF, December 9, 2021. www.missingwitches.com/2021/12/09/ep-113-wf-dr-phyllis-rippey-i-started -to-see-breastfeeding-as-central-to-the-construction-of-gender/.

Robinson, Margaret, Granddaughter Crow, Zoe Todd, and Chrystal Toop. "Beltane Special and Fundraiser 2022: Kinship with Margaret Robinson, PhD, Granddaughter Crow, Dr. Zoe Todd and Chrystal Toop." *Missing Witches,* Episode 138. June 2, 2022. www.missingwitches.com/2022/06/02/ep-138 -beltane-special-and-fundraiser-2022-kinship-with-margaret-robinson-phd -granddaughter-crow-dr-zoe-todd-and-chrystal-toop/.

Rosenberg, Gemica. "Poetry Is the Only Thing That Makes Me Feel Like I Am a Witch." *Missing Witches* (podcast). Episode 125 WF. March 17, 2022. www .missingwitches.com/2022/03/17/ep-125-wf-gemica-rosenberg-poetry-is -the-only-thing-that-makes-me-feel-like-i-am-a-witch/.

The Royal Society. "West Africans and the History of Smallpox Inoculation: Q&A with Elise A. Mitchell." *History of Science* (blog). October 20, 2020. https://royalsociety.org/blog/2020/10/west-africans-and-the-history-of -smallpox-inoculation/.

Rucker, Walter. "Conjure, Magic, and Power: The Influence of Afro-Atlantic Religious Practices on Slave Resistance and Rebellion." *Journal of Black Studies* 32, no. 1 (September 2001): 84–103.

Rutledge, Pamela B. "The Psychological Power of Storytelling: Stories That Leap-Frog Technology, Taking Us to Authentic Experience." *Psychology Today*. January 16, 2011. www.psychologytoday.com/us/blog/positively-media/201101 /the-psychological-power-storytelling.

Ryzik, Melena. "The Afrofuturistic Designs of 'Black Panther.'" *New York Times*, February 23, 2018. www.nytimes.com/2018/02/23/movies/black-panther -afrofuturism-costumes-ruth-carter.html.

Sacks, Oliver. *Migraine, Revised and Revisited*. Toronto: Vintage Canada, 1999. iBooks.

Samuels, Michael. "Dances as a Healing Force," afterword to *Returning to Health with Dance, Movement and Imagery* by Anna Halprin, 161–164. Mendocino, CA: LifeRhythm Books, 2000.

Sanchez, Nikki. "Decolonization Is for Everyone." TEDxSFU (YouTube post). March 12, 2019. www.youtube.com/watch?v=QP9x1NnCWNY&.

Sandberg, Patrik. "Genesis P-Orridge: Altar Everything." *Dazed.* June 17, 2016. www.dazeddigital.com/artsandculture/article/31620/1/genesis-p-orridge -altar-everything.

Schechner, Richard, and Anna Halprin. "Anna Halprin: A Life in Ritual. An Interview." *Tulane Drama Review (1988–)* 33, no. 2 (Summer, 1989): 67–73.

Schulke, Daniel A. *Veneficium: Magic, Witchcraft and the Poison Path.* Three Hands Press, 2018. https://threehandspress.com/.

Scientific American. "Sarcasm Spurs Creative Thinking: Although Snarky Comments Can Cause Conflict, a Little Verbal Irony Also Stimulates New Ideas." Scientific American Mind. May 1, 2016. www.scientificamerican.com/article /sarcasm-spurs-creative-thinking/.

Sender, Ron, Shai Fuchs, and Ron Milo. "Revised Estimates for the Number of Human Bacteria Cells in the Body," *PLOS Biology* 14, no. 8 (2016): e1002533. https://doi.org/10.1371/journal.pbio.1002533.

Shaw, Judith. "Cerridwen, Dark Goddess of Transformation, Inspiration and Knowledge by Judith Shaw." *Feminism and Religion.* October 30, 2014. https://feminismandreligion.com/2014/10/30/cerridwen-dark-goddess -of-transformation-inspiration-and-knowledge-by-judith-shaw/.

Shone, Sherry. "aka That Hoodoo Lady: Reclaiming The Bible." *Missing Witches* (podcast), Episode 66 WF. October 7, 2020. www.missingwitches.com /2020/10/07/ep-66-wf-sherry-shone-aka-that-hoodoo-lady-reclaiming -the-bible/.

Shulman, Alix Kates. "Dances with Feminists." Berkeley Library, University of California. Accessed August 28, 2022. www.lib.berkeley.edu/goldman /Features/danceswithfeminists.html.

Silverstein, Shel. "Invitation." In *Where The Sidewalk Ends*, 9. New York: Harper-Collins, 2014.

Simpson, Dave. "Genesis P-Orridge: 'People's Lives Should Be as Interesting as Their Art.'" *Guardian.* August 29, 2013. www.theguardian.com/music/2013 /aug/29/genesis-p-orridge-throbbing-gristle.

Sjöö, Monica, and Barbara Mor. *The Great Cosmic Mother: Rediscovering the Religion of the Earth*, 2nd ed. San Francisco: HarperSanFrancisco, 1991.

Skinner, Julia. "Collaborate with These Beings That Have Been Waiting to Support You." *Missing Witches* (podcast). Episode 83 WF. March 31, 2021.

www.missingwitches.com/2021/03/31/wf-dr-julia-skinner-collaborate-with
-these-beings-that-have-been-waiting-to-support-you/.

———. *The Hidden Cosmos: A Fermentation Oracle Deck with Recipes*. Available
from www.etsy.com/ca/listing/1060925658/the-hidden-cosmos-oracle
-recipe-deck.

Sklar, Jessica S., and Elizabeth S. Sklar. *Mathematics in Populare Culture: Essays
on Appearances in Film, Fiction, Games, Television and Other Media*. London:
McFarland and Company, 2014.

Smith, Beverly. "Anything That We Do to Help Each Other Is Resistance." *Missing Witches* (podcast), Episode 81. March 24, 2021. www.missingwitches.com
/2021/03/24/81-dr-beverly-smith-anything-that-we-do-to-help-each-other
-is-resistance/.

Social Science Space. "The Geographer of Space and Power." March 14, 2016.
www.socialsciencespace.com/2016/03/the-geographer-of-space-and-power
-doreen-massey-1944-2016/.

Sparkly Kat, Alice. *Post-Colonial Astrology: Reading the Planets through Capital,
Power, and Labor*. Berkeley, CA: North Atlantic Books, 2021.

Sparks, Amber. "Magical Thinking for Girls." *Gay Magazine*. October 25, 2019.
https://gay.medium.com/magical-thinking-for-girls-e04eaf934546.

Specter, Michael. "In Modern Russia, a Fatal Medieval Witch Hunt." *New York
Times*. April 5, 1997. www.nytimes.com/1997/04/05/world/in-modern-russia
-a-fatal-medieval-witch-hunt.html.

Sreechinth, C. *Thich Nhat Hanh Quotes*. Ballard, UT: UB Tech, 2017.

Starhawk. *The Spiral Dance: A Rebirth of the Ancient Religion of the Goddess*. San
Francisco: HarperOne, 1999.

Steblin, Rita. *A History of Key Characteristics in the Eighteenth and Early Nineteenth
Centuries*. Ann Arbor, MI: UMI Research Press, 1983.

Stewart, Madrone. *Feminist Weed Farmer: Growing Mindful Medicine on Your Own*.
Portland, OR: Microcosm Publishing, 2018.

Stine, Rachel. "A Modern Shaman in Seoul." *Huffpost*. Last modified December 8,
2016. www.huffpost.com/entry/a-modern-shaman-in-seoul_b_8747172.

Strand, Sophie. "I Will Not Be Purified." She On the Tip of Her Tongue
(Facebook Community post). June 29, 2021. www.facebook.com
/SHEonthetipofhertongue/posts/5997435740267367.

———. "We Are the Product of Anarchic Queer Love Making." *Missing Witches*,
Episode 114 WF. December 16, 2021. www.missingwitches.com/2021/12/16
/ep-114-wf-sophie-strand-we-are-the-product-of-anarchic-queer-love-making/.

———. "What Is Poison?" *Creatrix*. November 23, 2021. https://creatrixmag.com
/what-is-poison/.

———. "Your Body Is an Ancestor." *Braided Way: Faces and Voices of Spiritual Practice.* November 16, 2021. https://braidedway.org/your-body-is-an-ancestor/.

Thompson, Helen. "How Witches' Brews Helped Bring Modern Drugs to Market." *Smithsonian Magazine.* October 31, 2014. www.smithsonianmag.com/science-nature/how-witches-brews-helped-bring-modern-drugs-market-180953202/.

Time. "Folk Singers: Solitary Indian." December 10, 1965. Accessed online at https://content.time.com/time/subscriber/article/0,33009,898410-1,00.html.

Tolle, Eckart. "The Flowering of Human Consciousness." In *A New Earth: Awakening Your Life's Purpose.* New York: Penguin Books, 2016. www.penguinrandomhouse.ca/books/291884/a-new-earth-by-eckhart-tolle/9780452289963/excerpt.

Trent, William Peterfield. "Southern Writers: Selections in Prose and Verse." archive.org. Accessed December 16, 2022. https://archive.org/stream/southernwriters03trengoog/southernwriters03trengoog_djvu.txt.

Tsumura, Emmie. "You Have to Believe in Magic." *Missing Witches* (podcast), Episode 89 WF. April 21, 2021. www.missingwitches.com/2021/04/21/89-wf-emmie-tsumura-you-have-to-believe-in-magic/.

Uehleke, Bernhard, Werner Hopfenmueller, Rainer Stange, and Reinhard Saller. "Are the Correct Herbal Claims by Hildegard von Bingen Only Lucky Strikes? A New Statistical Approach." *Forschende Komplementarmedizin.* 19, no. 4 (2012): 187–90. https://doi.org/10.1159/000341548.

"United States' Child Marriage Problem: Study Findings (April 2021)." *Unchained at Last.* April 2021. Accessed January 19, 2022, www.unchainedatlast.org/united-states-child-marriage-problem-study-findings-april-2021/.

Utu, Witchdoctor. *Conjuring Harriet "Mama Moses" Tubman and the Spirits of the Underground Railroad.* Newburyport, MA: Weiser Books, 2019.

Valiente, Doreen. "All Acts of Love and Pleasure Are My Rituals." *Missing Witches,* Episode 24, April 14, 2019. www.missingwitches.com/2019/04/14/missing-witches-doreen-valiente-all-acts-of-love-and-pleasure-are-my-rituals/.

Varlow, Veronica. *Bohemian Magick: Witchcraft and Secret Spells to Electrify Your Life.* New York: Harper Design, 2021.

———. "Sometimes the World Will Trick You and You Think You Are Alone." *Missing Witches* (podcast), Episode 119. January 20, 2022, www.missingwitches.com/2022/01/20/ep-119-wf-veronica-varlow-sometimes-the-world-will-trick-you-and-you-think-you-are-alone/.

Vogt, Yngve. "World's Oldest Ritual Discovered. Worshipped the Python 70,000 Years Ago." *Appolon.* Last modified February 1, 2012. www.apollon.uio.no/english/articles/2006/python-english.html.

Walker, Monefa. "In the Next Ten Years Everything Will Change." *Missing Witches* (podcast), episode 131 WF. April 7, 2022. www.missingwitches.com /2022/04/07/ep-131-wf-monefa-walker-in-the-next-ten-years-everything -will-change/.

Warner, Andrea. *Buffy Sainte-Marie: The Authorized Biography.* Vancouver, BC: Greystone Books, 2018.

Waxman, Olivia B. "Where Do Zodiac Signs Come From? Here's the True History Behind Your Horoscope." *Time.* June 21, 2018. https://time.com /5315377/are-zodiac-signs-real-astrology-history/.

Wel, Marlynn. "The Healing Power of Sound as Meditation." *Psychology Today.* July 5, 2019. www.psychologytoday.com/ca/blog/urban-survival/201907 /the-healing-power-sound-meditation.

Wertheim, Margaret. "Wonderful, Mysterious, Beautiful 1.61803 . . ." *LA Times,* February 2, 2003. www.latimes.com/archives/la-xpm-2003-feb-02-bk -wertheim2-story.html.

West, Lindy. "Yes, This Is a Witch Hunt." *New York Times.* October 17, 2017. www.nytimes.com/2017/10/17/opinion/columnists/weinstein-harassment -witchunt.html.

Wigington, Patti. "Perfect Love, Perfect Trust." *Outside the Lines* (blog), May 13, 2020. www.pattiwigington.com/perfect-love-perfect-trust/.

Wikipedia. "Child Marriage in the United States." Wikimedia corporation. Last modified July 28, 2022. https://en.wikipedia.org/wiki/Child_marriage _in_the_United_States#cite_note-:1-12.

———. "Cremation of Care." Wikimedia Foundation. Last modified May 21, 2022. https://en.wikipedia.org/wiki/Cremation_of_Care.

———. "Emergence." Wikimedia Foundation. Last modified November 18, 2022. https://en.wikipedia.org/wiki/Emergence.

———. "Gebel el-Arak Knife: Similar Knives." Wikimedia Foundation. Last modified June 28, 2022. https://en.wikipedia.org/wiki/Gebel_el-Arak _Knife#Similar_knives.

———. "Kahina" Wikimedia Foundation. Last modified November 28, 2022. https://en.wikipedia.org/wiki/Kahina.

———. "Lozen." Wikimedia Foundation. Last modified November 7, 2022. https://en.wikipedia.org/wiki/Lozen.

———. "Mary Daly" Wikimedia Foundation. Last modified on August 21, 2022. https://en.wikipedia.org/wiki/Mary_Daly.

———. "Nevertheless, She Persisted." Wikimedia Corporation. Last modified February 8, 2022. https://en.wikipedia.org/wiki/Nevertheless,_she _persisted.

———. "Ojo Caliente Hot Springs" Wikimedia Corporation. Last modified July 28, 2022. https://en.wikipedia.org/wiki/Ojo_Caliente_Hot_Springs.

———. "Patience Worth" Wikimedia Corporation. Last modified July 7, 2022. https://en.wikipedia.org/wiki/Patience_Worth.

———. "Thelema." Wikimedia Corporation. Accessed August 28, 2022. https://en.wikipedia.org/wiki/Thelema.

———. "Tuareg People." Wikimedia Corporation. Last modified June 21, 2022. https://en.m.wikipedia.org/wiki/Tuareg_people.

———. "Victorio." Wikimedia Corporation. Last modified June 11, 2022. https://en.wikipedia.org/wiki/Victorio.

———. "Victorio's War." Wikimedia Corporation. Last modified June 7, 2022. https://en.wikipedia.org/wiki/Victorio%27s_War.

———. "Wendy Carlos." Wikimedia Corporation. Last modified November 16, 2022. https://en.wikipedia.org/wiki/Wendy_Carlos.

williams, Rev. angel Kyodo. *Radical Dharma: Talking Race, Love, and Liberation.* Berkeley, CA: North Atlantic Books, 2016.

Williams, Terry Tempest. *Erosion: Essays of Undoing.* New York: Farrar, Straus and Giroux, 2019. Kindle.

———. *The Hour of Land: A Personal Topography of America's National Parks.* New York: Sara Crichton Books, 2016.

———. *Red: Passion and Patience in the Desert.* New York: Knopf Doubleday Publishing Group, 2008.

———. *Refuge: An Unnatural History of Family and Place.* New York: Vintage Books, 1991.

———. *When Women Were Birds: Fifty-Four Variations on Voice.* New York: Picador, 2012.

Winton-Henry, Cynthia. *Dance—The Sacred Art: The Joy of Movement as a Spiritual Practice.* Woodstock, VT: SkyLight Paths, 2009.

Wise, Eryn. "This Is the Frightening Way Fossil Fuels and Violence Against Native Women Are Connected." *Bustle.* April 21, 2018. www.bustle.com/p/this-is-the-frightening-way-fossil-fuels-violence-against-native-women-are-connected-8858200.

———. "What Everyone Can Learn about Women's History from This Two-Spirit Love Story." *Bustle.* March 29, 2019. www.bustle.com/p/lozen-dahtestes-two-spirit-love-story-is-the-womens-history-month-narrative-that-needs-to-be-told-16996854.

Witch Camp (Ghana). *I've Forgotten Now Who I Used to Be.* BandCamp digital album. Accessed August 24, 2022. https://witchcampghana.bandcamp.com/album/ive-forgotten-now-who-i-used-to-be.

Woolfolk, Joanna Martine. *The Only Astrology Book You'll Ever Need*. New York: Taylor Trade, 2006.

Yeats, William Butler. "The Second Coming." *Poetry Foundation*. Accessed November 16, 2022. www.poetryfoundation.or/poems/43290/the-second -coming.

INDEX

Index

ABOUT THE AUTHORS

Amy Torok and Risa Dickens started the *Missing Witches* podcast in September 2018 and published their first coauthored work, *Missing Witches: Reclaiming True Histories of Feminist Magic*, in 2021. Both have a background in creative community-building and ran two different, interdisciplinary monthly arts performance showcases for years in the same town before meeting, forming their coven, and beginning the podcast.

Risa has a BA in literature and an MA in media studies, where she wrote about the communications history and impact of open source. For two decades, she has made magic and organized interdisciplinary community events, including advocating for a Universal Basic Income. She lives in a cabin on a lake in the woods north of Montréal with her husband Marc and daughter May Marigold.

Amy Torok is a Witch, teacher, counterculture enthusiast, musician, and visual artist/designer with a BA in English literature and a post-graduate diploma in journalism. She can be found atop a forest ravine in Quebec, with dirt under her fingernails and a song in her head at all times.

About North Atlantic Books

North Atlantic Books (NAB) is a 501(c)(3) nonprofit publisher committed to a bold exploration of the relationships between mind, body, spirit, culture, and nature. Founded in 1974, NAB aims to nurture a holistic view of the arts, sciences, humanities, and healing. To make a donation or to learn more about our books, authors, events, and newsletter, please visit www.northatlanticbooks.com.